Japan's Role in the Post–Cold War World

Recent Titles in
Contributions in Political Science

Japan's Role in the Post–Cold War World

Richard D. Leitch, Jr., Akira Kato, and Martin E. Weinstein

Contributions in Political Science, Number 361

GREENWOOD PRESS
Westport, Connecticut • London

Library of Congress Cataloging-in-Publication Data

Leitch, Richard D.
    Japan's role in the post–Cold War world / Richard D. Leitch, Jr.,
Akira Kato, and Martin E. Weinstein.
        p.   cm.—(Contributions in political science, ISSN 0147–1066 ;
no. 361)
    Includes bibliographical references and index.
    ISBN 0–313–29731–2 (alk. paper)
      1. Japan—Foreign relations—1989– 2. Japan—Foreign economic
relations. 3. Japan—Foreign relations—United States. 4. United
States—Foreign relations—Japan. I. Katō, Akira, 1951– .
II. Weinstein, Martin E., 1934– . III. Title. IV. Series.
DS891.2.L45   1995
327.52'009'049—dc20   95–9875

British Library Cataloguing in Publication Data is available.

Library of Congress Catalog Card Number: 95–9875
ISBN: 0–313–29731–2
ISSN: 0147–1066

First published in 1995

Greenwood Press, 88 Post Road West, Westport, CT 06881
An imprint of Greenwood Publishing Group, Inc.

Printed in the United States of America

∞™

The paper used in this book complies with the
Permanent Paper Standard issued by the National
Information Standards Organization (Z39.48–1984).

10 9 8 7 6 5 4 3 2

Contents

Figures and Tables

Acknowledgments

This project was made possible through a grant from the Japan Foundation's Center for Global Partnership, and the authors gratefully acknowledge their financial support and the full intellectual freedom given us to express our views. The opinions and views herein are those of the authors, and do not necessarily reflect those of the Government of Japan or the project's sponsors. Special appreciation is expressed to the National Institute for Defense Studies, Tokyo, which welcomed Weinstein and Leitch as visiting researchers, and graciously allowed nearly unlimited use of facilities and resources; to Ms. Sherry Petersen, Financial Officer of the Mansfield Foundation, for support rendered to Akira Kato during his work in Montana; and to Ms. Merrily Shaw, Assistant Director, Program in Arms Control, Disarmament and International Security, University of Illinois, for her generous help and for administrative support. Ms. Sato Chiharu of the Japan Information Center, Chicago, and Ms. Carol Murakami of the Japan External Trade Organization, Chicago, cheerfully provided assorted government documents in English and Japanese at a moment's notice. This study would not have been possible without the willingness of the interviewees to find time in their demanding schedules to meet with us, and to frankly express their views. Everyone needs a resourceful contact for a project like this, and we appreciate the helpfulness of Ms. Louisa Rubinfein while we were in Tokyo.

Introduction

In the history of the world, the bipolar structure of the Cold War was but a brief interlude that in a perverse way brought relative stability to the international order. The threat of nuclear war between the superpowers created a balance of terror and, combined with the commitment of the two superpowers to block the other's ideological aspirations, produced a continuously tense, yet relatively predictable, international environment. At the same time, this standoff between the United States and the former Soviet Union also provided a foundation upon which most nations could devise their short-term and long-term foreign policy objectives. Depending on geostrategic factors, some nations were greater beneficiaries of superpower budgets and security assurances than were others, and most (though not all) of these nations in turn aligned their foreign policy programs closely to the objectives of their ideological leader. In the post–Cold War world, however, that raison d'être upon which to construct a foreign policy, a foundation that at one time seemed nearly inviolable, has been lost for many foreign ministries throughout the world. Both the Soviet Union and the United States are now paying domestically for the price of a war that never transpired, and their ideological followers are left groping for a policy course that is coherent, flexible, and that can be gradually implemented. Japan is one of these nations.

Since the early 1960s, when then Prime Minister Ikeda Hayato
enacted his "income doubling plan" designed to raise the incomes
and standard of living of the Japanese to levels comparable to
those of other industrialized nations (particularly the United
States), Japan's relations with the rest of the world have characteristically been perceived in strictly economic terms. This pre-
dominance of Japan's economic image, in large part perpetuated
by the foreign media and popular press, has understandably intensified at times of trade disputes with other nations. It can also
be rekindled when the "subject" of Japan is revisited by foreign
reporters after a hiatus of Japan-related stories from the pages of
their dailies and weeklies, as if a certain issue in Japan or in Japan's relations with other nations has suddenly evolved. Although
it is true that today one is more likely than five years ago to find
a social, political, or "human interest" story on Japan in major
dailies and periodicals throughout the world, it is also true that
days can go by without any mention of Japan in the press or
broadcast media, and then it is most often an economic-related
story that will end the drought. The simple fact is that most people
outside Japan are naively ignorant of anything Japanese that is
not economic-related, and even then misinformation is widespread. On the other hand, relative to their European and American counterparts, the Japanese are keenly aware of what happens
outside their nation. The amount of information on foreign customs, society, and politics available to the typically voracious
Japanese reader-viewer is remarkable in comparison to the characteristic dearth of information about Japan available in the West.
It has been said time and again during the past decade that the
world has entered the information age, one in which knowledge
and manipulation of technology represent the keys to the treas-
ures of prosperity. If this is true, the rest of the world's ignorance
of Japan—or even worse, its imperceptions of Japan—is not only
appalling, but foolish.

Most academic disciplines in the United States and elsewhere
have their intellectual rifts and conflicts. In economics, for example, there are practitioners whose thoughts are influenced by
the neoclassical approach to the field, there are those who call
themselves "supply-siders," and there are still those, though their
numbers are now limited, who have adopted (and continue to

uphold) the writings of Marx, to name but three. Very rarely, if ever, do adherents of these three approaches see eye to eye. Intellectual disagreement is by no means absent among scholars from a range of disciplines who study Japan, but the fundamental division has primarily been one of perceptions and not of polemics. Perhaps this is because while theories abound in economics, international relations, sociology, and anthropology, to "theorize" about the workings of a nation in all its facets is a particularly unscientific practice. Nevertheless, there certainly is no dearth of proclaimed comprehensive theories about Japan. But rather than being based on previous theories, these theories are most often premised on perceptions.

There are those who study Japan (both foreigners and Japanese) who are enamored by the beauty of its landscape, by the grace and elegance of Japan's cultural traditions, such as the tea ceremony and flower arranging, or by the generosity of its people toward foreign travelers. These supporters of Japan (we refrain from using the term "Japan lovers") are guided by this "positive" side of Japan in their thinking and in their writing. The other distinguishable group of Japan scholars are generally more critical of Japan, and emphasize conditions or customs in Japan, or the actions of its people, that appear to be different or unexplainable by their own cultural standards. These people, recently referred to as "Japan bashers," predate this term that now includes many in the general public who know little about Japan except what they see and hear via the popular channels of information. To make a distinction between the group of scholars who are more critical of Japan than are Japan supporters, yet who are more informed than those labeled Japan bashers, we will use the term Japan detractors. Just as there are different reasons why some are enchanted by Japan and have chosen to relate this positive side of their subject to the rest of the world, there are a host of reasons why Japan detractors have focused their attention on those issues that represent Japan in a less than positive light.

The distinction between Japan supporters and Japan detractors is clear, so clear that one might believe that the field of Japan studies is polarized by these two groups. We believe otherwise, and join a growing rank of scholars and interested Japan watchers who could be termed Japan realists. Too many Japan detractors have readily criticized conditions in Japan that are equally evident in their own nations, or are too eager to transfer their cultural norms to Japan. And too many Japan supporters believe that they have to play the role of cultural ambassadors or "apologists" for Japan, or at least counteract the growing political influence of Japan bashers. We propose that Japan should be studied on its own terms, for no nation is "perfect." Nor should perfection be a standard by which to judge nations, for it is an ideal that none has yet to reach.

As suggested earlier, lately Japan's economic image has been negative, but it was not always that way. From the time of Ikeda's four years as prime minister, and until the first oil shock (1974), Japan was presented as a "miracle" of economic development to be admired and, if possible, emulated by the developing world. With the events of the early 1970s, however, two previous images were to be forever altered. First, the self-image of the United States (and the image of the United States held by most of the world) as a nation that dominated the course of world events was fundamentally challenged by its defeat in Vietnam. Moreover, actions in late 1973 and early 1974 reminded the world that a threat to the national interest of the United States (and the rest of the world) did not have to be encased in military hardware, but could take other forms (i.e., economic). Second, as an outgrowth of the oil embargo, U.S. industrial firms were for the first time faced with a serious challenge from abroad in the form of competitive, efficient, Japanese-manufactured goods. The image of Japan slowly began to change as it became an easy target for justifying a range of American economic and social ills. In short, Japan was transformed from a model Cold War ally to an economic menace to the United States.

There is a perception outside of Japan, particularly in the United States, that Japanese trade and contact with the United States is the lifeline that sustains the well-being of this "vulnerable" island nation. Many argue that it is a lifeline that should be kinked from time to time to elicit a response from a burdensome dependent, and this option is often held before Japan when it "misbehaves." Yet it would be unrealistic for anyone to believe that Japan is entirely dependent on the United States for its well-being, or that it has concentrated on fostering relations with the

United States at the expense of building relations with other nations. No nation is without contingency planning, yet in this post–Cold War world from no other nation is so much expected and anticipated yet so little thus far clearly formulated.

For more than four decades, Japan's foreign policy elite constructed a foreign policy course based on the assumption that friendly, working relations with the United States would form the basis of all policies emanating from the Ministry of Foreign Affairs, and relations with other nations would be a derivative of this assumption. Although there is no reason to believe that Japan's relations with the United States will no longer be a significant consideration, the once virtually unshakable alliance has been called into question on both sides of the Pacific. Japan has cultivated interests elsewhere in the world, and by all indications in the future it will follow a more independent, non-aligned approach in its foreign relations. Exactly what that policy course will be is still unclear, but it is the aim of this book to offer some suggestions. It is our belief that although Japan is being pressured to take part in shaping the "post–Cold War international order," it will do so cautiously and reluctantly because of the uncertainty of what that order will look like. While Japan is prepared to make practical, modest contributions in the post–Cold War order, for a number of reasons it will not play the major leadership role and it is unrealistic to think otherwise.

The history of Japan's foreign policy is as much a study of a nation attempting to achieve its national objectives as it is the story of a nation pursuing these objectives by following the laws and customs of an international system that it had limited input in creating. During the Cold War, other nations' expectations of Japan's role in the international system were limited; but with a rise in its economic presence throughout the world, the perception that Japan had benefited more than other nations from the imperatives of the Cold War, and its emergence as the world's second largest economy from its status as a developing nation in less than three decades, these expectations have increased. We agree with those who have argued that an understanding of the present and forecasting of the future require an appreciation of the past; therefore, the first part of this study will consider Japanese perceptions of the international system from its inclusion in that sys-

tem in the mid-nineteenth century to the end of the Cold War.
The analysis continues with the Japanese perception of the post–
Cold War international order, and the security considerations that
are facing Japan in the post–Cold War world. Our observations
are based on numerous interviews with members of the Japanese
political and bureaucratic elite, public surveys, and analyses of
both the official and public press. The conclusions reached in this
section will be applied to an analysis of Japan's future role with
its Asian neighbors; with Eastern Europe, Western Europe, and
the Russian Republic; and with the United States, for these are
what we and a majority of knowledgeable Japanese believe to be
the relationships that will define Japan's post–Cold War foreign
policy. Particular consideration will be paid to how these relations
have changed (if at all) with the end of the Cold War. By limiting
the scope of our analysis, we do not intend to imply that Japan's
interest in the developing world or other parts of the developed
world is insignificant, but we must leave this investigation to a
small yet growing number of specialists in these areas.

It is essential that policymakers in any nation have foresight
and not be controlled by short-term fluctuations and events, and
we believe that certain long-term trends are evident and are likely
to continue. Of particular interest, the chapter on the United
States–Japan relationship will discuss the implications for the
United States, of Japan's changing world role, and the extent to
which a "global partnership" is feasible in a changing international order.

I

HISTORICAL BACKGROUND AND ASIA

East and West in Japanese Foreign Policy

To have a sense of what course Japanese foreign policy will follow in the post–Cold War world requires an understanding not only of the history and development of previous policies, but of the motivations and objectives that inspired them. Even though an all-encompassing, detailed analysis of the history of Japanese foreign policy is beyond the scope and limits of this study, we believe that there are certain fundamentals and patterns which have characterized Japan's relations with the rest of the world. Broadly categorized, these can be termed identity, adaptability, and resolve. Each of these characteristics will be discussed briefly at the outset, and will then be considered in greater detail with reference to Japan's diplomatic-political history.

The first of these factors is that of identity. Its significance in Japanese foreign policy is either often understated by those foreign commentators who emphasize the negative history between Japan and its neighbors, or overstated by others who believe that a shared "Asian identity" implies common goals and values. Although there are clear distinctions between the Japanese public's perceptions of China and Korea and the nations of South Asia and Southeast Asia, and by extension the Japanese government's interest in these areas as well, Japan is an Asian nation. Historically as well as psychologically, most Japanese have an affinity for the region in the same way that many Americans may think of Europe.[1] During his October 1992 trip to the People's Republic of China, a visit that was significant for both its symbolism (the first postwar visit to that nation by a member of the Imperial family) and its timing (in the midst of Japan's legislative debate over sending peacekeeping forces overseas for the first time), Emperor Akihito stated, "Exchanges between our two countries continued in peace for long since ancient times, and the Japanese people entertained profound respect and a feeling of affinity for Chinese culture."[2]

Nor is it a coincidence that, unlike the world's earlier colonizing powers whose presence was often far from home, Japan's expansionist policy of the late 1800s and through World War II was focused on Asia; that its foreign aid disbursements have been heavily concentrated in the region; or that it chose Cambodia over Yugoslavia as the destination for its first post–Cold War peacekeeping operation under United Nations (UN) auspices. To a large extent Japan's involvement in Asia has been undertaken to secure what its leaders believe are (or believed were) its geostrategic and security interests, but Japan's ties to the region, and its actions within it, go beyond this explanation. Racially, culturally, and increasingly economically, Japan has developed stronger ties to Asia than it has to most other regions of the world. However, primarily because of the memories of Japan's policies from the late 1800s until the end of World War II, its presence in Asia has not always been welcome, and the feeling of affinity that many in Japan claim they hold for Asia is met by feelings of hostility that many Asians hold for Japan.

Another aspect of identity which has been a factor in shaping Japan's foreign policy has been its self-perception as a resource-poor nation that is consequently held vulnerable to the inherent instability of world affairs. This feeling of vulnerability has at times produced in Japan a sense of urgency in developing ties with the rest of the world, and in maintaining those already established. On the other hand, some have argued that Japan is an inward-looking nation plagued by geographic, historic, and psychological isolationism. These competing observations and attempts to define Japan's identity are attributable to the differences between opinions held by the elite level and those of the masses in Japan. At the national (elite) level, Japan's geographic isolation vis-à-vis the economic "power centers" of Europe and North America is reinforced daily (and will continue until the world's securities markets adopt a twenty-four hour trading day); one need only visit the New York or London office of a Japanese company in the middle of the night to see employees waiting for a telex or facsimile transmission from Tokyo to appreciate this point. Japan's geographic isolation is also reiterated politically, for even though many international meetings may be convened by *a* Japanese clock, few are convened by *the* Japanese clock. At the individual level, all communities in Japan are within seventy miles from the ocean, and few Japanese are not influenced to some extent by an "island mentality." On the one hand, therefore, large corporations and government agencies in Japan are incredible consumers of knowledge from the rest of the world (particularly that emanating from Europe and the United States) to compensate for this feeling of isolationism, and the concern of being "left out." On the other hand, however, for many individuals in Japan this feeling of isolationism justifies their belief that their nation can assume a position of noninvolvement in world affairs.

The second characteristic of Japan's foreign policy has been its ability to determine what is accepted practice (or expected of it) within the norms and rules of the international system, and to adapt its domestic policies accordingly to realize the goals that are valued within that system. This "national policy," which is a blending of foreign policy and domestic policy structured to achieve these objectives, is not unique to Japan, but Japan has been more successful than most other nations in linking the two concepts. Japan has never "made the rules" of international relations, but it has proven remarkably adept at following them and in prospering under them, often to the chagrin of the rule-makers themselves. Within the international system, Japan has not necessarily been a leader, but it has been a successful follower. Critics may claim that Japan's experience in World War II contradicts the idea that Japan was a successful follower, and may instead argue that it should be considered an unsuccessful leader (or maverick that challenged the status quo). But unlike the ideological rift that was to divide the Eastern and Western camps during the Cold War, when the adversaries could not always agree on the rules of the game, during World War II the rules of the game were clear; it was the interests that were in disagreement. As will be discussed, it was only after Japan became too successful that the rules of the game were reinterpreted, and Japan's achievements criticized in retrospect.

This factor of resolve and determination to succeed within the framework of the rules is the third continuity that has been present throughout Japan's relations with the world. Three examples will serve to illustrate this point. Japan was confronted by the Western powers in the mid-1850s, was "given" democracy and forced to demilitarize with the end of World War II, and in the postwar period was encouraged to construct an economy based on the ideals of the Bretton Woods system and under the GATT (General Agreement on Tariffs and Trade) rules of international trade. In all three cases, Japan was determined to follow the rules, yet for some of its critics it followed the rules too skillfully. As a more efficient empire builder than other expansionist powers, it was branded "imperialistic"; as a nation demilitarized at the end of the war by the Allied forces, it was later criticized for its relatively low military budget; as a capitalist nation that has become the world's leading creditor nation, its trading practices have been called unfair. With the end of the Cold War, Japan is now witnessing another threshold that may give rise to a new set of rules, and this is one of the central questions that will be examined throughout this study. What rules will be followed in the post–Cold War world, and what role will Japan play in shaping and defining those rules? Can or should Japan be expected to help define the post–Cold War international order? As we believe that any speculation of the future requires an appreciation of what came before, it is essential that through a reference to history, however limited, we retrace these characteristics of identity, adaptability, and resolve in Japan's relations with East and West.

While history is a continuum and any demarcation for the analysis of it therefore arbitrary, for convention or convenience scholars of Japanese history often choose the Meiji Restoration of 1868 as an appropriate, if not convenient, point from which to begin their analysis. Indeed, when compared with the more than two and a half centuries of virtually nonexistent "foreign policy" which preceded it, without question the Meiji period was both revolutionary and monumental. It was during this period that the ideas of "citizenship," "sovereignty," and "nationalism"—concepts that had already been well established in the West and articulated in the writs and practices of Western-created international law—were incorporated into the foreign policy of Japan, as well as formalized in the Meiji Constitution of 1889.

Yet, no matter how significant were the changes that the period ushered in, to review the evolution of Japan's foreign policy from 1868 assumes the events which preceded this change were inconsequential in the development of the policy that it inspired, as if the Meiji Restoration was a clean break from an inconsiderable period of Japan's history. True, once the inefficiency of the Tokugawa system was replaced by an oligarchy that ruled through the name of the emperor, essentially there was no turning back for Japan. However, it is only through an understanding of the challenges that Japan faced prior to its goal of "nation building" that we can appreciate why it pursued the foreign policy goals it did, or adopted the methods it believed would see those goals realized. It is therefore with some degree of justification that we have decided to relate the events of the latter Tokugawa period (1600–1868), since its demise served two purposes in the development of Japanese foreign policy.

First, confronted with the unmistakable threat of superior Western firepower and technology, Japan was forced to deal with the West on dictated terms and in accordance with a body of diplomatic laws that was developed in the West. To Japanese official and commoner alike, the arrival from the United States of Commodore Matthew Perry with his fleet of four smoke-spewing "black ships" against a backdrop of small wind-powered and manpowered vessels lining the shores of Edo (Tokyo) Bay blatantly represented the relative advancement of the West. But perhaps even greater than the technological symbolism of Perry's steamships, the purpose of his 1853 journey opened Japanese eyes to a type of statesmanship of which they had been ignorant. The ideology of the day for the Western powers was expansionism, and the formality that legitimized their actions was unequal treaties, with extraterritoriality and relinquishment of the right of tariff being two of the many injuries inflicted on Japan and other "uncivilized" lands of the world. Perry's visit forcefully awakened Japan to the necessary prerequisites of empire building—the self-assuredness of a great power destined to bring "civilization" to those less enlightened, and the military means to back up one's ambitions. Of course, one could not deny the inherent appeal of exerting influence over other nations, except this time Japan played the role of subordinate. Unlike other nations that became the target of Western designs, however, Japan neither meekly accepted its fate nor, save for a few isolated incidents, rebelled against the foreign presence. Instead, sensing what really mattered in the world of the day, its leaders were determined to see Japan overcome this inferior role and become like the Western powers themselves.

Second, the latter years of the period also witnessed the development of the modern Japanese state and concomitant expansion of "Western learning" regarding foreign technology, culture, and customs from a largely progressive and ambitious elite class to a broader segment of the Japanese population. In Japan's attempt to face the West on terms defined by the West—in effect, to play by the West's rules of "international relations" more efficiently and thoroughly than the West itself was able or willing—development of the talents and labor of the citizenry was done in the name of development of the state. Japan's defeat in World War II was the inevitable conclusion to this way of thought, but to understand what led to this ascendancy of the state and subordination of the individual, we must consider Japan's relations with the rest of the world at a time when these relations were officially proscribed.

Tokugawa Ieyasu's rise to leadership at the turn of the seventeenth century followed more than four centuries of diffused power with nominal control of limited areas by warlords, and nearly incessant civil war among them. After his military ascendancy, and even with two-thirds of Japan's land area under his control, Ieyasu was well aware that his claim to rule was rarely unchallenged, with support for his reign less secure the further one traveled from the capital of Edo (now Tokyo). On the domestic front, Ieyasu and his familial descendants enacted both schemes designed to drain the treasuries of their competitors and thus lessen the likelihood of their inciting a revolution, and policies intended to inhibit the growth and relative power of a despised merchant class. In the end, the Tokugawa rulers' elaborate efforts produced the very results that they were supposed to prevent, but of interest to our analysis here is the policy commonly called "national isolation."

Official efforts at restricting foreign travel and eradicating outside influences judged to be socially corrupting, most notably Christianity, are well documented.[3] As Seiji Hishida notes, Toyotomi Hideyoshi's edict of July 1587, which ordered the Jesuit missionaries to leave Japan, was not proclaimed because Hideyoshi was necessarily anti-European or anti-foreign. Indeed, "he did not propose to banish Portuguese who were merely engaged in trade; but he desired to exclude any foreign element which would menace the national existence."[4] As a monotheistic religion, Christianity challenged the pantheistic acceptance of both Buddhism and the indigenous religion of Shinto and, by extension, the ruling elite's claim of deification and their celestial right to rule. Stated somewhat differently, the political threat that Christianity posed through its preaching that "thou shall have no other God before me" was obvious to Hideyoshi and his successors, who promoted their claim to power with the establishment of a rigid class structure rooted in the notions of Confucianism, social conformity, and unquestioned leadership. The ban on Christianity and persecution of its avowed adherents in the early years of Tokugawa rule is perhaps the most graphic testament of the purge of foreign influences. Until recently, however, what has often been overlooked in this notion of Japan's "total" isolation from the early 1600s to Perry's arrival is the extent to which it was a policy that applied more to Japan's relations with the West than it did to its relations with the rest of Asia.

The readily accepted view of Japanese foreign relations during the Tokugawa period has been one of self-imposed seclusion from the outside world, save for the small island port of Deshima off the coast of Nagasaki, through which the nonproselytizing Dutch were granted trading privileges. In later years this region would attract a corps of young Japanese hungry for information about the West, and eventually many of these same individuals would play key roles in the transition from a feudal society to a modern state in Japan. There is also no denying the existence of proclamations and edicts of the Tokugawa government, particularly those issued in the 1630s, which prohibited the foreign travel (and even limited the domestic travel) of the Japanese masses, or the confusion that resulted with the appearance of unwanted foreigners within Japanese territory.

Laws that prohibited foreign travel were rarely challenged, nor was there any doubt that they would be enforced. According to a famous proclamation issued in 1638, accused or even suspected violators were subject to death, as were those Japanese who returned from abroad and the families that awaited them. And though a relatively less significant objective of his journey, it was with the intent of assuring the Japanese government's safe treatment of foreigners who arrived in Japan by happenstance—specifically shipwrecked American whalers—that Perry visited Japan in 1853. Considering that Perry "found that no fewer than ten thousand" Americans aboard eighty-six steamships engaged in whaling activities off the Japanese coast in 1850, the number of sailors affected must surely have been significant.[5] Indeed, the Tokugawa leadership had its motives for maintaining such a policy of isolation. Foremost among these was the belief that commoner contact with foreigners would destroy the carefully formulated class structure of Tokugawa society. It was feared that commerce would have a greater likelihood of flourishing with an unchecked foreign presence, and would lead to the ascendancy of the merchant class, a class that neither produced the grain of the peasant or the sword and essential products of the artisan, but simply prospered on the toils of both.

For decades, Western students of Japanese diplomatic history (and even most students in Japan) learned that Japan was "isolated" from the rest of the world for more than 250 years. In the past few decades, however, there has been a group of historians both in Japan and abroad who have questioned the extent to which this policy of "national seclusion" was in fact total.[6] While national isolation was the official government policy, one that held true in relations with the West (with, as mentioned, the exception of the Dutch trading post), it did not always apply in Japan's contacts with China and Korea. Documentary evidence has shown that on several occasions, delegations were exchanged between Japan and these Asian neighbors, while trade between Japan and the two nations was significant enough to have produced trading enclaves on the western coast of Honshu (Japan's largest island) and on the island of Kyushu (in addition to Nagasaki and the island port of Deshima). Certainly, geographic proximity was a large reason for this interaction between nations, as the ties between China, Korea and Japan can be traced prior to the first millennium.

Chinese coins and objects of worship from the Han dynasty (202 BC to 9 AD) have been unearthed in Japan, and it is hardly coincidental that burial mounds similar to those found in Korea, and dating from the third century, can be found in Japan. In the eighth century, China served as the source of reference and inspiration for Japan's early legal and governmental systems, and the writing system that Japan adopted is a direct descendant of that used in China. Confucianism, which still influences social conduct and social expectations in Japan, is also a distinctly foreign notion that has been successfully adapted to the needs of Japan, and the same can be said of Buddhism. Introduced in the sixth century from India and China via Korea, Buddhism was as much a transport of culture from the continent as it was a religion that provided answers for the meaning of life and death, and to this day Japan is considered to be a predominantly Buddhist nation.

These are but a few examples to illustrate the point that when Japan was "discovered" for the first time by the Western world, Japan's ties with both China and Korea were already in place, and when it was "rediscovered" (or, as some refer to the engagement, "opened") by the West in the 1800s, for more than two hundred years following the expulsion of foreigners, Japan had maintained, though limited, its dealings with its neighbors. In other words, there is no denying that although scaled back during the Tokugawa period, Japan's interaction with Asian nations had never totally ceased, while the cultural bond between Japan and Asia was already more than one thousand years old before the first Europeans arrived in the 1500s. For foreigners to discount this aspect of Japan's identity, or to ascribe more "Western-ness" than "Asian-ness" to Japan because of its relatively developed economy vis-à-vis its neighbors, is clearly deficient. But unlike Japan's relations with China and Korea, which were based on paying tribute to the dynastic leaders of the former and maintaining at least an equal, if not at times a self-perceived superiority over the latter, while engaging in commercial and diplomatic relations with both,

Japan's initial relations with the West were unquestionably based on inequality.

Perry's arrival in 1853 received curious stares from those manning boats in Edo Bay, but caused a great uproar among officials in the Tokugawa government.[7] His unwanted appearance was not the first attempt by Westerners to open Japan's ports to foreign trade, but it was surely the most significant. Indeed, the debate on how to properly deal with the foreign menace had been raging for some time in Japan's intellectual circles. One of the most influential and widely published groups that advocated total rejection of Western customs and beliefs was known as the Mito school. As early as 1825, one of the group's members wrote that with the influence of "Dutch learning,"

the weakness of some [in Japan] for novel gadgets and rare medicines, which delight the eye and enthrall the heart, have led many to admire foreign ways. If someday the treacherous foreigner should take advantage of this situation and lure ignorant people to his ways, our people will adopt such practices as eating dogs and sheep and wearing woolen clothing. And no one will be able to stop it. We must not permit the frost to turn to hard ice.[8]

The reaction among the leadership to foreign demands for trade was divided between those who were absolutely determined to reject foreign advances, by force if necessary, and those who urged the opening of the country and its participation in international trade. The political struggle between these two forces gradually became more antagonistic, but in the end those who favored or realized the inevitability of relations with the West were successful in their arguments. One senior Tokugawa official cogently presented this view:

Not to enter into friendly relations entails war and not to wage war entails entering into friendly relations; there is no other way, and there is not a single country which avoids both friendly relations and war, which spurns diplomacy and yet enjoys peace and maintains its independence. By behaving now as though the foreigners were our enemies, unreasonably rejecting offers of friendship and alliance, we are clearly making ourselves a hindrance to all countries; and it is certain that all countries, which are now divided among themselves, will on that account unite their forces and one after another send warships to demand explanations and open hostilities. After incurring the enmity of all countries in the world, we could not long hold out in this remote and isolated island of the East. Such a policy would not only be to fold our arms and humble our spirit. It would be to inflict destitution on the innocent people of our country, and would leave us virtually no prospect of restoring our national strength.[9]

For statesmen like Perry, who proclaimed their venture to Japan was in the name of peace and or the promotion of trade, it was hardly certain that their overtures would be welcomed if accompanied solely by diplomatic discussion. Without push nor shove directed against them, they were practitioners *extraordinaire* of "gunboat diplomacy," a concept first adopted by Thomas Jefferson in his dealings with pirates on the Barbary coast. But the Japanese were not suspected criminals and they had not challenged anything of the West except, unwittingly, its claim to moral superiority. On his mission to Japan, Perry wrote,

It is true that, in all negotiations with China and other eastern nations, the display of a respectable armed force is necessary to satisfy those people of the power of the foreign contracting party to protect its rights and enforce its just claims; but, in most cases, the mere presence of such force will answer all the purposes desired.[10]

Commodore Perry's expedition laid the groundwork for relations between Japan and the West, but it was the arrival to Japan and efforts of the American emissary Townsend Harris that would serve to formalize for the next forty years the first impressions that each side had of the other. Like many diplomats of the time, Harris was unabashedly biased in favor of civilization and culture as he knew it, and regarded any people who deviated from this ideal as barbarians and heathens. Learning of the persecution that claimed the lives of many Christian missionaries and their Japanese converts in the early years of Tokugawa rule, Harris proclaimed,

if I succeed in establishing negotiations at this time with the Japanese, I mean to boldly demand for Americans the free exercise of their religion in Japan with the right to build churches. . . . I shall be both proud and happy if I can be the humble means of once more opening Japan to the blessed rule of Christianity.[11]

Harris was also a man who spared no threat in his dealings with the Japanese. His hosts were already well aware of the fate that befell their Chinese neighbors a little more than a decade earlier in their efforts to rid their nation of opium, and in his meetings with Japanese officials Harris emphasized the inevitability of Japan's opening to the rest of the world or "Japan would suffer the miseries of war"[12] and a defeat similar to that of China. Irritated that "the Japanese do not decide important affairs until after long deliberation" (an opinion shared by many foreigners since 1856), Harris concluded that "no negotiations could be carried on with them unless the plenipotentiary was backed by a fleet, and offered them cannonballs for arguments."[13]

The Meiji Restoration of 1868 brought to power an oligarchy of former samurai-turned-bureaucrats with a decidedly outward-looking perspective. Many of these new leaders had earlier traveled to Deshima and read of the inventions of the West, and of the Western system of international affairs, prior to Perry's arrival in 1853. With this perspective the government began with abandon its policy of *fukoku kyohei* (rich country, strong military) in an effort to not only emulate the West, but if the future necessitated, to defeat the West. This strategy would undoubtedly require the acquisition of foreign sources for raw materials and foreign markets for goods. Yet it was never forgotten that equal relations with the West, and the restoration of Japan's right of tariff and freedom from laws of extraterritoriality, were impossible without elimination of the treaties that Japan had been forced to accept during the later years of Tokugawa rule. This Japan set about to do. The first such mission to the United States, known as the Iwakura mission, had the dual aim of persuading the Americans to repeal the treaties and providing leading Japanese statesmen with the opportunity to see America firsthand. This 1871 venture was unsuccessful in its diplomatic aims, but in exposing the Japanese leaders to life in the West it proved invaluable. The Japanese delegates to the United States and Europe must have had impressions similar to those of Fukuzawa Yukichi, who traveled to the United States in 1860 with the first Tokugawa mission.

I am sure that our attentive hosts thought they were showing us something entirely new, naturally looking for our surprise at each new device of modern engineering. But on the contrary, there was really nothing new, at least to me. I knew the principle of the telegraph even if I had not seen the actual machine before.... Rather, I was surprised by entirely different things in American life. First of all, there seemed to be an enormous waste of iron everywhere. In garbage piles, on the sea-shores—everywhere—I found lying old oil tins, empty cans, and broken tools. This was remarkable to us, for in Yedo [later renamed Tokyo], after a fire, there would be hundreds of poor people swarming in the ruined district, looking for nails in the charred wood, so valuable was metal in Japan.[14]

Fukuzawa was but one of many Japanese of his time who realized their nation was resource-poor, but even more telling in his account was the perception of the relative wealth, and complacency that it breeds, of the United States. For the most part, these perceptions continue in Japan more than a century after Fukuzawa's account. Japan is now a nation of affluence and highly equal income distribution (though as in any nation, one can find the homeless and poor), and it is true that economic success and a lower birthrate have spawned a younger generation that at times seems more concerned with consumer values and brand names and less with slavish work than were their ancestors. Yet even during Japan's real estate market boom of the late 1980s, among the class of *nouveau riche* landholding families who became millionaires virtually overnight there was still a sense of hard work and frugality. A fancy imported automobile may have looked out of place in the driveway of a rural farming family, and the woman of the house may have had a diamond necklace, but neither husband nor wife would impulsively quit their job or by newly acquired habit pour a half-full glass of milk down the drain. A psyche inspired by Japan's resource paucity is one explanation for conservation among those who most Americans would think would be in a "position" to waste or to become complacent; the psyche of Japan's experience in war is another, though considering the consumerism of successive generations removed from the memories of war, this explanation may be more meaningful only among older Japanese. Nevertheless, it is to these experiences that we now turn.

Although the subsequent (and more elaborate) Iwakura mission was not able to persuade the Western nations to reverse the unequal treaties that Japan had signed from a position of relative weakness, it would not be the last contingent of Japanese sent overseas for this purpose. Patient diplomacy finally paid off, and just two weeks after the Western nations had agreed in 1894 to repeal the provision of extraterritoriality within five years, Japan began its own expansionist program with the Sino-Japanese war. Ten years later, the world seemed less unconquerable with its victory over a highly regarded Russian navy. All the while Japan's leaders believed they were merely following a *de jure* set of rules of international affairs, rules that nations more experienced with this type of diplomacy had adopted or at least threatened to apply in their dealings with Japan and the rest of the unconquered world. For those nations which considered themselves to be "great powers,"expansionism was the ideology of the day. The ambitions of the United States, Britain, Spain, France, Germany, and the Netherlands knew no geographic limits for colonies and markets, and once they arrived often thousands of miles from their homelands, these foreigners did little to develop the infrastructure of their newly claimed territories. Often they fought amongst themselves as much as they did with the natives in their claim to these "new" territories,[15] but in the end the victor's claim was routinely given the legitimacy of approval by the others. Learning from the experiences of these nations, Japan was much more calculated and efficient in its expansionist ambitions and its aspirations to be included among the world's great powers. It did not extend its imperialist reach to regions of the world other than its own, and its presence was accompanied by a plan of development for these territories that bettered the characteristically piecemeal efforts of its Western counterparts. Yet these powers were not ready to accept Japan among their group, or acknowledge the similarities between Japan's ambitions and methods and their own.

Following its defeat of China in 1895, Japan's leaders anticipated that the world's "great powers" would not let Japan realize all of what it believed were its rightful claims to concessions and reparations in the name of war. Their premonition proved accurate. With the three-power intervention of Russia, France, and Germany, Japan was " 'advised' to return the Liaotung Peninsula to China for the 'peace of the Orient,' "[16] while the United States refused to mediate at Japan's request. These earlier expansionist nations based their argument on the logic of a "balance of power," an inherently European concept that was suddenly being applied to China, yet ultimately these same nations, together with Britain, Belgium, Italy, and the United States, would advance their own claims and become the beneficiaries of territorial leases, railway concessions, and mine exploitation from a partitioned China. In 1898, Japan's renunciation of its claim to the Liaotung Peninsula was made more painful, and the hypocrisy of "international law" made clearer, as it watched Russia gain a twenty-five-year lease of the territory that three years earlier it had forced Japan to relinquish. Writing forty years later, when the Japanese occupation of his homeland was met with limited resistance of the Western powers, Ching-chun Wang observed,

If it has served no other good purpose, the whole Sino-Japanese crisis [of the 1930s and 1940s] has at least taught students of international affairs to realize more than ever the importance of being constantly on guard against a too ingenious use of established terms of international usage, and popular reference to such special conditions in international relations as the Monroe Doctrine, the Panama Canal Zone, the American intervention in Mexico, and the British position in Egypt for the justification or explanation of acts and situations in the Far East, because in many cases the Western nomenclature simply does not fit the Eastern conditions.[17]

Japan surveyed the unified opposition mounted against its claims to the spoils of war, and began to appreciate the necessity of another Western convention—alliances—if it was to realize its vision of a unified empire. With a conviction that it too would one day be a great power, and determined to see that its own still undefined "sphere of influence" would be recognized by the West, between 1902 and 1908 Japan entered formal alliances with each of the major powers—the Anglo-Japanese Alliance, the Franco-Japanese agreement, the American-Japanese agreement, and the Russo-Japanese convention. Whether an alliance, agreement, or convention, surely Japan must have rationalized, since these pacts were concluded with the creators of "international law" themselves, its ambitions of empire-building would now have a degree of legal authority. Each of the four documents specifically recognized Japan's interests in China (with the Anglo-Japanese Alliance also recognizing Japan's interests in Korea), while the interests of the Western powers in China were reciprocally recognized by Japan.

Japan's claim to what it believed were its inherent rights in Asia loomed large in its decision to pursue militarily against Russia the respect it thought it deserved but failed to gain in its dealings with the West, for to Japan, Korea and Manchuria were clearly within the Japanese "sphere of influence." The Western powers did not see things in quite the same light as Japan, however, and what the Japanese viewed as Russian meddling in its interests in Korea, combined with Russia's intransigence in withdrawing from Manchuria following Japan's 1895 victory over China, led to the outbreak of war between Japan and Russia in 1904.

Japanese victory against the Russians was assured after only nine months of battle, and although the war was a severe drain on the treasury of the potential victor, for the potential loser the resultant domestic upheaval served as an igniting force against the government of the Tsar. The final naval battle in the Japan Sea saw speedier Japanese torpedo boats "swarming like angry hornets" around the Russian fleet, sinking twenty-six of thirty-seven ships.[18] Although the Japanese loss of life was less than one-tenth of that of its opponent, and its navy lost only three torpedo boats, neither side wanted to prolong the war. With the intermediation of President Theodore Roosevelt, Russia and Japan were able to resolve their differences at the indemnity table. The agreement, known as the Portsmouth Treaty in honor of the American site of negotiations, earned Roosevelt the Nobel Peace prize in 1906 for his part in bringing the disputants together. But it also earned the Japanese plenipotentiaries censure from the public back home, and caused the resignation of the Katsura cabinet.

By the result of this conference Japan, perhaps, got as much as she had expected, although not as much as she wanted. The Japanese envoys went home somewhat disgruntled—at least outwardly so—and when they reached home they had to have police protection from howling mobs. Japanese dailies made bitter comments to the effect that Japan won all the battles in the war, and lost all the spoils on the green table. Later, when the anti-American feeling was high as an echo of the anti-Japanese sentiment in California, more than one periodical in Japan referred to the diplomatic "loss" sustained by Japan at the Portsmouth conference as the result of American intervention.[19]

It is somewhat ironic, though understandable, that the Japanese chose Roosevelt to broker peace between the two combatants. His reputation as an outspoken advocate of the Monroe Doctrine was well known in Japan, and while it has been suggested that Roosevelt envisioned Japan adopting an "Asiatic Monroe Doctrine,"[20] in the end his belief was that the concepts were appropriate as long as they only applied to the United States. The Western response to the actions and audacity of this "new" expansionist power, which had the brazenness to force an ultimatum of twenty-one demands on a recently defeated China, was designed to limit the growth of the Japanese empire, yet it was a case of a group of status quo empires rebuking a maverick that threatened their interests. The Washington Naval Disarmament conferences of the early 1920s are a case in point. As William Woodruff relates, "Japan's conduct in the immediate post-war [World War I] years left the other nations little to complain about. It remained loyal to the League [of Nations], was conciliatory toward China, and cooperated with the United States and Britain in the Washington Naval Disarmament conferences of the early 1920s. . . . In contrast to Japan's behavior, the United States seems to have gone out of its way to irritate [Japan]."[21]

In the United States, concern over the "yellow peril" intensified into legislation—both national and local—to confront the Japanese threat. As Theodore Roosevelt wrote in his autobiography, "It is eminently undesirable that Japanese and Americans should attempt to live together in masses; any such attempt would be sure to result disastrously, and the far-seeing statesmen of both countries should join to prevent it."[22] With passage of the Gentlemen's Agreement in 1908, Japanese laborers were restricted from emigrating to the United States, and in 1924 the U.S. Congress passed the Japanese Exclusion Act. Legal discrimination against Japanese in property ownership and education (particularly the move by the San Francisco Board of Education in 1906 to segregate students of "Asiatic descent") also served to inflame racist hatred on both sides of the Pacific.

These legislative efforts at confronting Japanese expansionism did little to quell it, and it should come as no surprise that both Korea and China were less than eager to become subsumed within the Japanese empire under the guise of a "Greater East Asia Co-Prosperity Sphere." In 1939, Chiang Kai-shek exhorted, "The Japanese are to do as they please: to have power among us over life and death, the power of binding and loosing: we are then to become their slaves and cattle, and to have our substance devoured beneath the lash of tyranny."[23] For Japan, on the other hand, its Asian policy was justified as a response to the established powers of Europe and the United States, which were perceived as threatening its interests and not acknowledging its newly earned stature in the international community. The writings of an anonymous Japanese are interesting in that they reflect a sentiment similar to that held by Asia vis-à-vis its relations with Japan at that time.

The new Asia fully realizes the situation. It knows that the Orient has nothing more to lose. It has grown desperate in the consciousness that the only future that awaits the peoples of Asia is an extermination like that of the dodo or the bison. It has, therefore, accepted the challenge and ultimatum of Europe and America. It has also formulated its own demands in response. These are being pressed into the world's notice not indeed loud enough, for yet Asia is unarmed and disarmed. But humanly speaking, it cannot remain armless for an indefinite period. The day of reckoning is not far off.[24]

Japan's ambitions of uniting Asian strength against a Western imperialist foe were almost simultaneous with its appreciation for the technological and military superiority of the West, which were expressed by Perry's arrival. One of a number of young Tokugawa officials to understand the connection between the two was Katsu Kaishu. Destined for a career in military service, at a young age Katsu was trained in Dutch and Western learning and eventually earned appointment as the captain of the first Japanese ship to sail across the Pacific, bound for America and ratification of the Harris Treaty. While in the United States, Katsu quickly understood the importance of supremacy of the seas, and when he returned to Japan became the driving force for a Japanese naval power. An 1863 entry in Katsu's diary during the interlude between Perry's arrival and the imminent Meiji Restoration reveals his military program and advocacy for a consolidated Asia.

[A]ll through Asia no one is offering any resistance to the Europeans; everybody is just imitating them in a petty manner, and none of us is pursuing a far-sighted policy. What we ought to do is send out ships from our country and impress strongly on the leaders of all Asian countries that their very existence depends on banding together and building a powerful navy, and that if they do not develop the necessary technology they will not be able to escape being trampled underfoot by the West. We should start with Korea, our nearest neighbor, and then go on to include China.[25]

Katsu's exhortations may have been a call for unified Asian resistance against the West, but more likely they were suggestive of Japan's own expansionist adventures to come. However, these were not competing images for Japan. Reflecting the latter course, in which Japan's role was not one of partnership with the rest of Asia, but more appropriately one of domination, Japan did not promote the interest of the region as a whole to face the challenge of the West, but considered how the region could be developed to Japan's advantage to face that same challenge. The reason for Japan's policy was clear, as expressed by a Japanese writer on the eve of America's entrance into World War II: "East Asia is to become a vast self-sustaining region where Japan will acquire economic security and immunity from such trade boycotts as she has been experiencing at the hands of western powers."[26] Yet, were not the other nations of Asia also concerned with the "threat" of the West? Undoubtedly the thoughts of their leaders were as anxiety-filled as those of Japan's, but they either concluded they were powerless to resist or, as China showed, they faced the certainty of punitive concessions in defeat. Japan was not anointed the nation to confront the West on behalf of Asia, but Asia was indispensable for Japan to confront the West. In its relations with both the West and with Asia during the Meiji period, the blunt statement of an official in the latter years of Tokugawa rule still held true: "[I]n dominating men or being dominated by them, the issue turns simply on who has the initiative."[27]

This notion of Japan ensuring its economic security by developing relations with Asia is a third component of the identity factor mentioned earlier, and it is one that is often heard in Japan today. No nation is without contingency planning, and as will be examined in Chapter 3, Japan has realized for some time that diversification in diplomacy is the basis of economic and national security. In short, it has been strengthening its ties to Asia in response to the same concerns as those raised fifty years earlier, though it is not employing similar methods to meet the same objectives.

Eastern Siberia was to be included within Japan's designs for a "Greater East Asia Co-Prosperity Sphere," and Japanese war planners realized that if their goals were to be met, war against the Soviet Union over this territory would be inescapable. Of course, few Japanese officials were direct in stating their plans or motives for regional hegemony, but they were not reluctant to mask their ambitions in rhetoric that promoted Japan as a liberator and fellow brother of all Asians. According to the draft of the basic plan for the establishment of the Greater East Asia Co-Prosperity Sphere, "The ultimate aim in thought construction in East Asia is to make East Asiatic peoples revere the imperial influence by propagating the Imperial Way based on the spirit of construction, and to establish the belief that uniting solely under this influence is the one and only way to the eternal growth and development of East Asia."[28]

Japan's relations with the rest of Asia would never be the same following its "opening" by the West, and whether Japan would have followed the same course in Asia if its introduction to the West would have been one of equality and not domination is impossible to determine. Yet the similarity between Japan's imperialist ventures and those of the Western powers in Japan less than a century before is apparent. In both cases, the justification used by the foreign power, whether Western or Japanese, is analogous. The reverence of the subjugator to a higher being that was foreign to the subordinated land—whether a Christian God or a deified emperor—is one similarity, as was the justification that the designs of the more powerful nations were for the benefit of those who would ultimately be "opened." In both cases, the objective was basically the same—commerce, whether a search for markets or a search for raw materials—and it was only the methods used and the degree to which they were applied that distinguished one from the other. But all similarities end there. The following quote could have been uttered by a Japanese confronted by the specter of "the West" in the last years of the Tokugawa period, as it was, but it is unlikely that it would have been a Chinese, Korean, or other Asian absorbed into the Japanese empire during its fifty-year existence.

When those barbarians plan to subdue a country not their own, they start by opening commerce and watch for a sign of weakness. If an opportunity is presented, they will preach their alien religion to captivate the people's hearts. Once the people's allegiance has been shifted, they can be manipulated and nothing can be done to stop it. The people will be only too glad to die for the sake of the alien God.[29]

Reverence in the Western notion of God was, and remains, a voluntary decision by a certain, though limited, percentage of the Japanese population, and some Westerners ventured to Japan in Perry's wake with the express purpose of converting Japanese to their religion. As noted earlier, even among American officials sent to "open" Japan, a governmental pledge of religious toleration, specifically Christianity, was one of the agreements sought of the Japanese. In contrast, winning (or forcing) allegiance to the Japanese emperor among those subsumed into the Japanese empire was not a priority of the Japanese government. Emperor worship was for Japan a central doctrine by which to devise and pursue foreign policy, but it was also promoted by the Japanese government to reinforce a sense of Japanese superiority vis-à-vis the rest of Asia by virtue of their birth in a nation ruled by a perceived divinity. Most Japanese were "only too glad to die for the sake of their Emperor"; few who lived in nations that capitulated to Japan, and by extension became subjects of the emperor, were themselves possessed of the same reverence, nor could this have been realistically expected.

Japan's defeat in World War II witnessed a historically unprecedented benevolence by a victorious power over a defeated nation. The two objectives of the Allied Occupation—democratization and demilitarization—were legalized in the postwar constitution of Japan (1947), and became ideals that most of the Japanese public have held as nearly sacrosanct. In essence, after defeat the Japanese were given a new set of rules that would not only affect domestic matters, but Japan's relations with the rest of the world. Once again these codified manners of conduct were largely determined by outside forces. And the Japanese were resolute that they would follow them with the same determination that they had the previous set of rules introduced less than a century earlier. Being able to adapt to these new circumstances was hardly a difficulty for the Japanese. Writing in 1921, former Japanese Foreign Minister Goto Shimpei noted, "I believe that the Japanese are a race that is particularly susceptible to the influence of environment. The Japanese history is, in fact, one series of assimilation of different civilizations."[30]

It is clear that the Japanese postwar constitution was written under the influence of wide-eyed post–New Deal idealism, as it incorporates many of the "democratic ideals" that evolved in the United States since 1789. Even a perfunctory reading will show why many Japanese at the time believed some of the articles seemed a bit awkward.[31] But rather than feeling an injustice had been committed with this near-unilateral transfer of cultural norms on their nation, the Japanese have played by this new set of rules. Unfortunately for some, they have done so with the same efficiency and wholeheartedness that they had the previous set of rules. Whether the rules in the post–Cold War world will be as clear as those which preceded them, and in what ways Japan will design its foreign policy under this new set of rules, are points to which we now turn our attention.

NOTES

1. This sentiment is often emphasized in Japanese writings analyzing the Japan-China relationship, and was reiterated during an interview with Kuroda Makoto, November 27, 1992.
2. *Japan Times*, October 24, 1992, p. 6.
3. Perhaps the most compelling account is Endo Shusaku's historical-based novel, *Silence* (New York: Taplinger Publishing Co., 1969).

4. Seiji G. Hishida, *The International Position of Japan as a Great Power* (Ph.D. thesis, Columbia University, 1905), p. 85.

5. William Elliot Griffis, *Matthew Calbraith Perry, a Typical American Naval Officer* (Boston: Houghton Mifflin, 1890), p. 274.

6. For example, see Ronald P. Toby, *State and Diplomacy in Early Modern Japan* (Princeton, NJ: Princeton University Press, 1984); Oba Osamu, *Edo jidai ni okeru Chugoku bunka juyo no kenkyu* [The Demand for Chinese Culture in Tokugawa Japan] (Tokyo: Shohan, 1984); Marius B. Jansen, *China in the Tokugawa World* (Cambridge, MA: Harvard University Press, 1992). As Jansen points out, among early Western scholars of Japan the notion of *sakoku* (closed country) "became the most remarked-upon aspect of the Tokugawa system (2)," but the depth and breadth of subsequent studies has made the notion "[begin] to seem more symbol than fact (3)."

7. For a detailed account of Perry's expedition to Japan and his reception upon arrival, see Francis L. Hawks, *Narrative of the Expedition of an American Squadron to the China Seas and Japan*, vol. I (Washington, DC: U.S. Senate Printing Office, 1856), esp. ch. 12–25.

8. Aizawa Seishisai, "Preface to the New Proposals *(Shinron)*," as cited in Tsunoda Ryusaku et al., *Sources of the Japanese Tradition* (New York: Columbia University Press, 1958), p. 601.

9. "Hotta Masayoshi's Memorandum on Foreign Policy, Undated [Probably late December 1857]," as cited in W.G. Beasley, *Select Documents on Japanese Foreign Policy 1853–1868* (London: Oxford University Press, 1955), p. 167.

10. "Remarks of Commodore Perry Upon the Expediency of Extending Further Encouragement to American Commerce in the East," in Hawks, *Narrative of the Expedition*, vol. II, p. 175.

11. Townsend Harris, *The Complete Journal of Townsend Harris* (New York: Charles E. Tuttle, 1930), pp. 466–468.

12. Ibid., p. 485.

13. Ibid., pp. 495–496.

14. Fukuzawa Yukichi, *The Autobiography of Fukuzawa Yukichi*, trans. Kiyooka Eiichi (Tokyo: Hokuseido, 1934), p. 124.

15. For an excellent account of the many facets of European imperialism, see Prosser Gifford and William Roger Louis, eds., *France and Britain in Africa: Imperial Rivalry and Colonial Rule* (New Haven, CT: Yale University Press, 1971).

16. Takeuchi Tatsuji, *War and Diplomacy in the Japanese Empire* (Garden City, NY: Doubleday, 1935), p. 117.

17. Ching-chun Wang, "Theodore Roosevelt and the Monroe Doctrine," *Pacific Affairs*, vol. 9, no. 1, 1936 (Reprinted edition), pp. 5–6.

18. Sydney Tyler, *The Japan-Russia War: The Greatest Conflict of Modern Times* (Philadelphia: P.W. Ziegler, 1905), p. 553.

19. Henry Chung, *The Oriental Policy of the United States* (New York: Fleming H. Revell Co., 1919), p. 59.

20. Wang, "Theodore Roosevelt and the Monroe Doctrine."

21. William Woodruff, *The Struggle for World Power, 1500–1980* (New York: St. Martin's Press, 1981), pp. 180–181.

22. Theodore Roosevelt, *Theodore Roosevelt, an Autobiography* (New York: MacMillan, 1914), p. 396.

23. *Generalissimo Chiang Assails Konoye's Statement* (Chungking, China: China Information Committee, 1939), p. 5.

24. Anonymous, "The 'White' Problem in Asia," in K.K. Kawakami, ed., *What Japan Thinks* (New York: MacMillan, 1921), p. 186.

25. As cited in Marius B. Jansen, *Sakamoto Ryoma and the Meiji Restoration* (Princeton, NJ: Princeton University Press, 1961), pp. 164–165.

26. Royama Masamichi, *Foreign Policy of Japan, 1914–1939* (Tokyo: Japanese Council, Institute of Pacific Relations, 1941), p. 12.

27. Matsudaira Shungaku, as cited in W.G. Beasley, *The Meiji Restoration* (Stanford, CA: Stanford University Press, 1972), p. 111.

28. "Draft of Basic Plan for Establishment of Greater East Asia Co-Prosperity Sphere," as cited in Tsunoda et al., *Sources of the Japanese Tradition*, pp. 804–805.

29. Aizawa Seishisai, "The Source of Western Unity and Strength," as cited in Tsunoda et al., *Sources of the Japanese Tradition*, p. 602.

30. Goto Shimpei, "The Anti-Japanese Question in California," in *Annals of the American Academy of Political and Social Science*, January 1921, p. 106.

31. Article 9, Japan's "renunciation of war" clause, is the most cited (and its intent the most debated) of all the sections of the 1947 constitution. Yet there are other articles whose inspiration was clearly that of American-held democratic ideals (i.e., Article 23, academic freedom; Article 24, mutual consent for marriage and "equality" of both partners; and Article 25, the right of all people to "maintain the minimum standards of wholesome and cultured living," to name but three).

2

Defining and Pursuing a Post–Cold War Role

The world is divided on what Japan should do, and it would perhaps be much easier for Japan if they were unified. But listening to these opinions is not what we should do—we should find our own way.[1]

As we related in the first chapter, for most of Japan's post-1853 contact with the West, and until its defeat in World War II, Japan was a follower of the established rules, not a creator or guarantor of them. But in the post–Cold War world, Japan has been asked to take part in shaping the rules and formulating the policies that will come to the fore in this new international environment, and to assume a share in international leadership. This gives rise to the questions that will form the analytical focus of the remaining chapters of this book. To what extent is Japan able, or willing, to help create the rules that will define the post–Cold War international order? More fundamentally, what challenges do influential Japanese see in a world in which Cold War hostilities have been replaced by different forms of hatred within and between nations, and in which the near certainty of continued American amity and Communist enmity have been called into question? What do they envision as Japan's role in this new international order and, with an analysis of the policies it has undertaken since the end of the Cold War, what policies might Japan pursue in the future?

TOWARD THE END OF THE COLD WAR?

The end of World War II witnessed increasing East-West tensions that were to become the basis of the Cold War, and in this new environment Japan's postwar leaders and voters quickly realized their nation's role would be to serve as a bulwark against the spread of communism in the Pacific. With a corps of anti-communist bureaucrats who had been purged from office during the war because of their antiwar views returned to their government posts, and their calculation that in a conflict between the United States and the Soviet Union only the former could protect Japan from the latter and not vice versa, aligning with the United States was as much a pragmatic decision as it was one of ideology. Japan dutifully fulfilled this role in the name of upholding the tenets of the U.S.–Japan Security Treaty, which provided for an explicit American defense guarantee if Japan were attacked, and the use of military bases on Japanese soil by American forces. This reciprocal arrangement allowed the United States to efficiently launch its military operations during both the Korean and Vietnam wars from a strategic vantage point, and created a boom to the rebuilding Japanese economy. American military operations in Asia were an extension of Cold War competition, and may have prevented the Cold War from becoming a full-blown hot-war. Nevertheless, as the American economy planned for war, and successive national budgets reflected the diversion of capital from other deserving programs and productive enterprises, Japan was literally positioned in the backyard of hostilities. For the East and the West, the Korean and Vietnam wars were a clash between totalitarianism and democracy, but for the citizens of the nations where these clashes played out they were also a reaction against foreign intervention as well as an expression of nationalist sentiment. Japan distanced itself even further from the other nations of Asia with its production of wartime necessities for U.S. forces, an undertaking that generated an enormous profit for all types of industries in Japan—a trend that went unnoticed by most of the world. For those who bothered to take notice, Japanese economic development was welcomed in political terms as the stabilization of an ally, and in economic terms was not begrudged so long as the American economy maintained a respectable level of growth.

With the end of the Cold War, and in a climate of increased economic tension between Japan and its trading partners, particularly the United States, there was speculation in Japan that the United States might regard the U.S.–Japan Security Treaty as no longer necessary.[2] The logic was simple and the argument persuasive, as it was a concern not without precedent.

Even as early as the Allied Occupation of Japan, the Japanese were aware that among both the electorate and the elected in the United States, many believed that Japan was unappreciatively getting a "free ride" for its defense. These criticisms heightened as the guarantor of that defense—the United States—earmarked a considerable portion of its national budget for both advanced hardware and skilled personnel even during periods of depressed economic growth, while Japanese economic success appeared to gallop along unabated. Calls from Washington for Japan to assume a greater burden for its own defense in the form of larger defense appropriations, greater host-nation support, and defense of an expanded area which to patrol, were nothing new.[3] For example, in 1988 the Burdensharing Panel of the U.S. House of Representatives Committee on Armed Services concluded that,

[g]iven the substantial limits on what Japan is willing to do for defense, the Panel believes it imperative that the Japanese Government, at a minimum, accelerate its ability to perform the self-defense, "1000-mile" and "closing of the straits" missions and prepare to carry-out those missions if needed without direct U.S. assistance.[4]

Nor could an American military presence in the Asia-Pacific region be taken for granted, as epitomized by President Carter's campaign statement turned presidential proposal that U.S. forces be withdrawn from South Korea. But even if these challenges to the treaty's continuity could not always be met by Japanese agreement, American sensibilities, or a combination of the two, Cold War events would always deflate and overshadow any arguments that jeopardized the arrangement. Reversions to the hostility of the Cold War as expressed by the Soviet invasion of Afghanistan, the Vietnamese invasion of Cambodia, and the downing of Korean Airlines flight 007 off Sakhalin Island served to disguise the problems in the U.S.–Japan relationship, and solidify a shared Cold War mentality for these proclaimed allies.

The U.S.–Japan Security Treaty, which since the closing days of the Allied Occupation has provided the framework for U.S.-Japan relations, was drafted and enacted in the early years of the Cold War. As mentioned, many Japanese commentators predicted that with the end of the Cold War the United States would no longer have any "need" for Japan, and the treaty would be abrogated by the United States. Japanese knowledgeable about the United States believed this scenario was made even more likely with a rise of three related factors: a growing tide of "Japan-bashing" and protectionist sentiment in the United States; the twin deficits of trade and federal debt which plagued the United States, which, it was believed, would dictate a scaling back of its military commitments abroad; and a generally held view in the United States that with the end of the Cold War the world would be a "kinder, gentler" place. The general sense of euphoria felt in the United States with the collapse of the Soviet Union, a sentiment which momentarily colored the U.S. view of international affairs until Saddam Hussein's invasion of Kuwait, was a perception not shared by those in Japan, who instead viewed with concern the upheaval of an order that they had grown accustomed to for the last forty years. To quote an editorial from 1989 that appeared in the Japanese newspaper *Nihon Keizai Shinbun*, "To live through a time of confused peace like the present is far more difficult than to follow a world order predicated on the Cold War structure."[5] And so, too, were there doubts in Japan that the Cold War was actually over.

Save for relatively minor communist movements in Central and South America, and what is generally agreed to have been an overblown reaction against a communist insurrection on the island of Grenada, for the better part of the Cold War the perception of communism in America's backyard was confined to the Soviet client state of Cuba. With the pipeline of aid to the Castro regime virtually terminated with the dissolution of the Soviet empire, taken with news of the disparate conditions that challenged both the legitimacy of communist ideology and the longevity of Castro's claim to rule, this sole hostile communist threat to America's security became less menacing.

The United States could breathe somewhat easier, but for Japan there was little indication in its own backyard that the Cold War had ended. The resistance of the Chinese leadership to move toward a more democratic political system—highlighted by the June 1989 events in Tiananmen Square, the rounding up of suspected leaders and informants, and the execution of some of the most vocal and visible—graphically proved to the Japanese (and the rest of the world) that an increasingly liberalized economy could not usurp all totalitarian governments throughout the world. Troop and weapons movements from the Soviet east to the Soviet west, if only done by the Russians in the name of consolidation and protection of their military assets, effectively placed these potentially hostile resources closer to Japan. And of course, the simmering feud between the competing ideologies of North and South Korea was far from resolved, nor were the North Koreans cooperative, or have they since been, in revealing their plans to build a nuclear weapon. These realities which faced Japan led a significant number of Japanese to argue that there was now all the more reason to push for a continued American military presence in their nation, even if it meant compromising on trade issues for which Japan's position was near sacrosanct.[6]

It is often said that in the calculations which become Japanese foreign policy, the "U.S. factor" not only predominates, it overwhelms. "What will the United States do?" has for nearly fifty years been the most commonly asked question in policy debate that takes place in bureaucratic agencies, think tanks, scholarly journals, and mass circulation newspapers. At times concern with the United States has been so overwhelming that Japanese foreign policy has been portrayed as "reactive," suggesting that it lacks its own initiative and objectives other than satisfying U.S. demands. While this characterization may be somewhat of an exaggeration, considerations of the U.S. factor have been as much a mainstay for the Japanese policymaking process as was the Cold War. But this prioritization of the U.S. factor does not imply that Japan is, or has ever been, an American "lackey." The Japanese have always realized that selective accession to U.S. demands, often veiled as requests, is part of the price to be paid for access to the U.S. market and the maintenance of workable relations with its most significant military and trading ally. Will another nation, or perhaps a certain ideology, assume the role that the U.S. factor has played in Japan's policy formulation process since the end of the war? While this is a question which will be raised in the following chapters, for the moment it must be noted that the U.S. factor continues to be the most important external variable in Japanese foreign policy considerations. But as evidenced by the criticism that several bureaucratic institutions in the United States have been slow in changing from a Cold War mentality, difficulty should also be expected for Japan to suddenly rearrange its world view and abandon or replace the U.S. factor as predominant, especially if there does not appear to be a comparable substitute.

For example, although no one in Japan is taking the course of relations with the United States for granted, predictions of an end to the U.S.–Japan Security Treaty, common shortly after the fall of the Soviet Union, are now rarely heard in Japan. Even the opposition political parties (with the exception of the Japan Communist Party) have backed away from their insistence that the treaty be terminated,[7] which challenges intuition in that their decades-long criticism of the treaty would seem to have more validity since the primary threat to Japan's security, the Soviet Union, has been reduced. Some observers believe the opposition parties—primarily the Social Democratic Party of Japan ([SDPJ] formerly called the Japan Socialist Party in English)—finally realized that their traditional opposition to the treaty and calls for its abrogation were unpopular positions among the electorate, a majority of whom have favored continuing the treaty since it was enacted. In this sense, the SDPJ could be criticized as pandering for votes by reversing their position on the issue.[8] But one could also argue that on the issue of security, for Japan the U.S. factor—which in this case takes the form of continuation of the U.S.–Japan Security Treaty—is a virtual given, and opposition to it near heresy, especially if those in the opposition have not suggested a viable alternative. In the words of Kuroda Makoto, managing director of the Mitsubishi Corporation,

People in Japan are beginning with the assumption that what role Japan plays will depend on what role the United States plays. For example, they start with the assumption that the United States will stay in the region. But we can't simply try to give host nation support fully—

you don't want to become mercenaries. I'm arguing that it is a good idea to tell the United States to stay here, but the final decision comes from them. If they withdraw, what should we do? We aren't prepared to argue this. . . . [9]

There is no indication that Japan has clearly formulated (or at least made public) an adequate contingency plan for its own defense in the event of a U.S. withdrawal, because most believe that scenario unlikely. But whether the issue is one of security, participation in international organizations, or its relations with other nations, does Japan's assumption of a share of "world leadership" imply that prioritization of the U.S. factor will continue? One could foresee an international order in which the leading nations of the world confer with each other on international issues, and arrive at a consensus for the appropriate policy course. Consensus would imply consideration of the other parties' positions, and with the United States as one of the role-sharing nations, the United States would continue to weigh heavily in Japan's policymaking decisions. But one could also foresee a scenario in which shared leadership and the notion of consensus masks disagreements over values and priorities. This would be a scenario in which Japan's prioritization of the United States does not necessarily have to continue, while other considerations may gain in relative importance to the U.S. factor in Japan's foreign policymaking process. In this new role, it would be virtually impossible for Japan not to follow a policy course that is more independent of the United States, one which is more initiative-driven than what has been judged to be reactive-based. And the likelihood of disagreement between the two nations would be that much greater.

Bilateral trade disputes are an inevitable by-product of deepening interdependence between all nations, not just between the United States and Japan, and it is naive to believe that trade disputes between the two nations—or any pair of trading nations—will ever totally cease. Even during the Cold War, whether the American charge was cheap textiles or canned tuna dumped on the U.S. market, trade friction ebbed and flowed. The onus of unfair trade has usually rested with the United States, and the emphasis of the U.S. position has shifted from access to the American market (importation of Japanese goods) to penetration of the

Japanese market (exportation of American goods). Ultimately, perhaps, whether years or decades into the future, it may just be bilateral trade friction which causes irreparable damage to, or cessation of, working relations between the two nations. But during the Cold War, even with an underlying constant of trade friction coming between them, Japan and the United States could always agree on a "world vision." That was the case for two reasons: the existence of the Soviet threat and East-West rivalry, and just as significant, agreement was virtually assured since Japan had a minimal role in defining that vision. Leadership was the purview of the United States. But with an increased Japanese role, will there still be agreement with the United States over what is "important" in the world, on issues that transcend trade disputes? In other words, will Japan's world view and that of the United States complement each other, and even if they do, will they be in agreement over what are the best means to achieve the desired ends? In the words of Tsukuba University professor Sato Hideo,

the problem is that Americans will have to share leadership, including political leadership, but this may be difficult for them to do. The U.S. mentality is still that of hegemony; it still suffers from what [international relations scholar Hans] Morgenthau called "nationalistic universalism." This idea went well with the leadership of the 1950s and 1960s, but there is a disparity between that and the reality of today.[10]

On issues of trade and defense the United States has frequently sought Japanese "leadership," which often is another way of saying acceptance of the U.S. position. But on non-bilateral, non-trade issues, what indications have there been of a "new look" Japanese foreign policy since 1989, one that incorporates this aspect of international leadership, and what are its characteristics?

JAPAN'S "NEW" DIPLOMACY

It was obvious to Japan's leaders that even though from their nation's perspective the Cold War may not have ended, Japan could not for much longer continue to act as, or believe it was, a minor player in the international system. A member of the Upper House of the Japanese Diet, one often consulted and quoted on

Japan's international role, Shiina Motoo has often been called an "internationalized" Japanese. As he eloquently stated in an interview,

After 1960, for Japan it was like finding the entry to an expressway—we ran without thinking where to turn. The speed and safety of the expressway was the first priority. In fact, a big vehicle can be saved even if there is an accident. But now we have to define what our goal is and how to get to that route. I think that the bureaucrats, politicians and academia are all off the expressway, but they don't realize it.... But it is important to remember that someone else had built that expressway. What we in Japan have to realize is that there is something called "international public goods"—tangible and intangible ones. How to be a part of the participation of building international public goods is the task facing us now.[11]

Instead of the question being, "what will the United States do?" in Japan the question has become, "what will Japan do?" As evidenced by a plethora of books and scholarly articles published in Japan, the Japanese believe that the world is waiting for its "agenda." Did the United States feel this same sense of urgency in defining its role in world affairs following World War II, a time when its position vis-à-vis the rest of the world was unchallenged and its leadership assumed? World events dictated the role that the United States would play, and there was no need, nor did the United States have the luxury of time, for it to ponder what it believed its "world role" should be. Then again, following World War II American supremacy was acknowledged, and the United States was in a position to define its leadership role. But in the transition to the "new world order," Japan's expectation, whether real or imagined, that it must present to the international community some coherent sense of its role in world affairs is unprecedented. It is also unrealistic for the world to expect from Japan a dramatic shift from previous policy, or for the new policy to be totally coherent and without flaws.

One of the first indications of what role Japan would define for itself, and for its place in the international order, was advanced by Kuriyama Takakazu in a May 1990 article in the Ministry of Foreign Affairs journal, *Gaiko Forum*.[12] Subsequently translated into English as "New Directions for Japanese Foreign Policy in the Changing World of the 1990s: Making Active Contributions to the Creation of a New International Order," it was a position paper that for several months was often disseminated by Japanese officials to their foreign audiences. As such, it represented the "official" line of what Japan planned, wished, and or desired to be its role in the "new international order." But it was also significant for both its timing—just a few months after the collapse of the Berlin Wall—and for the bureaucratic standing of its author. At the time, Kuriyama was a career civil service official who had attained the position of administrative vice minister of foreign affairs, which was, for a non-political appointee, the highest post in the foreign affairs hierarchy. Subsequently he was appointed to what most agree is Japan's most important diplomatic post, that of ambassador to the United States. In any government, position papers are rarely an expression of personal reflection or opinion of their stated authors, but rather serve to "personalize" the views of the government and subject potential policy to discussion and debate. Although Kuriyama must have played a role in drafting this article, the intent of putting out "feelers" is doubtless no different for this document than those which came before, and as such it deserves our attention.

NEITHER A FACELESS NOR A HEGEMONIC FOREIGN POLICY

In his article, Kuriyama envisions a trilateral of international leadership among the United States, the European Union (EU) and Japan, all of which share democratic values and operate market economies, and notes that cooperation between these three leaders will be the "key to world peace and prosperity." Previously Japan took "maximum advantage of the international order maintained by the United States," and Kuriyama admits that Japan is no longer a minor power and must realize its position and accept its international responsibility. But he is very explicit that Japan's realization of its new role does not imply that it is, or seeks to become, a "superpower." As Kuriyama points out, perhaps it is merely coincidence that in 1922 the Washington Naval Conference fixed the tonnage of the naval forces of the United States, Britain, and Japan in the ratio of 5 to 5 to 3, the same ratio of the present day gross national products of the United States, the EU and Japan, respectively. It was with disastrous results that Japan tried to upset that previous balance, and argues that it must not upset that order again. The point is clear: relative to the other two members of the leadership coalition, Japan is in no position to lead, and it is only with cooperation with the other two members of this envisioned post–Cold War trilateral that Japan can "fulfill its responsibility in rule-making."

The components of Japan's international role as envisioned by Kuriyama were in fact nothing new, as they had been stated the previous March by then Prime Minister Kaifu in a speech before the Diet.[13] In the earlier version, it was proposed that Japan would participate in the creation of an international order that ensures peace and security, respects freedom and democracy, guarantees world prosperity through open economies, preserves an environment in which people can lead decent lives, and creates stable international relations based on dialogue and cooperation. Kuriyama defends this policy from charges that it is vague, idealistic, and in his words "faceless," by stating that fulfillment of each of these goals has a specific policy component for Japan. At the time, Kuriyama reiterated that none of the goals would be achieved by military means. "Japan has pledged never to become a military power, and in this sense, Japan's international role will be exclusively limited to non-military contributions." In this way, Kuriyama believes, Japan will be able to pursue "the diplomacy of a big power without appearing to be a big power." This was not the first time that Kuriyama used this phrase,[14] an unfortunate choice of words that for Japan's detractors reveals that Japan's true intentions are not all benevolent, but instead border on underhanded hegemony. Regardless of the accusations by Japan's Asian neighbors,[15] or those who sensed something sinister and conspiratorial behind Kuriyama's phrasing, it is very unlikely that Japan could become, or aspires to become, a true hegemon for two reasons.

First, even though notions of Japanese hegemony seemed to gain some merit with the declared "end of history," the world has not yet seen its last ideological struggle or last war. The Cold War was but a relative blip in the struggles of mankind, and in its place the longest lasting conflict has returned to center stage—that of

religious and ethnic intolerance. Although economics may indeed
supersede strategics in the new world order, the role of a military
power able to ensure world peace and stability will still be necessary. This role that was once played by the United States is
increasingly being assumed by the United Nations, and true hegemony would be impossible with military decisions reached by
compromise and agreement, and proclamations upheld by coali-
tions. To lend legitimacy to military action, as well as to share the
cost of military operations among the beneficiaries of those actions, it is doubtful that even the United States will be in a position
to any longer unilaterally engage in prolonged military conflict.
Nor is it certain that the American public would tolerate another
large-scale war unless it was clear that American efforts were part
of a "united" coalition of nations. With the breakup of the Soviet
Union, Japan's defense budget became the second largest in the
world by default. Since the end of the occupation, the percentage
of Japan's national budget allocated for defense has hovered
around 1% of gross national product, as compared to 5% for the
United States, and on paper this is a considerable sum because of
the scale of its economy. Realistically, however, this appropriation
of funds does not translate into military might, for the size of all
branches of Japan's Self Defense Forces (ground, air, and maritime) at present stands at approximately 85% of the authorized
limit of slightly more than 273,000 (153,000 of these ground
troops), a figure that pales in comparison to the PRC's estimated
three million troops. Training and quality of non-officer personnel
is also notoriously inadequate for a nation that would harbor any
plans of remilitarization, nor has the SDF ever been successful in
the postwar era in meeting its troop authorization limit. The quality of Japan's military equipment is on the whole modern, with
many weapons state of the art, as equipment acquisition accounts
for 27% of the 60% of Japan's defense budget allocated for supplies (compared to 40% allocated for personnel), figures that are
comparable to those of the United States. However, the quantity
and range of Japan's arsenal is limited by either budgetary restrictions, intention, or both. For example, Japan's Maritime Self Defense Force is largely a fleet of destroyers, submarines,
minesweepers, and support aircraft, characteristic of its mission as
a defense-oriented force, and is one notably without an aircraft

carrier and battleships, which are essentials of an offensively-minded military. Military watchdogs (both domestic and foreign) add to these factors that argue against a Japanese military hegemony. Each increase in Japan's defense budget, no matter how slight, or acquisition of new hardware, no matter how common, is routinely reported by the Japanese press and scrutinized (and criticized) by Japan's neighbors. It is difficult to believe that as long as the U.S.–Japan Security Treaty is maintained, Japan will become a military force with which to be reckoned.

Second, as Kuriyama notes, for all its economic strength, at present Japan is hardly the world's leading economy. Nor is it likely that with its level of economic resources Japan could, or would be willing to, single-handedly maintain the relatively smooth functioning of a global trading system, and absorb the losses when necessary, much like the United States did in the past. International politics, specifically the stability of its democratic allies, was a prime motive of U.S. willingness to assume the role of banker to the free world from the initiation of the Bretton Woods system in 1947, through cessation of the gold standard in 1971, to the Plaza Accords of 1985. As Robert Solomon notes, by assuming the role of creator of international wealth, the United States increased the level of its financial obligations to the rest of the world. "Of the $8.5 billion increase in world reserves in the years 1949–1959, the United States provided $7 billion through the increase in its liabilities to foreign monetary authorities."[16]

Even if Japan were to be driven by an ideology similar to, or different from, that which guided the economic benevolence of the United States for forty years, in an era of deepening economic interdependence among nations, the notion that international economic relations is a "zero-sum" game in which all the benefits accrue to one nation or a group of nations and the deficits are borne by their trading partners is becoming obsolete. As Aoyama Gakuin University professor Komiya Ryutaro writes, "It seldom occurs that a nation with a high national income per capita 'rules' or 'exploits' other countries through economic relations, without political power and military power."[17] Nor does it appear that one nation any longer has the economic means to support such an arrangement. All of the leading economic nations are saddled with varying degrees of national debt, and each is experiencing anemic economic growth. Additionally, even though the rhetoric of the day implies that regional trade agreements which give preferential treatment to signatory nations and discriminate against the exports of outsiders will lead to a more open economic system (a doubtful outcome, at best), there will be less incentive for any nation not granted preferential treatment in every arrangement to sacrifice its economic growth for those of others.

No trading nation, especially one as dependent on trade as Japan, wants to see its trading partners languishing in economic straits. And in the past, perhaps because the extent of economic problems in the United States was relatively manageable, Japan was traditionally reticent in criticizing U.S. economic policy. But as economic problems in the United States have grown in both depth and scope, Japan has not been reluctant to call on the United States to reduce its federal budget deficit and encourage investment in plant and equipment through a hodgepodge of suggestions including lower interest rates, higher taxes, and incentives for personal savings, among others. Perhaps as a foreign observer, Japan believes it can be an objective critic. Or as a member of the G-7 group of industrialized nations, whose individual economic well-being is dependent on the economic health of its counterparts, Japan believes that it has a right to offer advice. It may also have become more critical of U.S. fiscal and monetary policy (especially the former) being used as a political tool to gain elected office as a counterweight of U.S. criticism of a closed Japanese market. Whatever the reason for Japan's more vocal stance, Japanese government officials and business leaders realize that a depressed American economy will have repercussions in Japan, and it is only with U.S. sacrifice and effort that these problems will be rectified. This does not resemble hegemonic thinking. Rather, it demonstrates Japan's concern for an ally, without whose cooperation it would be weakened.

Of course there is an unmeasurable factor that weighs against Japan becoming the world's next hegemon, but it is perhaps the most important factor of all—that of will. For what reason would Japan be willing to become the world's next hegemon? And on the other hand, how willing would the rest of the world be to see Japan in such a position? Japan has not yet demonstrated a willingness to be the sole leader of the world, and it perhaps never will during our lifetimes. As outlined in Kuriyama's article, Japan will become both a leader and a follower, a consultant as well as an initiator. In what way, and how effectively, has Japan pursued this new policy? And to what extent is this view of Japan's new "international role" shared by other Japanese?

Kuriyama's proposal is interesting for several reasons. First and foremost, it represents the first official statement of Japan's self-defined role in the post–Cold War world. Japan realized that the perverse sense of stability that accompanied the Cold War, which guaranteed its economic growth and a continued U.S.-backed defense commitment, had diminished. It was unlikely that conditions would ever again be so favorable for Japan. Second, Japan realized that in order to ensure its future prosperity, and to deflect criticism from abroad that it only benefited and never contributed to the guarantee of this system, its active participation in the creation of a post–Cold War international system was essential. Third, although Japan realizes the limitations of its ability to contribute to the construction and stability of the new international order (relative GNP, domestic difficulties, concerns from abroad of Japanese "hegemony"), its leaders understand that responsible leadership implies going beyond the pursuit of national interests and the maintenance and betterment of "public goods." In this regard, Kuriyama's appeal for Japan to willingly and not reluctantly accept a share of "world leadership" resembles that of an earlier American visionary, Harrison Brown.

A geochemist involved in the atomic bomb project at the University of Chicago's Institute for Nuclear Studies, Brown wrote most of his book *The Challenge of Man's Future*[18] with the white sand beaches of the island of Jamaica as a backdrop. Brown was no doubt captivated by his surroundings while reflective of his role in helping to create a weapon that threatened all that stood before him, if not man's survival itself. First published in 1954, and reprinted several times during the next thirty years, the book's thesis is that overpopulation and extermination of non-renewable resources are problems that face the world community, and it is up to those in the industrialized world (Brown specifically touted the United States) to find a solution. "A substantial fraction of humanity today," wrote Brown,

is behaving as if it were engaged in a contest to test nature's willingness to support humanity. . . . Man is rapidly creating a situation from which he will have increasing difficulty extricating himself. . . . [but] it is within the range of his ability to choose what the changes will be, and how the resources at his disposal will be used—or abused—in the common victory—or ignominious surrender of mankind.[19]

It is interesting to note that although Brown's predictions are dire, he does hold out some degree of hope for the survival of the human race. Writing shortly after the Allied Occupation of Japan, his foresight for Japan was less than positive, however.

Today Japan is confined once again to her home islands, and the pressure of her population is now far greater than it was prior to World War II. She must import a substantial portion of her food and raw materials, yet she is cut off from many of her sources of supply. In the long run her situation is unstable in the extreme, and it is highly likely that serious trouble lies ahead. The Japanese now express the desire to live in peace with other nations, but as time goes on and the pressures become still more intense, it is likely that they will attempt again to extend their area to the point where they can attain some measure of self-sufficiency.[20]

Whether the extent of Japan's more independent foreign policy will be to the extreme predicted by Brown is a matter better left to the pundits and prognosticators. What is interesting to note, however, is that Kuriyama's article mirrors Brown's book in its realization that international responsibility implies global vision and acceptance of global problems. It allows for neither maintenance of a problem-plagued status quo nor consistent pursuit of a parochial, national interest. Rather, genuine acceptance of international responsibility implies that the national interest will be realized only as a corollary of the solution of problems that are not confined to national borders, not as the desired goal driving the process. This is distinct from purely humanitarian gestures, from which the initiator may in the end also derive some national benefit. Humanitarianism is an infrequent, oftentimes stopgap measure usually driven by unforeseen disaster, and not a basis around which to construct foreign policy. International responsibility, on the other hand, is. The potential disasters are before us, and the solutions require both effort and commitment. In the end, perhaps in the unimaginable distant future, the national interest may benefit; but in the meantime, by shifting resources to problems that are international in scope, the national interest will suffer. This is the basis of accepting international responsibility, and the challenge that faces Japan. In the words of Yoshino Bunroku, "All in all, all democratic nations have their own weaknesses. The big question is how do we consolidate them?"[21]

IMAGES OF GILD

Except for a brief mention that "in the security area outside of the framework of the Japan–U.S. Security Treaty, Japan will fulfill its responsibilities through non-military means," security concerns are conspicuously absent in Kuriyama's proposal. Perhaps this is because, as Kuriyama states, "even though a major nation, Japan has pledged never to become a military power, and in this sense, Japan's international role will be exclusively limited to non-military contributions."[22] It could be argued that failure to mention military matters, except in the very broad sense of highlighting the Security Treaty's three roles of deterrence, dialogue, and a framework for stability of the Asia-Pacific, was a conscious effort by the Japanese government to avoid creating concern both within Japan and from abroad that Japan is harboring aspirations of remilitarization, which does not appear to be the case. It may also have been Kuriyama's wish to stay clear of the debate over constitutional interpretation which, never far below the surface in Japan, is most often revived in connection with the role of Japan's Self Defense Forces (SDF). The conundrum of what constitutes a "self defense" force, and the issue of whether or not that force can be assigned to overseas duty, was the focus of both parliamentary and public debate during the Persian Gulf War of 1991.

By skirting the security issue, for a paper that is intended to express the "new directions" of Japanese foreign policy, Kuriyama's contribution is clearly incomplete. Whether intentionally or unwittingly, the article understates Japan's self-defense role, the position of United States Forces in Japan (USFJ), and Japan's participation in international peacekeeping efforts. Yet these points, especially the third, are at the heart of the debate in Japan between pacifism on the one hand and realism on the other. Until the debate precipitated by the Persian Gulf War, with criticism from abroad (again, that of the United States was most severe and taken most to heart) leaving no alternative to tackling the issue head-on, the Japanese government had been constrained in its ability to commit forces overseas—even in the name of "peace-keeping" operations—because of the widely held beliefs among the public that peace is an ideal state that should not need to be "kept" or maintained to exist, and anything short of peace implies some state of war. This peace-war dichotomy therefore challenged the concept of "peacekeeping" operations, which according to Kuriyama's vision of a "harmonious" role for Japan, would be impossible. How could Japan *actively* contribute "to the mitigation of international tensions and to the settlement of regional conflicts"[23] while maintaining a "harmonious" role? The inevitable conflict in Japan between domestic public opinion and international pressure would necessitate a change of the former or an avoidance of the latter, and it was only a matter of time before one would win out.

Just three months after the publication of Kuriyama's article, Iraqi forces invaded Kuwait. While the United States formed a coalition of allied fighting forces to drive the Iraqi troops from Kuwait, in the name of upholding what was portrayed as a democratic government's legitimate claim to rule, Japan's absence in the form of fighting forces was all too glaring for many of the coalition participants. Japan relies on the nations of the Persian Gulf for 70% of its oil imports, and it was not long before many of the allied nations who assembled troops in Saudi Arabia to fight for some combination of democracy and oil wondered if they were not actually fighting for a steady supply of oil for Japan, which did not seem appreciative of the allied effort. Citing two of a stream of public opinion polls conducted in Japan at that time, Jeffrey Garten indicates in his book *A Cold Peace* that "a survey conducted by the *Nihon Keizai Shinbun* in November 1990 showed nearly 70 percent of the Japanese polled believed that the use of force in the Gulf was not justified under any circumstances. Three months later, surveys showed that only a third of the people approved of Japan's making any financial contribution to the allied effort."[24]

Arguing that they were constrained by the limits of military participation as stated in their constitution, Japanese officials provided a total of $11 billion in financial support for the operations.

Save for the amounts disbursed by the United States, Kuwait, and Saudi Arabia, in monetary terms the Japanese contribution was the most significant. Yet from those in the Japanese government to the person on the street, most believed that the world viewed Japan as selfishly content with leaving the fighting to other nations, while merely "writing a check" for its share of the operation. In this light, many Japanese argued that their contributions to this allied military effort against Iraq, and subsequent efforts if they were to come to be, would never be appreciated by the international community. To a large extent the Japanese view was accurate. The Japanese media enlightened the public that Japan's name was missing from a public "thank you" advertisement placed in the *New York Times* from the reinstated government of Kuwait to those nations that had participated in the international effort, while a monument constructed in Kuwait some months later for the same purpose of "appreciation" flew the flags of all coalition nations except for that of Japan.[25] The Japanese felt slighted, but realized the issue of their participation in international "peacekeeping operations" (which even in Japan took the abbreviation PKO) would have to be addressed.

For Japan, the Gulf War brought the conflict of prioritization between domestic politics and foreign policy into focus. Because of a lack of both legislation allowing it or precedent condoning it, Japan was hindered in its ability to contribute anything but financial support and limited supplies to the Allied effort against Iraq. As noted, Japan was criticized from abroad for contributing funds and ultimately encouragement, but not personnel, even though the financial pledge was significant. That was to be expected, even if the intensity of the reaction against Japan was not. But for Japan, the Gulf War was even more significant in that the diplomatic sequence of events which preceded the military operation—the discussion and debate, and the self-determined inability of the United States to take action until a UN resolution authorizing a military response was passed—convinced the Japanese public and government officials alike that the United Nations would from that point forward play a larger role in the course of events in the new world order. In short, the Gulf War created a subsequent rise in the stock of effectiveness of the UN, and more than ever Japan wanted a piece of the action. At the time, Japan felt shut out from

Table 2.1
Assessments for UN Member Nations, 1994 (as a percentage of total assessments)

United States	25.00%
Japan	12.45%
Russian Federation	6.71%
Germany	8.93%
France	6.00%
United Kingdom	5.02%
PRC	0.77%

Source: United Nations Handbook, 1994 (Wellington, New Zealand: Ministry of Foreign Affairs and Trade, 1994), pp. 281–282.

the inner circle of that process, and many of its leaders believed that criticism against their response could have been forestalled had they known earlier what would be expected of their nation, as well as be in a better position to predict when and in what way those expectations would change. The way to prevent a repeat of that embarrassing scenario was clear: inclusion among the world's decision-making elite, represented by a permanent seat on the UN Security Council. Besides bringing Japan closer to the formulation of policy, the position would also bring with it prestige in the world community and acknowledgment of Japan's stature as one of the world's major powers, even if this was already assumed. But Japan doesn't want an "assumption," it wants recognition. As the second largest donor of funds to the UN budget (see Table 2.1), Japan believes its aspirations for the post are not without merit.

Unlike the U.S. public's commonly held perception of the organization, which, whether or not valid, was generally one of ineffectiveness and frequently disregarded proclamations until the war against Iraq, the UN has traditionally held a somewhat gilded image among the Japanese as a forum where the fruits of negotiation and consultation can avoid the fatalities of armed irrationality. Largely for this reason, although initially the Japanese public was adamantly opposed to the thought of sending a Japanese contingent abroad (whether or not that contingent would be members of the Self Defense Forces), the PKO bill's stipulation that Japanese forces would only operate under the auspices of UN command, and especially that they would play a non-combatant role, were made more acceptable to the Japanese public. In the opinion of Sato Hideo,

In the area of security, the UN will—and already has, if you look at the Gulf War—play a greater role. For this reason, Japan should increase its association with the UN and its military activities. In this way, Japan can still maintain its security interests without arousing foreign hyper-sensitivity or Japanese public opinion.[26]

But even with Japan's sincerity and long-held belief in the effectiveness of the organization, its vision of the UN becoming a greater force in future dispute settlement and peace efforts, and even with its relatively significant level of funding, what is the likelihood of Japan assuming a permanent member post? In the words of Henry Kissinger, this scenario would open a "whole can of worms"[27] because of the likely (if not equally legitimate) demands by Germany that it, too, be given a seat. And Germany's request would likely be the first of several. As Sato Seizaburo analyzed the situation,

If Japan is given a permanent seat, the countries in the South [developing nations] will be unhappy. The Northern [developed nations] representation to the Security Council will be overwhelming if both Germany and Japan are extended these seats. Of course, among these nations of the South, India and Brazil are obvious candidates, but then we would have none from Africa, and none from the Middle East. Nigeria and Egypt might be the choices to represent these regions. But if we have Egypt, then Iran will protest that Egypt is not an Islamic nation, and Islamic nations have to be represented. But if we have more than 10 with veto power, the system will never work. We would have to eliminate the entire veto system and introduce a majority decision or 2/3 majority system or something like that. And then the whole structure of the UN will have changed. But of course, no existing permanent members are willing to agree on that proposal.[28]

The possibility of Japan becoming a permanent member of the UN Security Council thus becomes a conflict over whether Japan should be given a permanent member seat, and whether, because of other considerations (most notably the composition of the

Council), it can. Japan has clearly made attainment of this position somewhat of a priority. The *Nihon Keizai Shinbun* reasoned that Japan's decision to send peacekeeping forces to Mozambique, a nation in which Japan has limited interests, would make its humanitarian pledge seem more legitimate, would deflect criticism that Japan's peacekeeping presence in Cambodia proves it is only interested in its regional role, and would "strengthen Japan's argument and help it realize its long cherished wish of Security Council membership."[29] However, some observers, like diplomatic historian Nishizaki Fumiko, point out that the movement for Japan's obtaining the position has largely come from within Japan, while it should come from other countries.[30]

Beyond the merits and complications of Japan's aspirations for permanent member status on the Security Council, the real issue is the extent to which the United Nations will assume a greater role in the post–Cold War world, as well as provide a forum and the framework for future collaboration on the monumental problems that face the world. In the post–Cold War period, we have seen an increase in both the responsibility of the UN and the frequency of requests for its participation in activities both old and new. Will this trend continue or is it an aberration, and what is the limit of the capability and intent of the powers given to the UN? Is the UN merely filling a void, playing the role of a "seat-warmer" until the new world order takes shape? We can speculate that if this were the case the decision to include Japan among the group of the world's political elite, as represented by the UN Security Council, would be a foregone conclusion, and though Japan's power relative to that of other members (both of the General Assembly and of the Security Council) would increase, the power of the organization itself would be nominal. In somewhat oversimplified terms, if other nations did not believe the role of the UN would at least resemble what it is now, if not increase, Japan's (and or Germany's) inclusion among the UN's decision-making elite would find no objection. Japan would be granted elite status in an organization that people believe would have restricted or insignificant powers, solely to appease Japan's wishes. Yet since there appears to be no indication of a diminshed role for the UN, nor any policy of appeasement for Japan, how long will Japan be willing to serve as the UN's second-leading financial contributor without realizing what it believes is its valid claim to be included among the organization's decision-making elite? Sato Seizaburo half-jokingly noted the similarities between Japan's position in the UN and the American Revolutionary War which was fought on the injustice of taxation without representation.[31] Japan's position, as well as that of Germany, has been endorsed by President Clinton and some other world leaders whose nations are not represented among the permanent members of the Security Council. But Clinton's pragmatism that inclusion of Japan and Germany may be the only acceptable quid pro quo to assure funding of UN operations (which not coincidentally often reflect U.S. policy) will not go unchallenged by the other permanent members, each for their own reasons. If the veto system were to be maintained with the addition of two more members, the power of last resort for the present members would not be affected, but their power relative to the two inductees would be diminished. On the one hand, the European contingent would gain relative to the other members by having three representatives, but on the other Germany would now be included in decisions that had once included only Britain and France. And with the sensitivity of China toward anything that resembles a hint of Japanese militarism, even if only routine military preparedness drills, it is unlikely that the Chinese would readily welcome Japan as an equal in decisions that involve committing international forces to areas of conflict.

IMAGES OF GUILE

One of the biggest weaknesses (perhaps liabilities is a better term) confronting Japan in its search for a new world role is the present state of upheaval, relative to the preceding thirty-eight years of near predictability, of its domestic politics. The Japanese were well aware that the Gulf War was not the first time that the world expected their nation to play a more visible role in what was termed "international peace keeping operations."[32] But it was the protracted domestic political debate over the issue, and attention given to domestic political scandal which sidetracked the peacekeeping operations legislation, that convinced many outside observers that Japan was not serious in its pledge to assume greater international responsibility. In short, it was suggested from abroad that Japanese leadership allowed the seemingly superfluous, day-to-day scandals of corrupt politicians to detract their attention from what should have been the more monumental task at hand—defining their nation's international role.

Coordination between domestic and foreign policies is an imperative that faces the leaders of all nations, but at times prioritization of one over the other is inevitable, if not essential. It is the degree to which these leaders are able to convince competing groups of their sincerity and interest in their concerns, whether the domestic electorate or the international community, and their follow-through on promises, that is the essence of the quality of "leadership." Those familiar with Japan's political system and recent political scandals would lament that Japan has in large part been paralyzed from playing a larger role in the international sphere by the turmoil of its domestic politics, and by a low level of "leadership" among its elected officials.

It was because of this lack of leadership and commitment by politicians to what Shiina Motoo called "international public goods" that debate stalled on legislation which would allow participation of Japanese Self Defense Forces personnel in UN peacekeeping operations. There was also the question of the constitutionality of allowing Self Defense Forces personnel to participate in international efforts, and in the future, many Japanese believe, Japan's constitution may have to be amended to account for this new role. Yet even though from an international perspective the Japanese Diet of 1992 may be remembered for the peacekeeping operations bill, from a domestic perspective it will be remembered for the testimony over political scandal. Ultimately, even on issues of Japan's accepting or assuming a larger international role, it may be the latter which proves to have a greater overall influence. Diet sessions through the summer and fall of 1992 were initially distracted and then dominated by testimony over unfolding domestic political scandal, notably the Sagawa Kyubin bribery investigation which implicated the former general secretary of the ruling Liberal Democratic Party, Kanemaru Shin, and the charges of corruption and links to organized crime figures that faced former Prime Minister Takeshita Noboru. After an unsuccessful initial attempt at passage of the bill, a compromise bill eventually earned the endorsement of other centrist parties, and the peacekeeping operations law was enacted.

Was it possible that legislation which would ultimately become the PKO law was held up for as long as it was because Japan truly did not want it, and was instead once again responding to the demands of a foreign critic? This question was posed to Tokyo University Professor Tanaka Akihiko, who responded that there was

a sense of frustration that many LDP members of the Diet felt against the inability of Japan not being able to respond promptly in the Gulf Crisis. And on the part of the government—the Ministry of Foreign Affairs—there was a clear understanding that without certain legal mechanisms you can't do anything at the time of crisis. . . . I think that in Japan there was, and has been, an increase of a genuine desire to play at least some responsible role in international affairs, and the PKO law reflects this. But you know, it is very difficult to distinguish between this feeling of international contribution and how much was a feeling of U.S. placation. Even though the original starting point may have been to pay lip service to the United States, isn't it the nature of humans to believe in the message if you constantly repeat it?[33]

Because of the delay in passing the legislation, what genuinely may have been a Japanese initiative at the outset quickly appeared to be another reactionist response by Japan. It is clear that the delay was in no small measure attributable to a lack of leadership among politicians, especially then Prime Minister Kaifu. Kaifu was selected for the prime minister post by Liberal Democratic Party (LDP) leaders for his clean image in the wake of the Recruit scandal, a money for influence scandal which implicated most of the LDP's upper ranks and saw the party's loss of its majority in the 1989 election for the Upper House of the Diet. A member of the LDP's smallest faction, Kaifu's most significant leadership experience prior to being tabbed prime minister was a one-term appointment as minister of education. As prime minister, he was popular among the public for the image of honesty that he evoked, but behind the scenes it was assumed that he was a pawn of LDP party bosses. From the beginning, Kaifu's allegiance to a relatively insignificant faction (the Komoto faction) did not suggest that he would have much of a political position from which to bargain with members of other factions. Nor did the reputation of the Komoto faction as one not known for its ability to raise funds (or a need to raise funds for that matter, as all expenses are bankrolled by shipping magnate Komoto Toshio) endear Kaifu to other politicians for whom raising money for the faction, and for themselves, is a necessity of electoral survival. But even if the prime minister had hailed from the largest faction, it is uncertain that the legislation would easily have been pushed through the Diet. Simply put, the attributes or requisites of leadership among politicians in Japan may not resemble those found in other nations.

For the past several decades, a message propagated by the Japanese government has been the record of Japan's postwar economic achievement, and as long as economic growth continued, the LDP had always done its part to link this economic success with its tenure in office. As noted, for all but nine months of the postwar period (and even then in a climate of spiraling inflation and labor demands shortly after the war), the reins of government at the national level have been controlled by conservatives. And until creation of the LDP in 1955, which itself was a concerned response by business leaders to the unification of left-wing parties into the Japan Socialist Party less than a week earlier, national politics was dominated by the LDP's predecessors, the Liberal Party and the Democratic Party. But in Japan, national politics is also very much local politics. With the possible exception of former Prime Minister Nakasone Yasuhiro, limited have been the careers of politicians who have aspired to be "national" leaders, let alone international statesmen, and the number of either group who have succeeded is also limited. In short, Japanese politics could be called the ultimate in pork-barrel democracy, in which representatives to the national legislature (Diet) realize that meeting the local concerns of their constituents will return them to office, while dabbling in "national agenda" or "international role" debates may not.

On his way to the post of prime minister, and continuing the practice after he had "arrived," Tanaka Kakuei was legendary for seeing to it that his constituents in rural Niigata were provided with perks that would develop the region, and virtually assure his reelection. Tanaka's deftness in earmarking substantial funds for public works projects in his home district was unmatched, the most elaborate of which is the system of hot steam pipes that runs under the streets of the city. Niigata is famous for its snowfall, which would be plentiful enough to bury telephone poles anywhere else. Courtesy of its favorite son, however, the city has been blessed with the most efficient means of snow removal and ice prevention employed by man. But there are other pork barrel projects more visible than subterranean steam pipes. Perhaps the most extensive, and that which changed the image of Niigata as a rural outback, was the city's designation as a stop along the route of Japan's bullet train, which created hundreds of jobs and eventually gave birth to a "station town."

The most powerful member of the ruling LDP at that time, a skilled fund raiser, and gifted with a memory as sharp as a tack, Tanaka served as prime minister in the early 1970s, coincidentally corresponding to Richard Nixon's second term as U.S. President. The coincidence is the near simultaneous but unrelated fall from grace of both politicians, but all similarities end there. In 1974, Tanaka was forced to resign as prime minister following accusations tht he had personally benefitted from questionable land and financial dealings. Foremost among the allegations was that Tanaka's insider knowledge allowed companies in which he had an interest to purchase tracts of land that were guaranteed to appreciate in value because of their proximity to as-of-then unannounced government projects and expansion of the bullet train system.

But a more far-reaching scandal was revealed during a subcommittee hearing of the U.S. Senate Foreign Relations Committee in 1976. In what was to become known as the "Lockheed Scandal," officials of the U.S. aircraft manufacturer testified that they had transferred funds to Japanese politicians in 1972 and 1973 in return for their influence in awarding Lockheed a contract to supply twenty-one commercial aircraft to Japan's largest domestic carrier, All Nippon Airways (ANA). Tanaka was accused of accepting ¥500 million (approximately $2 million at the time), and his case plodded through Japan's legal system until he was found guilty of bribery in 1983. Although the LDP did suffer somewhat at the ballot box from the repercussions of Tanaka's dealings, most notably in the Lower House election of 1976, shortly after news of the transaction broke, and again in 1983, which was dubbed by Japan's press as the "Tanaka Verdict Election," the effects were not as pronounced as they were for Nixon and the Republican Party following the Watergate hearings. Unlike Nixon's case, however, the Lockheed Scandal did not permanently end the political career of Tanaka. Although he was forced to resign from the LDP, Tanaka was returned to the Lower House in 1983 as an independent, thanks to a record turnout of constituents in his home district, which resulted in a record margin of victory over his opponents. And even though he was no longer a member of the LDP, the Tanaka faction remained the largest and most influential faction in the Diet, with Tanaka exerting a significant role in both policy matters and the selection of Japan's prime ministers, up to and including Prime Minister Nakasone Yasuhiro in 1982. As subsequent events would prove, the Lockheed scandal would not be the last political scandal to confront the Japanese electorate.

Similar to this question of the leadership ability of Japanese elected officials, Japanese commentators have often remarked that Japan is a nation of first-rate economics and third-rate politics. While there is some measure of truth to every slogan, the representation has been more applicable to Japan's foreign politics than to its domestic politics. The ruling party may have been confronted by international challenges in the past to which it was unprepared—or unable—to respond, but on the domestic front, despite the charges of (and convictions) for political corruption, it was always a well-oiled-machine. Until July 1993, for all but nine months since the end of World War II, Japanese politics had been dominated at the national level by the LDP. Its near virtual control over the policymaking process led to charges of elitism and corruption, as many voters began to feel removed from their representatives. But there appeared to be no alternative to the political influence of the LDP. The efficiency and electoral success of the LDP was even more overwhelming when considering the virtual ineptitude of the opposition parties, most notably the SDPJ, which traditionally have been unable to capitalize on the LDP's lapses of political integrity. Recently, however, the oil on the LDP machine has seemed to lose some of its viscosity, while the role of the "opposition" parties has taken on a new face.

The national election held in July 1993 was anticipated as a "sea change" in Japanese domestic politics, for there was near universal agreement that the LDP would be unable to maintain its majority in the Lower House of the Diet. This was a significant prediction since political power at the national level is largely concentrated in this body, and it has served as the primary source of prime minister candidates. The predictions were not without justification. As already noted, LDP party bosses, most notably former Prime Minister Takeshita and former party chairman Kanemaru Shin, were indicted for their roles in two separate but equally complicated plots involving a trucking company, members of the underworld, and undeclared political contributions. But these two scandals were different than others which came before them for two main reasons. Both the brazenness of the accused, and the media coverage of everything from the trivial to the speculative, were unprecedented. First, forced by subpoena to testify before the Diet and national television (even if Japanese law only allows a still photograph of accused public officials to be shown, rather than the live footage of one possibly uncomposed), Takeshita denied paying off gangsters to cease their methodical campaign against his reelection bid. Eventually his testimony was proven false, but he added insult to injury by refusing to resign his Diet seat. Previously, Japanese politicians convicted (and sometimes only accused) of wrongdoing have made the first move in resigning, but Takeshita—a former prime minister no less— broke precedent. For days, Takeshita's face and accompanying testimony were broadcast in nearly every home, and editorials criticized his audacity.

The case of Kanemaru was perhaps even more intriguing, and it, too, differed from previous political scandals. Sometimes referred to as "the Don," and other times simply called the "king maker" of Japanese politicians, Kanemaru was reputedly the largest recipient of illegal funds from one of Japan's several delivery companies. It was alleged that he had received approximately $5 million from Sagawa Kyubin, an allegation which he denied and subsequently recanted. After confining himself to a hospital for more than two weeks for eye surgery, and thus avoiding testimony, Kanemaru testified that he distributed the money among LDP politicians to be used for their reelection campaigns. Accused of tax evasion, Kanemaru—the public servant with a low six-figure income (U.S.)—was arrested when a search of his estimated $10 million home in one of Tokyo's elite districts revealed a secret room filled with cash, gold, and stock certificates. Kanemaru's troubles became an all-consuming media event, as news cameras were staked out at his home both morning and night, and television viewers watched as Kanemaru's Mercedes limousine drove in and out of his brick mansion which, viewers were often reminded, was his second home. His bail, set at the equivalent of $2.5 million, was the highest ever set for an accused in Japan, and he paid it in cash. Though the accusations of 1992 tainted fewer politicians than the Recruit scandal of 1989, by this time, it seemed, the public had reached its limit of corruption tolerance. These two scandals, with their intricate plots, revelations, intrigue, and the sense of public contempt for politicians that they helped reinforce, were only the crust of the subsequent political upheaval that was to face Japan and the LDP. Their timing also lent credence to a ground swell of public opinion that believed the LDP was not serious in its pledge of undertaking "political reform," even though articulation of what would constitute reform was not yet clear.

Japanese are generally risk-averse, and when given the chance to "sweep out" corruption in politics through the ballot box, voters have not expressed the same vote-for-change attitude to the extent that is common among their American counterparts. Japanese are similar to Americans in the generally low level of respect that they hold for politicians,[34] but even if many U.S. voters express distrust or suspicion of their elected officials, politicians are routinely held by the American electorate to a higher moral standard than the American public applies to itself. If that standard is violated, or is merely perceived by the voter to have been violated, often the politician has spent his or her last term in office, regardless of the track record. Japanese have generally been more tolerant and pragmatic relative to Americans in the extent to which they assume corruption is an inevitable outgrowth of politics, and though they do not encourage the dishonesty of their elected officials, there is a distinction between whether the politician was corrupt for personal aggrandizement on the one hand or for the benefit of the constituency on the other. Japan is a

society in which seniority and experience are the primary deter-
minants of power, and the political system, as an extension of that
society, reflects many of the same attributes and priorities. There
are a host of election campaign laws in Japan, and specified limits
regarding political contributions, but the latter are routinely violated, as we will see. If an incumbent raises or accepts funds for
a reelection campaign in a less-than-legitimate way and then wins
reelection, not only will his or her rank and power rise within the
party hierarchy, but the payoff for the district will also likely increase. And as long as the representative can continue to deliver
to the home district, constituents will be more accepting of corruption than if the politician is perceived as breaking a law that
will accrue more of a benefit (or the sole benefit) to the politician
and not to his or her district. This was the case with the Recruit
scandal, in which politicians from the LDP and to a lesser extent
the SDPJ were implicated in accepting shares of a company before
its stock was publicly traded (which is a violation of securities
control laws in both Japan and the United States). The Recruit
scandal was regarded as one of three reasons, if not the main
reason, for the LDP's defeat in the 1989 Upper House election.
Similarly, the Sagawa Kyubin scandal was also one reason for the
LDP's loss of its majority in the Lower House—and thus the reins
of government—in the election of July 1993.

In Japan, massive amounts of money—which is fertile ground
for massive amounts of corruption and scandal—have always had
to be raised for two reasons. First, the allocation in the national
budget for support staff and office space in the representative's
district is relatively meager, especially by American standards.
This means that a representative aspiring to reelection must meet
the expenses for anything but the bare minimum of outward ap-
pearances of representation out of his or her own pocket. There
are also constituents' expectations that their representative attend
or acknowledge the funerals, weddings, and rites-of-passage
events of anyone living in the district, and the representative is
practically obliged by social-turned-political custom to present a
monetary gift expressing anything from celebration to bereave-
ment (with the amount varying depending on the standing of the
constituent).

But these demands for funds are superficial compared to what

many believe was the real source for money-seeking among politicians: the institutional explanation, which attributed most of the
problems to Japan's electoral system of multimember districting.
Until legislation that addressed redistricting was approved by the
Lower House of the Diet in November 1994, all electoral districts
except one were represented by more than one politician, and
some by as many as six. This led to the awkward situation of party
mates having to run against each other, giving rise to factions
within parties, and the necessity of political contributions to win
the favor of faction bosses. The result was a progression of money-
for-influence scandals as favor seekers on the outside, well know-
ing that money is the lifeblood of a politician's career, used access
to funds as a means to have their demands considered in the political arena via a politician (or several politicians), and unwittingly
onto the front page of newspapers. Corruption became an assumed consequence of a multimember district electoral system for
national representatives. Although corruption makes for good
press and interesting reading, and is the easiest to identify as a
cause of the LDP's downfall, there were other factors that suggested the LDP would have nevertheless had a difficult time maintaining its Diet majority.

First, as mentioned, Japanese electoral pragmatism in large
measure has been intertwined with the notion, largely advanced
by the LDP, that Japan's economic success has been linked to
LDP leadership. This success, it was suggested, would be threatened with an unproven, and possibly anti-business, opposition
party in power. Whether or not there was a indeed a correlation
between the LDP's longevity in office and Japan's rate of economic growth is impossible to determine. But when Japan's "economic bubble" burst in the early 1990s and Japan faced its first
prolonged recession since 1974, this justification for reelecting the
LDP not only lost its legitimacy, but came back to haunt the LDP
when government initiative could not as easily stimulate an economic recovery as it claimed to have engineered economic growth.

The second reason for the LDP's electoral defeat was the decision by some of its most influential younger generation leaders
to break away from a party system in which rewards were based
primarily on seniority (and thus age), and in which innovation and
charisma were shunned in favor of the status quo. It is true that

the LDP has been remarkably adept at broadening the base of its support from a party dominated by rural, agrarian interests and those of big business to urban regions, a traditional stronghold of progressive parties. But even the most steadfast supporter of the LDP must admit their party's success has been attributable as much to the lack of a viable opposition party as it has to the vision of the LDP. At least in appearance, the formation of new political parties by former LDP loyalists represented a desire to find an alternative to the LDP. Their leaders called for electoral reform and an end to money politics, but even these parties have their LDP connections. More significantly, whatever their party or faction identification, these politicians realize better than anyone that votes are won on domestic issues, not by honing the skills necessary for, or fostering one's aspirations of, statesmanship in the international arena. Even though it lost its majority in the 1993 election, the LDP is still the most powerful party in the Lower House. The party which lost the most support was the SDPJ, which in the past was always the strongest of the opposition parties. The biggest winners were the "new" opposition parties, the Japan New Party, and the Japan Renewal Party, the latter of which is comprised of former members of Tanaka's faction, among others. With the loss of the LDP Diet majority, it appears that domestic politics will occupy center stage in the trade-off between national and international priorities as newly formed parties vie for their claim of leadership, and the LDP fights to minimize its losses.

Despite their relative success in the 1993 elections, the Japan New Party and the Japan Renewal Party were disbanded in the fall of 1994, and joined forces with other minor parties and parliamentary groups to create a "new" political party. With former Prime Minister Kaifu as its first leader, the Shinshinto (literally, "New Frontier Party") was formed in late 1994 as an opposition party to the LDP. Unification of these smaller parties under one diverse, disjointed party banner that, at least publicly, bases its existence on an anti–LDP line has propelled Shinshinto to the status of primary opposition party in the Diet, subsequently intensifying the always latent calls by SDPJ party members that their ideologically divided party disband. Whether the creation of the Shinshinto will ultimately lead to the breakup of the SDPJ remains to be seen, and even then the correlation may not be clear. Domestically, in the short term it can be expected that the Japanese voter will continue to witness the rise and demise of political parties whose existence is based more on idealism, political faddishness, and anti–LDP rhetoric than on realistic, attainable goals. In the long term, voters may even see the rise of a new two-party system in Japan (contingent, of course, on the survivability of the Shinshinto or its reconstituted successors), with the eventual ruling and opposition parties less opposed in their policies and prescriptions than was the case for thirty-eight years, thereby representing acceptable choice for the risk-averse Japanese voter.

But there are also two possible implications of the "sea-change" 1993 election for Japan's role in the international community. The first is that with this diffusion of domestic political power, it is doubtful that in the short term Japan will be in as favorable a position as before to conclude significant agreements with the rest of the world or find its leaders occupied with anything but the domestic power struggle. The second suggests that although in the short term change may be unlikely, the stage has been set for Japan to assume a new role in international affairs with the rise of a new generation of politicians, and the dispersion of power away from an older generation that was unwilling to change or assume greater leadership in world affairs. Japan's "new" leaders are nevertheless still in the minority, and for the most part they were elected mainly on domestic issues. Even if this latter scenario is realized, it remains to be seen whether they will have the ability to consolidate power, and then if they will be able to direct an even greater degree of effort than in the past to this notion of international leadership. In the words of Okamoto Yukio, himself a member of Japan's Ministry of Foreign Affairs for twenty years,

In the government there is often a feeling of "why should I get involved?" The Ministry of Foreign Affairs is responsible for the day-to-day workings of diplomacy, and is not in a position to propose major changes in Japan's foreign policy. These major breaks will require political initiative.[35]

NOTES

1. Interview, Yoshino Bunroku, November 19, 1992.
2. Characteristic of this argument was Tahara Soichiro, *"Nichibei an-*

pojoyaku wa ippotekini haki sareru [The U.S.–Japan Security Treaty Will Be Abrogated Unilaterally]," *Ushio*, January 1990.

3. For representative writings on requests for Japan to increase its patrolling of waters around the Japanese islands, see the *New York Times*, May 8, 1991, p. 1, in which it was stated that the United States wanted Japan to increase "antisubmarine warfare patrols and naval patrolling and surveillance of Soviet naval movements in the Sea of Japan"; on requests for Japan to increase the percentage of its national budget targeted for defense, see the *New York Times*, January 14, 1981, p. A6, which noted that the United States sought an 11% increase in Japanese defense expenditures; on the issue of host nation support, see U.S. House of Representatives, *Report of the Defense Burdensharing Panel of the Committee on Armed Services*, August 1988, which also discusses the self-defense responsibilities requested of Japan.

4. U.S. House of Representatives, *Report of the Defense Burdensharing Panel of the Committee on Armed Services*, pp. 8–9.

5. *Nihon Keizai Shinbun*, May 7, 1989, p. 2.

6. Sato Seizaburo is among the most "pro-American" scholars in Japan, and has always been an outspoken advocate of Japan "doing whatever it takes" to continue its alliance with the United States. Although published before the "official" ending of the Cold War, see Sato Seizaburo, "Imakoso nichibei domei no kyoka o [Now is the Time to Strengthen the U.S.–Japan Alliance]," *Chuo Koron*, June 1988, pp. 110–119, in which he states that Japan must display a "self-sacrificing initiative" in opening its markets to foreign goods (p. 119); and also "Jidaino henka ga yori kyokona domei o motomeru [Changes in the Times Call for Still Stronger Alliance]," *Chuo Koron*, March 1990, pp. 125–134.

7. Opposition to the treaty had been an ideological pillar for the Japan Socialist Party since its founding in 1955, but their calls for abrogation changed to "continuation with simultaneous review," as stated by then party chairwoman Doi Takako. See *Asahi Shinbun*, July 24, 1989 (evening edition), p. 2, for Doi's position.

8. The *Sankei Shinbun* (February 11, 1990, p. 2) published an editorial that was critical of the JSP's position, and in the end Doi changed her position somewhat by suggesting the military aspects of the treaty be replaced with a Japan–U.S. Peace and Friendship Treaty. See *Asahi Shinbun*, July 6, 1990, p. 2.

9. Interview, Kuroda Makoto, November 27, 1992.

10. Interview, Sato Hideo, November 17, 1992.

11. Interview, Shiina Motoo, November 19, 1992.

12. Kuriyama Takakazu, "Gekido 90 nendai to nihon gaiko no shintenkai [The Great Upheaval of the Nineties and Japan's New Diplomacy]," *Gaiko Forum*, May 1990.

13. For the transcript of Kaifu's speech, see *Asahi Shinbun*, March 2, 1990 (evening edition), p. 3. It is interesting to note that even though Kaifu's Diet speech preceded the *Gaiko Forum* article by Kuriyama, similar proposals for a more global oriented, "new look" diplomacy that would address problems such as the environment, drug trafficking, and terrorism, were unveiled earlier in the year in a speech by Kuriyama, as summarized in a *Tokyo Shinbun* article, January 23, 1990, p. 2.

14. See the *Tokyo Shinbun* article mentioned in note 13, above.

15. Allan Whiting's *China Eyes Japan* (Berkeley: University of California Press, 1989) is one of several works that examines the issue of Japanese hegemony and the basis for Chinese claims.

16. Robert Solomon, *The International Monetary System, 1945–1981* (New York: Harper and Row, 1982), p. 31.

17. This point is made by Komiya Ryutaro, 'Nihon kyoiron' no meimo [The Fallacy of the 'Japan Is a Threat' Argument]," *Chuo Koron*, January 1991, p. 70.

18. Harrison Brown, *The Challenge of Man's Future: An Inquiry Concerning the Condition of Man During the Years that Lie Ahead* (Boulder, CO: Westview Press, 1954).

19. Ibid., p. 221.

20. Ibid., p. 235.

21. Interview, Yoshino Bunroku, November 19, 1992.

22. Kuriyama Takakazu, *New Directions for Japanese Foreign Policy in the Changing World of the 1990s* (Tokyo: Ministry of Foreign Affairs, 1990), pp. 18–19.

23. See Kuriyama, "Gekido 90 nendai to nihon gaiko no shintenaki," p. 19; translated version, p. 21.

24. Jeffrey E. Garten, *A Cold Peace* (New York: Times Books, 1993), pp. 164–165.

25. This issue was so "popularized" that a picture of the monument, sans Japanese flag, was even published in a woman's magazine better known for fashion and makeup advice than for political commentary. See "Bush kusen no amerika daitoryosen. Matamata chutoga kinakusakunatte kita! [Bush's Hard Fight in the American Presidential Election. Once Again, Something Smells in the Middle East!]," *More*, December 1992, p. 405.

26. Interview, Sato Hideo, November 17, 1992.

27. Henry Kissinger, "Kissinger-Nakasone Forum," Tokyo, October 22, 1992.

28. Interview, Sato Seizaburo, October 27, 1992.

29. *Nihon Keizai Shinbun*, March 27, 1993, p. 2.

30. Interview, Nishizaki Fumiko, October 6, 1992.

31. Interview, Sato Seizaburo, October 27, 1992.

32. The issue first received serious attention, and caused debate among government officials and politicians, in connection with the Iran-Iraq War and the bombing by the two nations of neutral ships in the Persian Gulf. See *Asahi Shinbun*, April 20, 1988, p. 2.

33. Interview, Tanaka Akihiko, October 28, 1992.

34. An *Asahi Shinbun* public opinion poll found that 82% of respondents had no trust in politics following Kanemaru's indictment for tax evasion. *Asahi Shinbun*, April 6, 1993, p. 2.

35. Interview, Okamoto Yukio, November 20, 1992.

3

China and Asia Loom Larger

Japan has traditionally emphasized economic cooperation with [the Asia-Pacific region] from the perspective that economic development is most important for regional stability. For instance, top priority has been placed on the Asian region in Japan's programs. Such Japanese efforts have contributed greatly to the peace and prosperity of the region, and Japan will continue the endeavor. In addition to these efforts, what must be strengthened are the political and diplomatic endeavors on direct and indirect contributions toward solutions of regional conflicts and confrontations, such as the Cambodian problem or the Korean Peninsula problem. It is also essential to play a positive role in multilateral cooperation and consultations in the region as symbolized in the Asia-Pacific Economic Cooperation (APEC) and to support each country's efforts to democratize, open up the economy and transform it into a market economy. Amid the evolving world order, the international contribution expected of Japan is not confined merely to the economic area but also increasingly includes the political dimension as well. Japan, with the correct recognition of history, will have to make positive contributions appropriate for a peace-loving nation.[1]

The above passage, from Japan's first *Diplomatic Bluebook* to reflect a post–Cold War outlook, succinctly summarizes Japan's perception of the issues that it faces in the Asia-Pacific region, as well as its envisioned regional role. The linkage between the economic development of neighboring nations and Japan's security is explicit, as is Japan's prioritization of foreign aid appropriations to enhance the development of Asia. Trade, foreign direct investment, and technology transfer have represented the major means employed by Japan to bring stability to the region, and they will continue as the basis of Japan's relations with Asia in the future. Joined by what the Foreign Ministry has termed the "political and diplomatic endeavors" of increased diplomatic activity and peace-keeping operations, there is every indication to believe that Japan's regional relationship will be strengthened over time, possibly superseding in importance its relationship with other regions of the world. This scenario raises a number of questions, each of which will be addressed in this chapter. First, what has been the record of Japan-Asia interdependence in recent years, and in what way has it and will it continue to intensify? The second issue concerns the implications of this interdependence for the United States, and whether the U.S. perception of, or commitment in, the region has changed. And the third issue focuses on Japan's history in the region, the forces at work in keeping the memories of a turbulent past alive, and the potential for overcoming these memories with a future based on mutual respect and trust.

To reiterate, there is no reason to believe that Japan's perception of Asia and its role in it as outlined at the outset of this chapter will change in the foreseeable future, while there is every reason to believe that Japan will strengthen its conviction through action in the next several years. Japan's acceptance of a larger role in the security of the region would imply no less than active participation in peacekeeping activities, and a more visible diplomatic role as a mediator of regional disputes or an initiator in bringing disputant nations to the bargaining table. But the Japanese government realizes that both the roles of economic stimulant and active diplomat will be tempered and weighed against the Japanese experience in Asia. For fifty years, commencing with the Sino-Japanese War of 1894–1895 and culminating with Japan's World War II defeat in 1945, the Asian perception of Japan was generally one of bitterness and hatred tinged with fear. And though it is nearly fifty years again since the Japanese empire in Asia was liberated, it is the history which most Asians never experienced that they will not allow Japan to forget, a source of contention which today still colors Japan's relations with the rest of Asia.

AN ASIAN NATION, A WESTERN NATION, OR BOTH?

Japan has struggled with the question of its self-identity since the Meiji Restoration of 1868, and since that time the rest of the world has followed suit in the inconsistency with which it has applied a label to Japan. For several recent decades, Japan's "non-Westernness" provided researchers with an atypical case study of a developed, democratized nation, and for countless books and articles it remained the customary sole exception, the asterisked entry, or for those studies that sought a global approach, the convenient representative of Asian nations. But even for scholars of the latter stripe, Japan seemed different from other Asian nations, even if at the same time it did not necessarily seem very Western. Indeed, Japan had succeeded for the most part in emulating the political, economic, and social institutions of the West, while it appeared that the other Asian nations had failed or had not even tried.

Yet for all of Japan's successes at adoption and adaptation from abroad, one could not label it a Western nation. Its social customs were too "different," and its religious foundations were based on Buddhism and Confucianism, both imported from other parts of Asia, and an indigenous religion of spirit possession and ancestor worship known as Shinto. Society was not organized on the ideals of a Judeo-Christian ethic. Nor, many argued, could its government system be labeled "democratic," at least in the tradition of Western democracies, even if Japan had adopted its own version of many of the institutions of the West.

To borrow a phrase from Mao Tse-tung, for most of Japan's Cold War relations with the West and with Asia, Japan had been "walking on two legs." The problem was that depending on from whose perspective one was looking, at times Japan's legs appeared to be of different lengths, resulting in a cumbersome, plodding gait that emphasized one over the other. As Japan painstakingly played the role of both Western camp ally and member of Asia, when the two roles came into conflict, more often than not Japan attached primary importance to ideology rather than to geography. North Korea, the People's Republic of China (PRC), and Vietnam each represented potential markets for Japanese goods and eager recipients of Japanese technology, aid, and investment, but in the calculation of the East-West confrontation, each to differing degrees also represented a security threat to Japan, a threat that was met by the deterrent presence of U.S. forces on the Japanese islands.

Japan is not the only Asian nation that has played host to American troops, but charges of consenting to a contemporary form of American "imperialism" were rarely leveled at the Philippines, South Korea (except by North Korea), or Taiwan (except by the PRC). It appears, therefore, that the American military presence in Japan has had two effects on Japan's relations with Asia. Japan has, for the most part, been overwhelmingly supportive and in favor of the American military presence, and this presence has in turn quelled Asian concerns of a rearmed Japan. Yet even if American forces are based in Japan solely for U.S. security concerns, their presence suggests to other Asian nations that an independently armed Japan cannot be trusted. This distrust then extends to all levels of Japan-Asian relations, and reminds the rest of Asia of a history that most present-day Japanese and most citizens of Asia never witnessed. Paradoxically, it will be nearly impossible for Japan to present itself as a "peace-loving nation" to the rest of Asia as it so aspires, as long as the American forces either *are* or *are not* in Japan. In the short term, the American military presence is a no-win situation for Japan vis-à-vis its relations with Asia, and only by expanding its still nascent record in international peacekeeping activities and the like will it have any chance of regaining the trust of the region. But this is a long-term endeavor.

The second effect was that even if Japan may have had no conflict with certain Asian nations during the Cold War, the American presence reinforced an image that certain Asian nations *should* represent a threat to Japan, even if in retrospect they might not actually have posed much of a threat. The greatest threat actually came from a nation that considered itself to have been more European than Asian—the former Soviet Union—but perceiving the other nations of the region as either friend or enemy was the price that Japan had to pay for choosing sides in the Cold War. Could anyone argue in retrospect that Vietnam represented a serious threat to Japan's security? Or, for that matter, Cambodia or Laos? One could also make the case that for most of the Cold War, the PRC and North Korea were minimal security threats, at best. (It has been only since the end of the Cold War, when issues of nuclear proliferation have come to the fore with the dissolution of the Soviet Union, that North Korea has been regarded as a direct, primary threat to Japan.) Japan's alliance with the United States has in many ways been beneficial for its development, especially during the years of America's military involvement in Asia, first in Korea and then in Indochina, when for the United States Japan served as a central location from which to conduct military operations and purchase supplies. But this close association and subsequent economic success removed Japan even further from the rest of Asia. In Asian eyes, therefore, Japan was somehow not one of them, yet at the same time it was one of them.

The same can be said of Japan's Cold War relations with the West. Japan was admittedly the West's most loyal Cold War ally in the Pacific, and although its trade and contacts with "our" mutual Communist foes in Asia were curtailed, these relations never totally ceased, which for many in the West called into question Japan's commitment to principles over profits. For example, Richard Nixon may have "historically" opened a door when he visited the PRC, but the Japanese had all the while, and with less fanfare, maintained a cracked window. The reason is that the Japanese government may have a different definition than the United States for the term security, and the economic development of Japan's neighbors may be perceived as the most effective basis for minimizing security threats. For the United States, on the other hand, the general belief is that the type of regime in power will determine whether a nation will be hostile to its interests. It follows that the means by which Japan seeks to ensure that stability may be different from traditional notions of "security enhancement" that we are accustomed to in the West. What may have been judged by foreigners as an effort by Japan to "gain profits" in China during the Cold War was probably undertaken in large measure in the name of security and actually did not amount to much in monetary terms, while it most certainly could have been larger if trade liberalization on both sides had taken place. On the other hand, it is doubtful that Japan could have considered that a relatively small amount of trade with the PRC would have transformed the regime of the nation; rather, the belief was that any type of contact would have brought the nations closer together. For Japan, this contact took the form of trade, limited though it was. In retrospect, notes Shiina Motoo, "In an economic sense, it was a good thing that China became a communist country, because we were forced to deal with other nations. Relations were different than with the China that we see now—that would have been going on since after the war, and Japan would have had a market so close to home, it probably would have focused entirely on that one nation."[2]

As Japan's relations with China (as well as with all nations of Asia) were conducted under the framework of the Cold War, they cannot be fully understood without taking into account the regional role played by the United States, the leader of the Western camp and, at least in nominal terms, for forty-five years the political and ideological inspiration for Japan. Since the end of World War II, the American military presence in Japan and other parts of Asia has provided stability, the basis for economic prosperity, and a brake against regional arms races, but it has also inhibited Japan's dealings in the region. Although the end of the Cold War did not eliminate all of the security threats in Asia, it is the changing American role in the region, as well as changes in the U.S.-Japan relationship, that as much as anything will continue to influence Japan's relations with the nations of Asia in the post–Cold War world.

JAPAN IN ASIA: MOVING BEYOND
A SECURITY TRIAD

Those travelers to the nations of Asia who have no doubt witnessed the Japanese economic presence might be inclined to conclude that the indirect, economic measures to ensure Japan's security are in fact more prominent than what Japan considers its "direct and indirect contributions toward solutions of regional conflicts and confrontations," or in other words, efforts of diplomatic negotiation and peacekeeping activities. As will be discussed further, there is no denying that economic relations are deepening the interdependence of the region, and Japan believes that with this increased interdependence comes a mitigation of threats to its security. The initiative to use economic means to keep Japan's neighbors from withdrawing from the international community can and often does come from the government. At present, this is most clearly the case in Japanese–North Korean trade, which for Japan is a negligible amount in the overall trade picture, but which by all estimates for North Korea represents its third largest trading link. The same can be said for Japan-PRC trade prior to U.S. contacts with Beijing in 1972, before the latter's moves towards economic liberalization in 1978, and again when Japan took the lead among the rest of the world's democracies by resuming relations with the Chinese following the 1989 Tiananmen uprising. Of course, for Japanese businesses these ties are also a source of potential profit and are not necessarily viewed in strictly commerce-for-security terms, but business realizes just as well as government that long-term investment derives long-term gain, regardless of the likelihood of short-term loss.

Nevertheless, it did not take the end of the Cold War to raise the level of economic activity, and thus the interdependence, between Japan and its neighbors. The steady progression of trade between Japan and the rest of Asia had Cold War antecedents, which were based in large part on the economic reality of a strengthened yen following the 1985 Plaza Accords. But these ties may also have been spurred on by Japan's realization that the politics of fair trade and threatened retaliation by its largest trading partner—the United States—represented a new form of concern to Japan's *economic* security. It was neither an empty threat nor a sentiment that was suppressed because of the necessity to maintain an alliance based on the existence of the Cold War, as the 1988 Omnibus Fair Trade and Competitive Act made clear. In short, for Japan the end of the Cold War may have led to less restrictive channels for economic transactions, but it was hardly a dam that was opened, soon to be followed by trade that had been repressed for forty-five years. Increased regional economic activity was inevitable and should have come as no surprise, and a climate of protectionism in overseas markets merely served to accelerate this trend. On the other hand, what can be considered revolutionary and hardly inevitable, at least in the light of Japan's previous foreign policy, have been Japan's politico-diplomatic security-linked initiatives in the region.

Unlike the cooperative security arrangement of Western Europe, the success of which has also been dependent in large measure on American participation, there is no framework for cooperative security in the Asia-Pacific which corresponds to NATO. As the *Nihon Keizai Shinbun* reminded its readers with the first indication of reduced East-West tension, in Europe during the Cold War there was the Warsaw Pact and NATO—a framework for confrontation followed by détente with the collapse of the Soviet Union—but "there is no framework for détente in Asia."[3] These sentiments were echoed by former U.S. Secretary of Defense Dick Cheney during his trip to Japan for the U.S.–Japan Defense Top Leaders Consultations in February 1990 when he remarked, "We must remember that the situation in the Asia-Pacific region is different from that in Europe."[4] Cheney's comments left the Japanese government optimistic that the United States had no intention of closing its foreign bases, even though the downsizing and elimination of domestic bases was at that time being considered. The reason for the Japanese concern is clear. In the domain of Asian security, there is the U.S.-Japan Security Treaty and other bilateral and a limited number of multilateral security agreements—most of which involve the United States—but nothing that is truly regional in organization and participation. In the past, Japan and most of the other nations of Asia (with the notable but understandable exceptions of the PRC and North Korea) have consistently acknowledged the significance of the American military presence for the economic success and relative political stability of the region, and for nearly fifty years this presence has been an assumed factor.

When analyzing Japanese-Asian relations, therefore, it could be argued that since the "American factor" has represented a third element in the equation for so long, for most of the past fifty years Japan has not experienced true bilateral relations with its neighbors. At first reading this statement may seem anomalous, for it is indeed a unique situation. One would be hard-pressed to say that when Britain and France engage in discussions on bilateral issues, the "American factor" influences the content and success of their talks, or that Spain and Belgium, Australia and New Zealand, or even Mexico and Venezuela give as much consideration to the role of the United States as do Japan and the rest of Asia when these nations' representatives meet. Part of the reason is that whether totalitarian or democratic, the Asian nations have welcomed the U.S. military presence in Japan to temper their concerns of a return to Japanese militarism, real or imagined, and without American forces stationed in Japan, it is difficult to imagine that Japan-Asian relations would have reached the level they have. For most Asian nations, the American military presence represents the primary restraint on the return of an independent, militarily capable Japan, and it is a situation that the Japanese government has itself acknowledged time and again. Former Foreign Minister Abe Shintaro was bluntly relaying the government line when he stated in 1990 that "the maintenance of the U.S.–Japan Security Treaty and Japan's not pursuing an independent defense policy will lead to the security of Asia."[5] The possibility of an American withdrawal would therefore have severe repercussions for Japan's relations with its neighbors.

As noted earlier, for Japan the presence of U.S. forces represents a paradox in its relations with the rest of Asia, but this presence is preferable to their withdrawal from the Japanese islands. Clearly Japan does not want to incite fear in Asia by contemplating the likelihood of an American withdrawal. But relative to previous issues of the Ministry of Foreign Affairs *Diplomatic Bluebook*, the 1991 issue cited at the outset of this chapter downplays the role of the U.S. military in the Asia Pacific. In this edition, failure to state the obvious, in this case the continued presence of American military forces, may also indicate that the obvious is less than certain. It is only further along, in a section entitled "North America" and under the subheading of "The United States," that mention is made of the "firm United States presence in the Asia-Pacific," and then again it is expressed in a mostly bilateral, U.S.-Japan context. Even if it seems more likely in the long term rather than the near future, perhaps Japan is slowly preparing itself and its neighbors for the possibility of a greatly reduced American military presence in the region, coming on the heels of marginal troop reductions in Korea and Japan, and the anticipated (and since realized) expulsion of American forces from the Philippines.

It should therefore seem to be no coincidence that the destination for Japan's first overseas dispatch of Self Defense Forces, if only to play a non-military role, was an Asian nation (Cambodia), even though this would have been unthinkable to many Japanese just a few years earlier and totally unacceptable to Japan's neighbors. Japan could have sent peacekeeping forces to Yugoslavia instead of Cambodia, for United Nations operations in Yugoslavia had been established before those in Cambodia. But the reason for Japan's decision should be clear. Logistically, Cambodia is relatively a stone's throw from Japan compared to the expense and preparation that would have been necessary if operations had commenced in Yugoslavia. Strategically, Japan would derive a much greater benefit from trying to maintain peace in a nearby nation that for years has been torn by civil war, and in which it plans to increase its economic presence, rather than sending forces to a nation which does not represent a security threat, or where efforts at peacekeeping would not result in as great an *economic* security benefit. Symbolically, the Japanese contingent of Self Defense Forces, which are viewed by the rest of Asia as Japan's "military," were joined by representatives of thirty-two other nations in peacekeeping activities under the auspices of the UN. No operation to send Japanese forces abroad for the first time since World War II could have been as controlled in its organization and peaceful in its intentions as the opportunity presented by the Cambodian conflict. Psychologically, a barrier was removed in Japan's relations with Asia. It was also somewhat of a watershed that Cambodian Premier Hun Sen personally requested Japan's peacekeeping presence in his nation, noting that the "unfortunate memories" of Japan's military actions in Asia "is a matter of the past."[6]

What was the impetus that spurred on Japan's participation in peacekeeping operations? Of course, one could argue that it was evidence that either Japan had accepted the call that it play a larger role in world affairs, and/or it believed its international contributions would never be fully appreciated by the rest of the world if it were to continue what was criticized as "checkbook diplomacy" without risking human life for what have been termed "universal values." The first explanation is more idealistic, and the effect of a changing mentality among the public (brought about by government prodding) that if Japan was to be a "global partner" it could no longer continue the posture of a "minor power" in world affairs. Though this argument is not incorrect, as one could point to the bitter, protracted, and sometimes physical disputes over legislation that ultimately authorized participation of the Self Defense Forces in UN peacekeeping efforts as a visible indication that Japan was struggling with these expectations for its "new world role," in any democratic nation groundbreaking legislation is rarely initiated without a livid battle over principles. Even over legislation less significant than the "PKO bill," Japan has never been immune from legislative squabbles. In fact, as previously noted, during the fall 1992 Diet session debate over the PKO bill was superseded by investigation into domestic matters—specifically political corruption charges brought against members of the LDP hierarchy. Yet if Japan had truly been struggling with the "conceptualization" of its still undefined role, debate over international issues, of which the PKO bill was one, would have dominated the legislative session.

Former LDP Secretary General Ozawa Ichiro, at times branded a "maverick" more for his style than his political independence, was one of the most visible and prominent politicians who argued that Japan could not continue telling the world that it was "special" because of the constraints of its constitution. "In other nations [participating in the war], there are some families receiving notification of the deaths of their husbands, sons, and boyfriends. Even with that, can we still say that Japan is special while they are fighting in the name of justice?"[7] This second explanation—that Japan had to abandon its checkbook diplomacy and risk the life of its citizens for it to gain international "respectability"—could be attributed to the criticism against Japan's strictly monetary contribution to the Allied efforts in the Gulf War, and would represent a more reactive explanation for the response by Japan. As with the previous explanation for Japan's initiation of "direct action" legislation (in the form of the PKO bill), this may hold some truth, but even a "reactive" foreign policy has its limits. In many respects, the PKO bill was monumental, but as with most

groundbreaking legislation in any country, an impetus from outside will at best serve to initiate the legislative process; it will not
guarantee its ratification.

The third explanation is more pragmatic, and in fact may have
weighed more heavily than the other two in Japan's decision. It
is clear that the PKO bill would have never been enacted without
public support, which in this case is indicative of a changed appraisal of Japan's role in Asia as much as it is the role of Japan's
Self Defense Forces. One could argue that the public would not
have supported the legislation had the initial destination been
anywhere *but* an Asian nation. For weeks, Japanese television
broadcast the work being done by UN forces in Cambodia, and
this constant coverage of bridge building and flood prevention
(among other "peaceful" actions) proved to the Japanese public
that peacekeeping did not imply fighting. Also influential were the
roles played by Ogata Sadako, formerly a professor at Tokyo's
Sophia University but at present UN High Commissioner for Refugees, and Akashi Yasushi, who was chosen to direct the UN's
Cambodian activities as head of the United Nations Transitional
Authority in Cambodia (UNTAC). As University of Tokyo Professor Tanaka Akihiko suggested,

In 1992, Akashi was appointed head of UNTAC. When he came back to
Japan, he spoke before the Diet and in front of television cameras several
times. In fact it was this—I believe his "lobbying"—was the most effective influence in winning support among the public for this law. He assured the Japanese that the type of activity that Japan would undertake
is not real military activity, but necessary activity to settle disputes.[8]

Japan deployed six hundred engineers of the Self Defense
Forces to offer assistance in the construction of bridges and roads,
along with seventy-five civilian police officers to assist in the mon-
itoring of the May 1993 Cambodian elections. However peaceful
the operations appeared to the Japanese television-viewing public,
the environment in which they were carried out was unstable and,
with retaliation against outsiders threatened by the Khmer Rouge,
still dangerous. In early May of 1993, eight of the police were
ambushed, leaving one dead. It was the second fatality of a Jap-

anese representative in Cambodia, the first being a Japanese United Nations volunteer in April. What originally was planned as a humanitarian mission of peace with minimal contingencies against attack was suddenly turned into a vicious reminder that making peace precedes keeping peace. The worst-case scenario predicted by the Japanese government in the legislation debate was realized, while opposition parties argued that one of the conditions for the dispatch of peacekeeping forces—a cease-fire—was non-existent, and therefore the forces should be recalled. Conscious that the world might be critical that Japan's somewhat noble objectives were in the end rather naive, Japan pledged that the SDF personnel would remain in Cambodia until their scheduled withdrawal date of September 1993.

Although Japan had hoped that it could participate in peacekeeping activities without loss of life, it is doubtful that this will be the last dispatch of Japanese non-combat forces in Asia, for SDF personnel have since been assigned to Mozambique. The dispatch of forces abroad—especially in a non-combat role—was made all the more possible by the factors stated above, but in large measure it was also made possible by the changing military role played in Asia by the United States and, as has been suggested, the increasing regional economic role played by Japan.

During the Cold War, the United States justified its military presence in Asia primarily as a counter to communist aggression, but this too has changed. Though it realizes that "increases in Japanese military strength undertaken to compensate for declining capabilities in the region could prove worrisome to regional nations,"[9] the U.S. government has stated that its military presence in the region is not maintained only "because we are concerned over the vacuum which would be created if we were no longer there.... Nor are we merely motivated by altruism. *Simply, we must play this role because our military presence sets the stage for our economic involvement in the region* [emphasis added]."[10] No one can predict what effects the North American Free Trade Agreement (NAFTA) and economic regionalism will have on the degree or rate of U.S. economic activity in Asia, but what if that economic interest should wane in favor of its own regional interests, and the world is faced with a system of economic trading blocs, as many have predicted? As Henry Kissinger offered to a large Tokyo audience of business leaders, government officials, and scholars in 1992,

given the fact that in the real world there will be some protection, how can there be trade-offs and how can you have rules that can then be followed? I suspect that over the next ten years, the real issue in this area cannot be expressed as GATT rules between nations, but as GATT rules between trading blocs. And what the role of trading blocs will be, whether they will reduce obstacles to trade or increase [them], whether they will become instruments of economic warfare, or means of more efficient economic organization, that will be the big challenge of the next decade.[11]

What therefore appears to be even more immediate for Japan-Asian relations than the issue of Japan's politico-diplomatic role, but also downplayed in the *Bluebook*, is this issue of regional economic integration. Save for a brief mention of the proposal by Malaysian Prime Minister Mahathir bin Mohamed for an "economic cooperation group in the East Asian region,"[12] this issue is glaringly absent from this edition of the *Bluebook*. Yet it is regional economic integration, whether by design or default, that may serve to change Japan's relations with Asia and with the rest of the world.

REDISCOVERING ASIA

Liberated from conducting relations under a Cold War framework, Japan is now developing those contacts in Asia that it refrained from developing for the past four decades. This increasing interest in Asia represents Japan's reprioritization of its Asian interests and, since the end of the Cold War, its more frequent self-identification as an Asian nation. During the Cold War, only occasionally did Japan's leaders refer to their nation as "Asian," or claim to represent the interests of the region. Recently, however, the frequency of this identity and representation has increased, in large part as an awareness of the region's economic dynamism, and a reaction to formal agreements in North America and Europe that enforce the identities of these areas. For example, in 1990 former Japanese Ambassador to China Nakae Yosuke reminded the readers of the *Asahi Shinbun* that the world is not only Europe and the United States, and since Japan is the only Asian nation that has been invited to international summits, it has to "advocate the stability of Asia," not just allow the United States and the European nations to push their own agendas.[13] This fear of being "left out" was clearly illustrated during GATT negotiations over agricultural subsidies in the fall of 1992, which became a bilateral debate between the United States and the EU, with minimal solicitation of Japan's opinion though Japan would directly be affected by the outcome. From a somewhat different perspective, though also illustrating Japan's "Asian-ness," when confronted with a conflict in scheduling his own foreign trips with the announced but still not finalized plan of U.S. officials to visit Japan, former Prime Minister Kaifu Toshiki was reportedly "agonizing," because a cancellation of his planned Asian trip would "once again cause ASEAN [Association of South East Asian Nations], which is considered closest to Japanese diplomacy," to believe that it had been treated lightly.[14] Similarly, in a speech before the Diet in October 1992, Kaifu's successor, Miyazawa Kiichi, stated that, "as Japan moves to take part in the buildings [*sic*] of a new international order for peace, it is important that we develop new foreign policy initiatives consistent with our basic position as an Asian nation, and this in turn means that we must work to build closer relations not only with our immediate neighbors but with the rest of the Asia-Pacific region as well."[15]

This policy is indeed what Japan has been pursuing, and it is doing so ten paces ahead of the United States. The two nations' post–Cold War experiences in Asia are indeed a study in contrasts, with the United States clinging to Cold War ideology and Japan bingeing on its appetite of Asian economics. For example, as reported by the *Asahi Shinbun* in the fall of 1991, "the [Japanese] government has proposed the strengthening of relations with Vietnam as a pillar of its Asian diplomacy after the signing of the Cambodia reconciliation proposal. It intends to support political stability with economic development in the Indochina region with Vietnam as a core."[16] According to a Foreign Ministry official, regardless of what course Japan followed in the debate over aid to Vietnam, it knew that it would be criticized.[17] The anticipated source of criticism—the United States—responded as expected, questioning Japan's move. A 1991 *Washington Post* article implied that Japanese observance of the American embargo against Vietnam was nominal at best, and Japanese companies were poised to exploit the economic opportunities once the embargo was lifted.[18] During his 1991 visit to Japan,[19] then Secretary of State James Baker received a "lukewarm" response to his call that Japan continue withholding aid to Vietnam "until the issue of U.S. soldiers taken as prisoners of war or missing in action is resolved."[20] Japan responded that it would continue to seek Vietnam's cooperation on behalf of the United States, but reminded Baker that Vietnam was "having trouble on meeting payments on its debts to Japan."[21] Ultimately, the United States reached the same conclusion and announced that it too would provide aid to Vietnam. Similar but more complex is the Japanese decision to resume loans to China following the events of June 1989 in Tiananmen Square.

When it was announced several months after the fact that Brent Scowcroft, former U.S. Presidential Assistant for National Security Affairs, had traveled to China in July 1989 and then again in December of the same year, the *Yomiuri Shinbun* reported that the United States had once again followed a diplomacy of "going over Japan's head."[22] The comparison with President Nixon's 1972 decision to recognize the government of the Chinese mainland, without first informing Japan of the move, was clear. (The other Nixon "shock" of the same year was to take the United States off the gold standard and apply tariffs of 10% to all imports.) As the *Nihon Keizai Shinbun* remarked at the time of this revelation, "Is it any wonder that a consortium of 67 Japanese banks agreed to a request by the Bank of China to resume providing loans to China in December 1989?"[23] Nevertheless, the United States was not about to support Japan's decision without a protest. Regardless of the objections raised at the Houston Summit of 1990 over the Japanese plan to lift the freeze on loans to China, the *Tokyo Shinbun* reported that there would be no change in Japanese policy.[24] In the end, the Houston Summit Political Declaration approved Japan's decision to resume loans to China,[25] but it was not the first conflict between the United States and Japan over the ideals and objectives of foreign aid.

JAPANESE FOREIGN AID: DEEP POCKET DIPLOMATS OR TROJAN HORSES?

One of the major vehicles by which Japan believes it is contributing to the construction of a new international order, and endeavoring to meet the goals of the Kaifu proposal, is through its foreign aid program, the only policy explicitly stated in the Kuriyama proposal outlined in the previous chapter.

In contrast to the beginnings of U.S. foreign aid appropriations, which followed on the heels of Allied victory in World War II, in the 1960s Japan was still the world's second largest aid recipient after India. In fact, it has become somewhat of a cliché among Japanese aid officials to point out the world famous Japanese bullet train was possible only because of foreign economic assistance received during those years. Indeed, after the war United States economic rehabilitation funds to Japan amounted to $2.1 billion, which represented "the first condition for Japan's magical economic restoration."[26] In this light, Japan "truly understands just how powerful a tool aid can be,"[27] and in the past three years its foreign aid expenditures have either surpassed those of the United States or have been closely behind. Similar to the experience of the United States, since the end of World War II Japan's foreign aid program has undergone several changes, most notably from its position of a major net recipient to a major provider of foreign aid. It is this change in policies, and an examination of the post–Cold War record of Japanese foreign aid, that bears investigation.

Japan's first foreign aid expenditures were in the form of postwar reparations payments to eleven nations of East Asia, with a high percentage of appropriated funds in the form of "tied" aid. One early analyst of Japan's foreign aid policy wrote that "Japanese aid is allocated with little regard to the requirements of the recipients. It is given on Japanese terms and in Japanese ways."[28] There is no denying that in the initial stages of its development, Japan's foreign aid program (which Japan calls "overseas development assistance") was a means of stimulating an export economy.[29] Determining what constitutes aid and what percentage of this figure is tied is certainly not an exact science, because nations differ on their definitions. But it is important to note that although the United States also disburses tied aid, and in fact its percentage of tied aid has been calculated by one knowledgeable source to be higher than that of Japan,[30] this characterization of Japan making aid allocation contingent on the recipient nation undertaking projects determined by Japan, or purchasing Japanese equipment or employing Japanese personnel, is largely inaccurate.

All aid donors are sensitive to charges of misdirected aid or aid approved for the benefit of the granting nation, but Japan seems to be targeted more than most. For example, widely publicized criticism came from developing countries at the first meeting of the United Nations Conference on Trade and Development in 1964, known as UNCTAD I, for Japan's stated "economics first" aid posture. It was a charge that the Japanese appreciated, and they pledged to consider more fully the needs of recipient nations. Even though it has become one of the world's leading donors of foreign aid, and now considers aid more a diplomatic tool than an economic pry, Japan is always prepared for foreign criticism of its aid policy. The difference between now and thirty years ago, however, is that the anticipated source of criticism is its fellow aid-giving nations, not the recipients of aid. Japan has been particularly conscious of its aid levels relative to those of the United States, which has served as the prime source of recent criticism. For example, the following article appeared in the *Yomiuri Shinbun* in July 1991, when it was announced that Japan's foreign aid expenditures made it the world's second leading donor behind the United States, not the first, as was previously announced.

This is because the OECD lowered the exchange rate of the yen against the dollar by about 5%, which still means an increase in Japan's ODA [overseas development assistance] of 6.4% [over the previous year's budget] in terms of yen. As a result, our country, which came to rank first in the world in ODA in 1989, has relapsed into the world's second biggest aid-giving nation, following the United States.... On this occasion, ranking or the amount in dollar terms is not a problem. It is worrisome that our country's ODA will once again become the object of criticism by international public opinion because of the decrease brought about by the difference in exchange rates.[31]

Japan has also been criticized for its targeting of aid to Asian nations, yet to Japanese policymakers, these appropriations are a way of maintaining the security of an area in which its strategic interests are apparent.[32] Nor does it appear that Japan is about to alter its Asian-centered foreign aid policy. In an article, Matsuura Koichiro, Director General of the Ministry of Foreign Affairs Economic Cooperation Bureau, proclaimed in 1989,

> we shouldn't simply throw money around in random directions. Aid must be steered to places where it will bring long-term benefits back to its donor.... As an Asian country, Japan's ties with its neighbors are naturally of central importance. Our foreign aid policy reflects this reality, the bulk of Japanese aid being channeled to other Asian countries. There is no pressing reason to alter that policy now."[33]

This policy of Asian prioritization in the allocation of foreign aid was reaffirmed by then Prime Minister Kaifu in 1991, following his visit to ASEAN nations.[34]

In 1989, 63% of Japanese aid was disbursed to the nations of East and South Asia, which dwarfed the amount appropriated by the United States for the region. Even taking into account the amount appropriated to the Philippines, which is the third largest recipient of U.S. aid (following Israel and Egypt, respectively), the total amount for the nations of East Asia was only 8.8% of the total U.S. aid budget.[36] For Japan, the largest recipient of aid in 1992 was Indonesia, followed by the PRC, the Philippines, India, and Thailand. Vietnam, to which aid was appropriated for the first time in fourteen years, ranked sixth with a total of more than United States $280 million.[37] But as noted earlier, the first real challenge for an "international role-seeking" Japan to consider its aid appropriations in political terms came with the events in Tiananmen Square. Although Japan joined the United States in suspending aid allocations to China, it was more eager than other aid-donor nations to resume these appropriations.[38] The issue of aid to China, together with outside pressure (*gaiatsu*) by the United States, led to the April 1991 declaration by then Prime Minister Kaifu of a new set of guidelines for foreign aid. Though as was true with previous guidelines, these have not been formalized and are interpreted as mere suggestions by the four bureaucratic ministries[39] primarily involved in the aid decision-making process. These four considerations of the Kaifu proposal are:

1. Is the recipient nation developing and manufacturing weapons of mass destruction?
2. Is it promoting democracy?
3. Is it making efforts to move toward a market-oriented economy?
4. What is its human rights record?

Of course, a violation of one or more of these conditions does not necessarily invalidate a request for aid. In the case of China, the Japanese government believes that aid is assisting in the creation of a market economy. Government officials do not publicly state their wish, but they believe that with greater economic liberalization, the move towards democratic reform will increase, thus bringing stability to the region. In Japan's view, to cancel aid would only serve to further isolate China from the international community, and reduce any hopes of improvement on issues that other donors (particularly the United States) have prioritized in their aid decisions.

As part of its pledge to assume an international leadership role, Japan announced in 1993 that its foreign aid policy for the next five years will send more funds to those developing regions (particularly Africa and Latin America) that had been relatively minor recipients in the past. Nevertheless, the prioritization of Asian nations in Japan's aid decision-making process will continue for the same reason that certain regions and areas have been prioritized by the United States and other donor nations: it is believed that these regions have derived for the grantors the greatest benefit, whether humanitarian, strategic, or economic. And, as the *Nihon Keizai Shinbun* commented in early 1993, the United States will attempt to divert Japan's influence in Asia, which far outpaces its own, by strengthening its relations with individual nations of the region, and will encourage Japan to recycle its funds through international organizations rather than bilateral.[40]

FOREIGN DIRECT INVESTMENT

As mentioned at the outset of this chapter, foreign direct investment is perhaps the most visible means by which the interdependence between Japan and Asia has been strengthened since the end of the Cold War. As David E. Sanger related in the *New York Times*, "Piece by piece, corporate Japan has created a startling replica of itself, not only in look and feel but also in culture. As a result, a region that only 15 years ago was seen by the United States as on the brink of Communism has instead embraced a decidedly capitalist model."[41] But increased investment in Asia by Japanese corporations was not guided by the politics of the Cold War's end; rather, in large measure it was determined before the end of the Cold War by the economics of deliberate revaluation of the yen intended to decrease industrialized nations' trade imbalances with Japan (particularly that of the United States), and the politics of protectionism in the United States brought about by that trade imbalance. As a paper by the Organization for Economic Cooperation and Development (OECD) noted, the devised appreciation of the yen agreed upon by the 1985 Plaza Accords "compelled Japanese firms to make rapid adjustments to remain internationally competitive. A large number of Japanese firms responded by relocating noncompetitive production processes or sub-processes in East and Southeast Asia through foreign direct investment (FDI) and by 'outsourcing' parts and components from low cost countries."[42] With a relative rise in the price of their exports, Japanese firms have looked to Asian nations as a source of relatively cheap labor in their efforts to cut costs. But Asian nations also represent a haven from protectionism, as goods manufactured in foreign factories have been exempt from trade legislation of final destination nations, even if the "local content" (percentage of parts manufactured in the nation of final production) for many of these products may be relatively low. Nations serving as ultimate markets for these products have tightened their local content laws to take this scenario into account, and we may see an increase in the presence of Japanese manufacturing enterprises abroad to circumvent this new legislation. It should have come as no surprise that corporate Japan's American presence blossomed in 1981, shortly after Japan was "advised" by the United States to restrict annual exports of automobiles to the United States to 2.3 million units. As illustrated in Table 3.1, through the end of the 1980s the United States represented the single largest destination for Japanese foreign direct investment, while the nations of Asia were far behind. In large measure this

Table 3.1
Actual Reported Direct Foreign Investment of Japan by Region and Main Countries (unit: $ million)

	1987		1988		1989	
	Amount	Component Ratio (%)	Amount	Component Ratio (%)	Amount	Component Ratio (%)
North America	15,357	46.0	22,328	47.5	33,902	50.2
United States	14,704	44.1	21,701	46.2	32,540	48.2
Canada	653	2.0	626	1.3	1,362	2.0
Central & South America	4,816	14.4	6,482	13.8	5,238	7.8
Panama	2,305	6.9	1,712	3.6	2,044	3.0
Brazil	229	0.7	510	1.1	349	0.5
Cayman	1,197	3.6	2,609	5.5	1,658	2.5
Bahamas	734	2.2	737	1.6	620	0.9
Mexico	28	0.1	87	0.2	36	0.1
Asia	4,868	14.6	5,569	11.8	8,238	12.2
Indonesia	545	1.6	586	1.2	631	0.9
Hong Kong	1,072	3.2	1,662	3.5	1,898	2.8

Singapore	494	1.5	747	1.6	1,902	2.8
Korea	647	1.9	483	1.0	606	0.9
China	1,226	3.7	296	0.6	438	0.6
Thailand	250	0.7	859	1.8	1,276	1.9
Malaysia	163	0.5	387	0.8	673	1.0
Middle East	62	0.2	259	0.6	66	0.1
Europe	6,576	19.7	9,116	19.4	14,808	21.9
United Kingdom	2,473	7.4	3,956	8.4	5,239	7.8
Netherlands	829	2.5	2,359	5.0	4,547	6.7
Luxembourg	1,764	5.3	657	1.4	654	1.0
W. Germany	403	1.2	409	0.9	1,083	1.6
Africa	272	0.8	653	1.4	671	1.0
Liberia	267	0.8	648	1.4	643	1.0
Oceania	1,413	4.2	2,669	5.7	4,618	6.8
Australia	1,222	3.7	2,413	5.1	4,256	6.3
Total	33,364	100.0	47,022	100.0	67,540	100.0

Figures derived from Japan External Trade Organization (JETRO), *Japan Economic Data Book* (Tokyo, 1991), p. 95.

trend was attributable not only to the location of manufacturing facilities closer to destination markets and under the protective barriers they had erected, but also to a rise in foreign affiliates of service sector firms (securities, insurance, banking) that reflect Japan's emphasis of these tertiary level businesses and a corresponding move from manufacturing enterprises, a shift that began with the first OPEC oil shock.

The recent downturn of the Japanese economy has been expressed by the decision of Japanese corporations to downsize their foreign operations or cease them altogether in favor of concentrating on domestic operations. Although the overall level of FDI has thus decreased, and the United States is still the most frequent destination for Japanese foreign direct investment, the share of FDI located in Asia as a percentage of the total has increased, while that for the United States has decreased. Compared to 1991, Japanese FDI in the United States fell 23.3%, representing 40.5% of the total, while FDI in Asia increased 8.2% during the same period, accounting for 18.8% of the total.[43]

What has been the recent record of United States FDI in Asia? According to Kuriyama Takakazu, who served as ambassador to Thailand among his many diplomatic posts, "I think there is a sense in Southeast Asia that the Americans kicked themselves out. . . . In the 60s and 70s the United States understood its strategic interests in the area. But it is not clear now that it always understands its economic interests."[44] The extent to which foreign direct investment shifts job opportunities from the domestic market to foreign factory workers is at the heart of the debate in the United States over the implications of NAFTA, and the role that will be played by Mexico in the arrangement. For the United States, Europe has been prioritized for some time as a destination for foreign direct investment, while Mexico and the nations of Asia account for a small percentage of the total. One could argue that a large percentage of United States FDI in Europe is concentrated in finance and services, sectors that are relatively undeveloped in Mexico and Asia. And so too, American corporations may feel more comfortable dealing in Europe, and may also be trying to position themselves in an integrated European market. In the long term, American companies may indeed reap the benefits of concentrating their resources in that region.

But the first principle of investing, whether the investor is a company or an individual, is diversification of assets. It would seem that the same should apply to direct foreign investment.

Japanese interest in Asia is not uniform, for there is a contrast between the amount of foreign aid, technology transfer, and foreign direct investment allocated to the ASEAN nations, the NICs, and the PRC on the one hand, and South Asia (India, Pakistan, Bangladesh, Sri Lanka) on the other. As Kitaoka Shin'ichi pointed out, "We have to combine altruism and self-interest in trying to solve global problems, and maybe ODA is one way to do this. You know, Korea may become an ODA giving country in a few years. So too Singapore. But Japan's level of trade, direct investment, and ODA in South Asia are a contrast to Southeast Asia."[45]

As noted, Cambodia and Vietnam have recently assumed increasing political and economic importance to Japan following a period of limited contact, and this interest will likely increase. As the home of some of the world's most dynamic economies during the past five years, opportunities for growth in Asia are plentiful. On the other hand, although the United States has for some time reaffirmed the significance of Asia to U.S. economic interests, most recently with President Clinton reminding the American public during the November 1993 APEC Summit in Seattle that more than 50% of U.S. trade is with nations of the Asia-Pacific region, the U.S. economic presence in Asia pales in comparison to that of Japan. A decided concentration of resources in Europe by U.S. corporations has indirectly served to deepen the interdependence between Japan and its neighbors. David Sanger notes that corporate Japan's presence in Asia is so overwhelming, and the absence of its American counterpart so glaring, that "after five years of intense investments, Japan's economic reach through the area is nearly all-encompassing, challenged only by a recent investment spurt from other Asian countries, particularly Taiwan."[46] Of course, in the future American companies can redirect their priorities and intensify their investments in Asia if they so decide. But the longer they delay their decision, the more difficult it will become to compete with Japan in these nations. And, as suggested earlier in this chapter, the region will become more economically interdependent, with Japan playing a leading role. In the opinion of political critic Tanaka Naoki, writing in 1991, the

United States feels "deprived" by Japan's new found influence in Asia.

Accompanying the increasing power of Japan's influence in Asia, and a corresponding American decline, voices are heard in the United States saying "we were not prepared for this type of situation." The U.S. government's trying to make Japan forego participation in the East Asia Economic Caucus (EAEC), which excludes the U.S., is one expression of this. In the 1990s, Japan will be asked what position it will take toward both Asia and the U.S.[47]

With such a scenario, might not the U.S. public and officials alike reconsider their nation's military commitment to the region? Especially with the loss of Subic and Clark naval bases in the Philippines, from a military efficiency standpoint, maintaining forces in Japan makes sense for the United States. The American presence allays Asian fears of Japanese militarism, and more than any other factor it has been attributed as the preventer of regional arms races and the promoter of economic stability. The host for that presence has also been a most willing provider of financial support to see that this arrangement is continued. As a nation the United States benefits from all of this, as does Japan. But in times of economic difficulty, as the United States is presently experiencing, and especially in times of economic competition, which U.S. firms are only beginning to experience in a third market (Asia) against Japan's own economic interests, how will the security arrangement be affected, if at all? Will the nations of Asia agree to some form of collective security, as has been promoted by the United States in the past?[48] Will a collective security arrangement—one whose participants are nations of competing interests and motivations—be able to provide regional stability to the extent that has been maintained by one regional military presence?

JAPAN-ASIA TRADE: INTERDEPENDENCE, INTENTIONAL OR CIRCUMSTANTIAL

While foreign aid and foreign direct investment are means by which Japan has increased the interdependence between itself and its neighbors, and thus believes it has mitigated (though in no way eliminated) its security threats, the initiative to pursue each of these measures in large part comes from Japan. In the end, both recipient and source may benefit, but even for foreign aid requests, without the approval of the Japanese government, the transaction will never take place. Basically, the decision to realize foreign aid, foreign direct investment, and technology transfer rests with the Japanese side. The same cannot be said for trade. Though controlled to a certain extent by governments, trade is more liberal in its application and more bilateral in its initiation than are the other three policies that link Japan and Asia, and in economic terms is even more significant in the degree to which it dwarfs the other means in economic terms. It is an interaction which therefore deserves our attention.

It is indeed true that the trading links between Japan and the nations of ASEAN (Malaysia, Singapore, Thailand, Indonesia, the Philippines, and Brunei),[49] the newly industrializing countries, or NICs (Singapore, Hong Kong, South Korea, and Taiwan), and the PRC[50] have progressively increased during the past decade. And although there is every reason to believe that this trend will continue, no matter how appealing or threatening the notion of an "Asian trading bloc" may be to some, at this time it is hardly a reality. Trite though it may seem, this is because regional economic integration is a two-sided equation, and to understand the dynamics of this interdependence, we must analyze both Japan's trading position and that of its Asian trading partners. Even if Indonesia-Thailand trade or Philippines-Malaysia trade is increasing, which would increase the inter-regional trade ratio, these ties should not be the primary focus of our analysis. For if any Asian "trading bloc" is to evolve, participation by Japan would be a necessity.

Table 3.2 illustrates the percentage of imports as a share of total imports for the individual countries listed. In 1985, Japan was the leading source of imports for each of these nations, with the exception of the Philippines, for which the United States held a share of the Philippine market nearly seventy-five percent greater than that of Japan.

Table 3.2 shows that as a share of total imports of the nine nations listed, imports from Japan have increased in six of the nations since 1985, while to a lesser degree four have increased their purchases from the United States. The difference is in the

Table 3.2
Imports from the United States and Japan as a Percentage of Total Imports

FROM	UNITED STATES			JAPAN			FROM
	1985	1989	1991	1985	1989	1991	
CHINA	12.0	13.3	12.6	35.6	17.8	15.7	CHINA
TAIWAN	23.6	23.0	22.5	27.6	30.7	30.0	TAIWAN
S. KOREA	20.8	25.9	23.2	24.3	28.4	25.9	S. KOREA
SINGAPORE	15.2	17.1	15.8	17.1	21.4	21.3	SINGAPORE
HONG KONG	9.5	8.2	7.6	23.1	16.6	16.4	HONG KONG
INDONESIA	16.8	13.1	13.1	25.8	25.6	24.5	INDONESIA
PHILIPPINES	24.9	19.0	20.2	14.4	19.6	19.4	PHILIPPINES
THAILAND	11.3	11.3	11.0	26.5	30.3	29.0	THAILAND
MALAYSIA	15.2	16.9	15.3	23.0	24.2	26.1	MALAYSIA

Figures derived from United Nations, *Statistical Yearbook of Asia and the Pacific; The Far East and Australasia; Japan Statistical Yearbook; The Economist, Country Reports;* all various years.

relative positions of Japan and the United States as a source of imports for these nations (or, inversely, as a market for the exports of the United States and Japan). Japan remains the main source of imports for each of these nations with the exception of the Philippines, but even there the gap is narrowing. Contrastingly, on the export side (Table 3.3) we see that in 1991 the United States was the major market for seven of the nine nations.

The numbers in the two tables above represent imports and exports as a percentage of total imports and exports of a given country, not the amount of trade in U.S. dollar terms or domestic currency. Nevertheless, in the calculation of trade balances, it should not require advanced math skills to conclude from the tables that unless the United States is exporting expensive items and importing relatively cheap items from these nations, it is experiencing a balance of payments deficit. In fact, in 1991 Japan had a trade surplus with each of these nations, with the exception of Brunei (not listed in the tables) and Indonesia, nations with oil reserves and with which Japan has historically had a trade deficit. The other exception is the PRC, which was initially a net debtor but since 1988 has become a net creditor in its trade with Japan. On the other hand, the United States had a trade deficit with each of these nations in 1991, with the exception of the PRC, with which it had a relatively insignificant surplus. In short, Japan has not replaced the United States as the primary destination for the goods of these Asian nations, and in 1991 Japan was the primary market only for China and Indonesia. Any notion, or formation, of an Asian trading bloc which excludes or discriminates against the United States would be economic suicide for these nations. This does not mean they have not considered the possibility, however.

Perhaps the most significant proposal for regional economic integration was advanced in December 1990 by Malaysian Prime Minister Mahathir. The regional trade grouping, which came to be known as the East Asian Economic Caucus (EAEC), was a response to the planned European Economic Area (EEA), and to an even greater extent the proposal for NAFTA. Mahathir's plan would exclude the United States, and its success would depend on Japan, though the Japanese were reluctant to support a proposal that was exclusionary. For Japan, the stated ideal has

Table 3.3
Exports to the United States and Japan as a Percentage of Total Exports

FROM	UNITED STATES			JAPAN			FROM
	1985	1989	1991	1985	1989	1991	
CHINA	8.6	8.4	8.6	22.3	15.9	14.3	CHINA
TAIWAN	48.1	36.3	29.3	11.3	13.7	12.1	TAIWAN
S. KOREA	35.5	33.1	25.8	15.0	21.6	17.2	S. KOREA
SINGAPORE	21.2	23.3	19.7	9.4	8.5	8.7	SINGAPORE
HONG KONG	44.4	32.2	27.2	3.4	5.8	5.0	HONG KONG
INDONESIA	21.7	16.0	12.0	46.2	41.7	36.9	INDONESIA
PHILIPPINES	35.0	35.8	37.2	18.9	20.3	20.0	PHILIPPINES
THAILAND	19.7	21.7	21.0	13.4	17.0	18.0	THAILAND
MALAYSIA	12.9	18.7	16.9	24.4	16.1	15.9	MALAYSIA

Figures derived from United Nations, *Statistical Yearbook of Asia and the Pacific*; *The Far East and Australasia*; *Japan Statistical Yearbook*; *The Economist, Country Reports*; all various years.

always been continuation of a nondiscriminatory international trading system conducted under the rules of GATT. As former Finance Minister Hata Tsutomu stated in 1992 at the Annual Meeting of the Board of Governors of the International Monetary Fund, "Regional cooperation and integration should not devolve into economic blocs or resurgent protectionism. It is vital to the development of the world economy that, while each region uses its own particular strengths to achieve development, it keeps its markets open to others, thereby promoting a multilateral free trade system."[51] Critics may contend that Japan has perhaps benefited more than most nations under this system, and that it realized the consequences of excluding its largest trading partner from any trade agreement would be severe. It simply would not make economic sense at this stage for Japan to trade only with Asia. Nevertheless, according to Tanaka Akihiko, Mahathir's proposal did win some sympathy in Japan because of the way that U.S. Secretary of State James Baker referred to Mahathir's proposal during his trip to Japan in the fall of 1991, calling it a wedge between Asia and the United States.[52] The Kyodo News Service reported at the time that Japanese government officials received a memorandum from Baker, "urging" the Japanese government to oppose the EAEC,[53] a decision that they would have likely reached on their own. The fact is that the United States is concerned about any trade grouping which excludes its interests, although Asian nations are similarly concerned about how NAFTA will affect theirs. In the words of Tanabe Yasuo, Director for North American Trade Policy Planning in Japan's Ministry of International Trade and Industry (MITI):

I think the United States is reacting too much to the EAEC—it is exaggerating the case a bit. Sometimes to us [Japan], the United States sounds like it has a double standard because while they are dealing in North America, they claim that the EAEC proposal will divide the Pacific from the rest of the world. But that is what the United States has done with NAFTA. This is not persuasive logic. I understand their concern, and I agree on the importance of U.S.-Japan relations, whether trade, political or security in the Asia-Pacific region, but I am afraid that in reaction to this contradictory policy and this type of logic, well, the East Asian countries might begin to feel sick of the United States.[54]

Table 3.4
Composition of Japan's Imports as a Percentage of Total Imports

	ORIGIN					
	ASEAN (A)	NICS (B)	PRC (C)	A+B+C	EEA[a]	NAFTA
1991	13.4	11.5	6.0	29.5	11.0	26.5
1990	12.5	11.1	5.1	27.1	12.5	26.7
1989	12.2	12.9	5.3	29.0	10.8	27.8
1988	12.0	13.3	5.3	29.3	10.4	27.7
1987	13.2	12.6	5.0	29.3	9.5	26.2
1986	13.1	9.9	4.5	26.3	8.9	28.0
1985	15.6	7.6	5.3	27.2	5.5	24.5

[a]Data for EEA only include U.K., Germany, France, and Italy percentages. Figures derived from United Nations, *Statistical Yearbook for Asia and the Pacific*; *The Far East and Australasia*; *Japan Statistical Yearbook*; all various years.

It appears unlikely that Japan will become a party to any regional trade grouping that excludes the United States, and approval of Mahathir's proposal among Asian nations is hardly certain. Thus far, we have only analyzed the Asian side of the Asian-Japan trade equation. Could it be that from Japan's perspective a de facto trade grouping already exists in Asia, and Japan is content with pursuing these "informal" trade relationships (as opposed to a formal multiparty trade agreement)?

Table 3.4 shows the composition of Japan's imports as a percentage of total imports for the period 1985 to 1991. The table shows three categories of Asian origin for imports, with the composite of these three represented in the column "A+B+C." The column labeled "EEA" has been included for illustrative purposes, and represents the percentage of imports from the four most significant European sources of Japanese imports (the U.K., Germany, France, and Italy). Even if we were to include all of the EEA nations in this analysis, the total would still be much less relative to the totals for the A+B+C column, and that labeled "NAFTA" (the United States, Canada, and Mexico).

As illustrated by Table 3.4, there has been an increase in the share of both NAFTA and Asian imports as a percentage of Japan's total imports, though the composition of the Asian share since 1985 has shifted somewhat from the ASEAN nations and to the PRC and the NICs. But the dramatic change is in the composition of Japan's export markets, as shown in Table 3.5.

As is clear from Table 3.5, since 1985 there has been an almost corresponding shift away from the NAFTA market and towards Asian nations. As noted, the revaluation of the yen was intended to make Japanese products more expensive for foreign (especially American) consumers and foreign goods cheaper for Japanese consumers. Ironically, however, the largest trade deficits that the United States experienced with Japan occurred after the revaluation, not before. Nevertheless, the percentage of Japanese exports to NAFTA nations has decreased since 1985. One could also argue that pending trade legislation prompted Japanese corporations to seek markets closer to home. Figure 3.1 is a consolidation of Japan's percentage of imports from and exports to Asian and NAFTA nations as a percentage of total imports and exports, from 1985 to 1991. For simplicity, we will call this measure the IEI, or combined import-export index.

The argument has been made that the nations of Asia are too diverse in their levels of both political and economic development to be able to consolidate their interests through a formal trade agreement, but from Japan's position it appears that integration is proceeding without the formalities of a trading "bloc." During the past decade, Japan has been able to expand its influence in Asia, and by not entering into exclusionary trade agreements, it has avoided alienating itself from the United States, its largest trading partner. Nor is it certain that Asian nations would agree

Table 3.5
Composition of Japan's Exports as a Percentage of Total Exports

	DESTINATION					
	ASEAN (A)	NICS (B)	PRC (C)	A+B+C	EEA[a]	NAFTA
1991	12.0	21.3	2.7	32.1	13.2	32.3
1990	11.3	19.5	2.1	29.4	13.3	34.6
1989	9.4	19.2	3.1	28.3	12.6	37.0
1988	8.1	18.8	3.6	27.3	12.9	36.9
1987	6.8	17.2	3.6	25.0	11.9	39.5
1986	5.8	14.4	4.7	22.7	10.5	41.6
1985	6.4	12.8	7.1	24.1	8.5	40.3

[a]Data for EEA only include U.K., Germany, France, and Italy percentages.
Figures derived from United Nations, *Statistical Yearbook for Asia and the Pacific*;
The Far East and Australasia; *Japan Statistical Yearbook*; all various years.

to any trade pact which they perceive would grant Japan, as the largest economy in the region, a formalized decision-making role. The words of Chiang Kai-shek more than fifty years earlier might echo the sentiments of a majority of those in ASEAN nations, who are less than certain that Japan is a trustworthy ally[55]: "[Japan] desires to reduce our resources by resorting to the machine of an 'economic bloc,' and to direct our politics and culture, with the extinction of our nation in view, through the medium of a 'unity of East Asia.' "[56]

Figure 3.1
Combined Import and Export Index (IEI) (1% = 1 IEI)

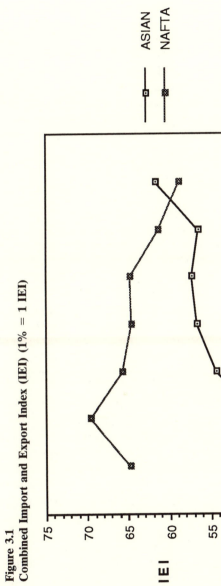

TECHNOLOGY TRANSFER

The transfer of technology from developed to developing countries is vitally important if the latter aspire to enjoy the benefits of an industrialized society. Although critics are often quick to dismiss the relationship between industrialization and development in favor of "indigenous" models of development (if not the definition of "development" itself), until alternate models are proven more effective in raising the living conditions and providing solutions for many of the problems that afflict the world's poorest inhabitants, industrialization will remain *the* development model. As one of the world's most industrialized nations, located in a region with some of the world's poorest, clearly Japan can play a role as a source of technology and expertise. Direct foreign investment is one way that technology is transferred to the host nation, as are educational exchange programs sponsored by both government and industry which allow Japanese researchers to travel abroad or foreign invitees to travel to Japan. These programs are offered by other advanced nations to developing nations, and are hardly unique to Japan. Nor is direct foreign investment and the subsequent transfer of technology exclusively Japanese. What is fairly unique to Japan's case of technology transfer, however, is a government program which allows foreign workers into Japan to receive training, and return to their nations with the skills they have learned.

As a nation develops economically, the composition and skill level of its labor force also undergo changes. Meeting the demands of an increasingly technological society requires advanced education, which creates aspirations for better-paying jobs. When an economy reaches the third and final stage of its development, there is a high proportion of "white-collar" workers (those holding jobs in service careers like finance, insurance, and high-tech) relative to the percentage of the labor force engaged in menial jobs, agriculture, and low-level manufacturing. Correspondingly, the willingness of service industry workers to accept jobs that their parents once held is decreased, as is the pool of undereducated workers to fill positions in non-white-collar fields. The shortage of workers in these low-level technology jobs is made more acute if the nation's population growth is decreasing, which is the case facing Japan, as parents are able to devote a greater share of their resources to the upbringing of fewer children. Japanese youth and those just entering the labor force have thus come to regard jobs in these non-white-collar fields as "the three k's"—in Japanese *kitsui* (demanding), *kitanai* (dirty), and *kiken* (dangerous). But buildings still have to be erected, holes still have to be dug, and bricks still have to be lifted. The result has been an acute demand for low-skilled workers, and an eager pool of foreigners who are willing to take these jobs for wages far higher than they would receive in their home market. The conflict, however, is between the reality of resource demand and economic growth, and Japan's cautious attitude towards allowing foreigners into the country.

On October 1, 1991, through legislative action, the Japanese Diet created the Japan International Training Cooperation Organization (JITCO), to "aid the less developed countries of the world while at the same time coming to terms with the labor shortage in Japan,"[57] according to one Ministry of Foreign Affairs official involved in the issue of foreign workers. As stated in an official document of the organization, while JITCO is technically a private corporation under the auspices of the Ministry of Justice, the Ministry of Labor, MITI, and the Ministry of Construction, it "aims to assist in the active transfer of Japanese technologies, skills and/or knowledge to developing and other countries by promoting and facilitating the acceptance of trainees, thereby contributing to the cultivation of human resources and socioeconomic advancement in these countries."[58]

Since Japan does not officially accept unskilled workers into the country, all of the trainees are classified as "semi-skilled" and the technology that they learn will technically be of that level. However, as a Ministry of Foreign Affairs official admitted, "It is not a purely 'trainee' position; it is 'on the job' learning actually. Of course, once an employer has a 'trainee'—even if technically semi-skilled—it isn't long before observation stops and they become like a regular employee, doing the same jobs and so forth."[59] But the problems encountered by the JITCO trainees, compared with those experienced by illegal workers (who make up the majority of menial workers in Japan), are minimal.

Presently, the official estimate of unskilled foreign workers in Japan is approximately 280,000, and all of these workers are violating their visa status by holding employment. In 1989, more than 16,500 people were discovered to be staying in Japan illegally, up from more than 5,500 in 1985, and nearly all of them are from Southeast and South Asia.[60] Many of them arrive in Japan on student visas with no intention of studying, while others have illegally overstayed their travel welcome. In the past, the number of females arrested for illegal status was far greater than the number of males (owing to the flourishing demand for foreign prostitutes). But reflecting the demand for foreign workers to fill jobs in the "*3k*" fields, notably construction, in 1989 more than 70% of the violators were male. Problems arise if these students-turned-workers are hurt while on the job, because they are not protected by Japan's labor laws or covered by its national health insurance system.

JITCO was created in response to these problems, though officially it does not arrange work opportunities in Japan for unskilled labor, and unofficially many government officials acknowledge that without this illegal foreign labor, many small- and medium-sized firms in Japan would have difficulty staying in business. Yet Japan is concerned should it actively recruit unskilled foreign labor from abroad, for it lacks the physical resources to accommodate what it believes would be a large scale influx of economic refugees.

In private discussions with Japanese officials, they admit that JITCO is not the answer to Japan's labor shortage or the transfer of technology abroad (in that order). Rather than formulate a plan which addresses the realities of labor demand and illegal immigrants, however, Japan has continued a stopgap policy while looking the other way. Many of its Asian neighbors would say Japan has taken the same approach in what the Ministry of Foreign Affairs has called "the correct recognition of history" (see the *Diplomatic Bluebook* excerpt in the opening to this chapter).

A HISTORY THAT CONNECTS, A HISTORY THAT DIVIDES

What does it entail for a nation, as distinct from an individual, to "recognize history"? Japanese textbooks have been a source of criticism both at home and abroad for their failure to present the "real" history of Japan, especially its actions during World War II.[61] But history is as much interpretation as it is fact. One would not expect to find similar accounts of the Vietnam War in textbooks used in the United States and Vietnam, for instance, nor would one find details of the slaughter of innocent Vietnamese in the textbooks used in U.S. schools. Yet because of Japan's highly centralized education system, organized under a Ministry of Education which approves all textbooks, there is an image of a government that is trying to hide its past from its own citizens, and predictions that the past is therefore bound to be repeated. To many Asians, the Japanese seem arrogant and chauvinistic, and believe that their strength lies in the "unity" of their nation, in contrast to the diverse populations of other Asian nations. This charge was supported by Japan's continued practice (recently terminated) of fingerprinting and treating as foreigners those second and third generation Koreans and Chinese born in Japan, whose ancestors were brought to Japan to fill the lowliest jobs during the war. Even though most of those affected by Japanese wartime policies are deceased, many in Japan (but many more outside of Japan) believe that the Japanese government is not facing its past. According to Nishizaki Fumiko,

Although the context was quite different, the way in which the United States dealt with the wartime internment of Japanese Americans was admirable in my view. President Bush, apologizing on behalf of the United States government, wrote to the former internees that a monetary sum and words alone could not restore lost years or erase painful memories, or convey the nation's resolve to rectify injustice and to uphold the rights of individuals. "We can never fully right the wrongs of the past," he said, "but we can take a clear stand for justice and recognize that serious injustices were done to Japanese Americans during World War II." The Japanese government has yet to do this, but if they moved toward this positon, I would be less opposed to their UN ambitions.[62]

Recently, Japanese leaders have included "remorse statements" for their nation's actions during the war in their speeches to Asian audiences. Prime Minister Miyazawa "reflected on past history" when he visited five ASEAN nations in April 1991, and emphasized that Japan had no plans to once again become a military power. The end of the Cold War had no bearing on Japan's decision to express the latter in its dealings with Asian nations, for this had been policy since the end of World War II. As the *Asahi Shinbun* quoted a Foreign Ministry leader in 1990, this policy will continue to be reaffirmed "time and again."[63] But the more significant recent change in Japan's foreign policy toward Asia has been the propensity of government representatives and officials to address Japan's wartime past in its former empire. Perhaps the most noteworthy "reflective" or "apologetic" pronouncement to date was that of Emperor Akihito, even though his position is that of symbol of the state and his 1992 trip to China was not considered to be a trip by a government official. He was quite frank when he declared that, "in the long history of relationship between our two countries, there was an unfortunate period in which my country inflicted great sufferings on the people of China. I deeply deplore this."[64]

Japan is experiencing a transition in its relations with Asia, and in the way that it appreciates the sensitivities of its neighbors' concerns that it acknowledge its past. As evidenced by the recent charges of Asian women that they were forced to serve as prostitutes for Japanese forces during the war, Japan will continue to be challenged by its history in its future relations with the rest of Asia. And as some believe that the motivation for such claims is based in large measure on Japan's economic success, the perception of a Japan that is somehow different from the rest of Asia will continue as well.

NOTES

1. Ministry of Foreign Affairs, Japan, *Diplomatic Bluebook 1991: Japan's Diplomatic Activities*, p. 204.
2. Interview, Shiina Motoo, November 19, 1992.
3. *Nihon Keizai Shinbun*, February 17, 1990, p. 2.
4. *Nihon Keizai Shinbun*, February 22, 1990, p. 2.
5. *Tokyo Shinbun*, June 10, 1990, p. 2.
6. *Asahi Shinbun*, March 23, 1992, p. 1 (evening edition).
7. *Asahi Shinbun*, January 23, 1991, p. 2.
8. Interview, Tanaka Akihiko, October 28, 1992.
9. U.S. Department of Defense, *A Strategic Framework for the Asian Pacific Rim: Looking Toward the 21st Century*, 1990, p. 6.

10. Ibid., p. 8.

11. Henry Kissinger, "Kissinger-Nakasone Forum," Tokyo, October 22, 1992.

12. *Diplomatic Bluebook 1991,* p. 205.

13. *Asahi Shinbun,* June 7, 1990, p. 5.

14. *Nihon Keizai Shinbun,* March 10, 1991, p. 2.

15. "Text of Prime Minister's Diet Policy Speech," *Japan Times,* October 31, 1992, p. 12.

16. *Asahi Shinbun,* October 25, 1991, p. 2.

17. Ibid.

18. *Washington Post,* January 2, 1991, pp. D1–D2.

19. During his entire term as secretary of state, Baker spent a total of one day in Japan.

20. " 'Noncommittal' on Withholding Aid," *Foreign Broadcast Information Service (FBIS),* EAS–91–218, November 12, 1991, p. 1.

21. Ibid.

22. *Yomiuri Shinbun,* December 20, 1989, p. 3.

23. *Nihon Keizai Shinbun,* December 19, 1989, p. 1.

24. *Tokyo Shinbun,* June 11, 1990, p. 1.

25. *Mainichi Shinbun,* June 11, 1990 (evening edition), p. 2.

26. Shidehido Toshio, *The Economic Development of Japan,* as cited in Zhang Peiji, "China's Strategy and Policy on Utilizing Foreign Capital," in Richard D. Robinson, ed., *Foreign Capital and Technology in China* (New York: Praeger, 1987), p. 3.

27. Hamada Takujiro (member of the Japanese Diet, House of Representatives), "Opinion: Japan's International Role," *Japan Economic Survey,* vol. 13, no. 6, June 1989, p. 15.

28. John White, *Japanese Aid* (London: Overseas Development Institute, 1964), preface.

29. This was clearly expressed in a 1961 MITI report: "Japan undertook economic cooperation not for political objectives arising from the Cold War, nor as support for developmental objectives resulting from decolonization, but in order to develop domestic industry." As cited by Joanna Moss and John Ravenhill, *Emerging Japanese Economic Influence in Africa; Implications for the United States,* Institute of International Studies, Policy Papers in International Affairs, Number 21 (Berkeley: University of California Press, 1985).

30. Alan Rix, "Japan's Foreign Aid Policy: A Capacity for Leadership?" *Pacific Affairs,* vol. 62, no. 4, Winter 1989–1990, esp. p. 464.

31. *Yomiuri Shinbun,* June 28, 1991, p. 13.

32. See Hanubasa Masamichi, consul general of Japan, "Fueling Success: Japan's Economic Aid Programs in Asia," speech delivered at

Princeton University, September 29, 1989, as reported in *Speaking of Japan*, vol. 10, no. 109 (Tokyo: Keizai Koho Center, January 1990).

33. *Economic Eye: A Quarterly Digest of Views from Japan*, vol. 10, no. 1 (Tokyo: Keizai Koho Center, Spring 1989), pp. 12–13.

34. *Asahi Shinbun*, May 7, 1991 (evening edition), p. 1.

35. *Japan Statistical Yearbook* (Tokyo: Statistics Bureau, Management and Coordination Agency, 1992), p. 361.

36. U.S. Department of Commerce, *Statistical Abstract of the United States, 1992* (Washington, DC: U.S. Government Printing Office, 1992), table 1329.

37. *Japan Times Weekly International Edition*, June 21–27, 1993, p. 3.

38. "China Aid to Be Resumed," *Japan Economic Survey*, vol. 14, no. 8 (August 1990.)

39. The four ministries charged with primary responsibility for aid appropriations are the Ministry of Foreign Affairs, the Ministry of International Trade and Industry, the Economic Planning Agency (which falls under the domain of the Office of the Prime Minister), and the Ministry of Finance.

40. *Nihon Keizai Shinbun*, March 3, 1993, p. 9.

41. *New York Times*, December 5, 1991, p. D 22.

42. S. Urata, "The Rapid Globalization of Japanese Firms in the 1980s: An Analysis of the Activities of Japanese Firms in Asia," as cited in Fukasaku Kiichiro, *Economic Regionalization and Intra-Industry Trade: Pacific-Asian Perspectives*, Research Program on Globalization and Regionalization, OECD Technical Papers, no. 53, February 1992, p. 20.

43. *Japan Times Weekly International Edition*, June 14–20, 1993, p. 14.

44. *New York Times*, December 5, 1991, p. D 22.

45. Interview, Kitaoka Shin'ichi, November 11, 1992.

46. *New York Times*, March 6, 1991, p. D 6.

47. *Nihon Keizai Shinbun*, November 20, 1991, p. 31.

48. See U.S. House of Representatives, *Report of the Defense Burden-sharing Panel*, August 1988, pp. 8–9.

49. For this analysis, however, the trade figures of Brunei are excluded because of the irregularity and infrequency with which they are announced; the major trade item between Japan and Brunei is oil, and Brunei is a secondary supplier to Japan.

50. In the calculation of both ASEAN and NICS trade figures, Singapore was counted for each category, but was only counted once for the Asian category.

51. International Monetary Fund, *Summary Proceedings of the Forty-Seventh Annual Meeting of the Board of Governors*, Washington, DC, 1992, p. 45.

52. Interview, Tanaka Akihiko, October 28, 1992.

53. "Foreign Minister Rejects Participation in EAEC," *FBIS*, EAS–91–218, November 12, 1991, p. 3.

54. Interview, Tanabe Yasuo, October 23, 1992.

55. According to a public opinion poll commissioned by the Ministry of Foreign Affairs and conducted in Indonesia, Malaysia, the Philippines, Singapore, and Thailand, no more than 25% of those polled (Thailand) responded in the affirmative, with most believing that Japan was "somewhat" of a trustworthy ally. Since 1983, the percentage who have responded in the affirmative has declined in Indonesia, Malaysia and Singapore. For the specifics of this poll, see Takeda Isami, "A New Dialogue for Japan, ASEAN and Oceania," *Japan Echo*, vol. XX, special issue, 1993, p. 75.

56. *Generalissimo Chiang Assails Konoye's Statement* (Chungking, China: China Information Committee, 1939), p. 13.

57. Interview, Ministry of Foreign Affairs official, October 13, 1992.

58. Japan International Training Cooperation Organization, *An Overview of the JITCO: Providing Information to Support and Promote Training Programmes in Japan*, 1992, p. 2.

59. Interview, Ministry of Foreign Affairs official, October 13, 1992.

60. Japan Ministry of Justice, *Summary of Statistics Related to Immigration Control*, as cited in Japan External Trade Organization (JETRO), *Japan Economic Databook*, Tokyo, 1991, p. 121.

61. For example, see *Washington Post*, "Keeping a Painful Past Both Dim and Distant," especially the textbook excerpt headed "Textbook Version: 'Japan Had No Choice,' " December 1, 1991, p. A 38.

62. Interview, Nishizaki Fumiko, October 6, 1992.

63. *Asahi Shinbun*, August 2, 1990, p. 2.

64. "Text of Emperor's Speech," *Japan Times*, October 24, 1992, p. 6.

II

POLICIES FOR A
TRIFURCATED EUROPE

4

Western Europe, Eastern Europe, and Japan

There are three distinct components to Japan-Europe relations, each of which continues to be influenced by a Cold War past. For more than forty years, Western Europe developed an infrastructure and economy far more advanced than those of its command economy Eastern European neighbors, while for the same period the former Soviet Union represented the greatest threat to Japan's security. Even though the Cold War has ended, neither the disparities of relative economic development nor the memories of distrust and tension will be removed as easily as was a wall which for many years symbolized the separation between East and West. Japan's business leaders see economic opportunity in all regions of Europe, but they are not about to reconstruct the former socialist states single-handedly. Nor are Japan's government leaders and bureaucratic officials in agreement over the potential longevity of Russian democracy and market reforms, the mitigation of its military threat, or its willingness to abandon a Cold War mentality in its relations with Japan.

To the reader, it may seem misplaced to consider Japan's relations with Russia under the same heading as those with Eastern and Western Europe. This ambiguity is understandable but, we hope, so is our rationale for doing so. The former Soviet Union was geographically situated in Asia as much as it was Europe, but throughout the Cold War it was identified by the West and Japan as a European power more often than it was an Asian power. The breakup of the Soviet Union and the independence of the Baltic states reduced this European component, and although Russia is by land mass more of an Asian nation, those in its center of power, namely Moscow, are more European than Asian in their outlook. Nor can one say that Russia is included in any plans for Japan's renewed cooperation with "Asia." In short, the categorization of Russia as a European state for the purposes of this study may be imprecise, but it reflects a Cold War past that still colors Japanese perceptions of the post–Cold War world.

Among Japan's three European relationships, those with Western (or developed) Europe have been the focus during the post–Cold War period, and there is no reason to believe this emphasis will not continue. Japan's relations with developing (or Eastern) Europe, long dormant economically and insignificant strategically, have increased for Japan since the end of the Cold War, and they will assume a greater though still limited role. The third component of Japan's Europe strategy, that of its dealings with the Russian republic, has a longer history than Japan's relations with the other two areas. Unfortunately, however, this longevity does not bode well for the future of Japan-Russia relations. Full normalization of relations between the two nations will be hindered by a territorial dispute that, until resolved, will prolong the animosities of the Cold War.

Chapter 4 will consider both the most developed of these three links (that of Japan–Western Europe), and the least developed (that of Japan–Eastern Europe). In Chapter 5, we will continue our analysis with the relationship that has the greatest obstacles to overcome (not only vis-à-vis the other two, but also compared to Japan's relations with most other nations of the world), that of Japan-Russia. While the Japan–Western Europe relationship is clearly the most significant of the three in terms of the stability of the global economic system, that between Japan and Russia is the most significant in terms of the global political system.

WESTERN EUROPE: CONFRONTING THE
SPECTER OF A FORTRESS

Even though Japan and the EU signed a joint declaration in 1991 covering issues as diverse as security, economics, and the environment,[1] each facet of the Western Europe–Japan relationship, particularly its political dimension, is not as significant as that between the United States and Japan or the United States and Western Europe. This relatively less-developed link has made the notion of a post–Cold War leadership trilateral of the United States, the EU, and Japan seem more like a two-sided arrangement, with the United States as common element. Both Japan and the nations of Western Europe are well aware that without the participation and cooperation of the United States, the international order as we know it would cease to function; nor can any future international order be conceptualized without the role to be played by the United States. But the acknowledged role of *primus inter pares* played by the United States should not overshadow the significance of both Japan and the EU to the world economic and political system, or the potential significance of the relationship between them. Yet until the Japan-EU bilateral component of this trilateral is developed, we will continue to see relations between the three conducted largely on bilateral terms, with the third member of the group always concerned that an agreement may be reached with the benefits only accruing to the other two.[2] For example, as a Chinese commentator notes, for Japan

there exist a lot of difficulties in forming a systematic East-Asian economic ring with Japan playing the leading role. Nevertheless, it works hard to set up an inseparable link with East Asia in down-to-earth economic matters, [to] promote the process of economic integration in the region, to lay the foundation for an East-Asian economic ring and to use it as a prop in dealing with the United States and the European community.[3]

Japan is understandably concerned about the possibility of being excluded from European integration and informal barriers to trade. However, in the opinion of the Ministry of International Trade and Industry's (MITI) European Division Deputy Director,

compared with NAFTA ... NAFTA is discriminatory. For example, with car import cases, NAFTA requires local content, while the EU market does not require this. Perhaps under the table they require a local content level, but it is not as outward as the NAFTA regulations. The local content rules are quite a barrier to us.[4]

The overriding concern confronting Japan in its relations with Western Europe is the extent to which European integration, when fully realized, will translate into discrimination for products of Japanese origin through local content laws and or quotas that restrict market access. But for Japanese business executives and the government, this concern was not always as acute as it has recently become. In 1990, it was the opinion of Bank of Tokyo Chairman Gyoten Toyoo that many Japanese were unconvinced that market integration of Europe would proceed as planned, a position that would be vindicated in light of the difficulty that faced passage of the Maastricht Treaty in national legislatures and through referenda during the fall of 1992.[5] This skepticism that a characteristically and historically divided Europe could agree on a shared vision, and in the process sacrifice a degree of their national decision-making autonomy, was combined with the reality of relations between EU member nations and Japan, which were conducted on bilateral terms more frequently than they were an aggregated Europe dealing with Japan. A German writer commented on Japan's initial uncertainty, an appraisal that he attributed in part to the nature of regional financing requests made to Japan. Prospective capital recipients "talked only about the advantages of their region and rarely missed an opportunity to speak negatively about other parts of the EU."[6] Another German writer related in 1991 that "the initial antipathy toward competition from the Far East has developed in several countries into going after Japanese investments. . . . No one is being stingy with attractive offers together with tax incentives or support in order to win the Japanese for their own country."[7]

But this doubtful evaluation of the likelihood of European integration slowly changed to one of belief as Japan and the rest of the world witnessed the reunification of East and West Germany. The division among EU members in their relations with Japan nevertheless remains, as does what Kuriyama Takakazu termed in 1991 Japan's "double-track relationship with the individual Western European countries and with the EU," noting that "for the strengthening of these relations, even still greater efforts than [those] between Japan and the United States will be needed."[8] It is clear that on certain economic issues involving Japan—notably Japanese automobile exports to the EU—the gulf of opinions among EU member nations is wide. France and Italy, and to a lesser extent Spain and Portugal, with the exception of Germany the EU's major manufacturers of automobiles, were the major opponents of replacing national barriers to Japanese auto imports with an EU quota. Under the agreements reached for EU economic integration, national quotas for automobiles would be phased out and replaced by a uniform EU quota, which would remain in effect until 1998. Relative to those of their EU counterparts, the stringency of these nations' trade agreements as they applied to automobiles is clear from Table 4.1.

Compared to the American presence in Europe, both in terms of political clout and economic activity, Japan is clearly in a secondary position. An increase in political influence will not be acquired overnight, if ever, and even though Japanese economic activity is not as strong as that of the United States, it is a presence that is hardly inconspicuous. In some European nations the response to this increased Japanese presence resembles that found in the United States in the early to mid-1980s, when Japan first intensified its level of foreign direct investment. The official opinions regarding Japan's economic activity in Europe are a study in contrasts, suggesting that, as with many issues before the EU, unified opinion is hardly guaranteed. For example, French Prime Minister Edith Cresson charged that Japan was "out to conquer the world" with its strategy of export diversification away from the recession prone American market.[9] Cresson reportedly said that she would "not allow France to bear the treatment inflicted by the Japanese car companies on United States industrialists."[10] While she personally—and her government officially—were strong opponents of the EU–Japan declaration, it was signed against the additional objection of Italy, which wanted the dec-

Table 4.1
Japanese Automobile Market Shares in Western Europe (percentages)

Country	1980	1985	1990
Austria	20.7	26.6	30.3
Belgium	24.5	19.8	20.1
Denmark	30.9	31.8	35.6
Finland	35.6	38.6	40.6
France	2.9	3.0	3.5
Germany	10.4	13.3	15.9
Great Britain	11.9	10.9	11.7
Greece	49.2	27.5	32.7
Ireland	0.5	33.8	40.9
Italy	0.1	0.2	1.6
Luxembourg	N.A.	15.4	14.8
Netherlands	26.4	22.4	26.8
Norway	39.1	34.1	44.1
Portugal	7.5	9.8	6.7
Spain	1.3	0.7	2.3
Sweden	14.1	16.1	24.9
Switzerland	23.0	25.5	28.1

N.A. : Not available

Source: Foreign Broadcast Information Service, WEU-91-120, June 21, 1991, p. 7.

laration to state specific market opening pledges from Japan, in contrast to Britain and the Netherlands, who argued that closer political dialogue would provide a forum to address trade issues.[11] Additionally, Jacques Delors, the president of the EU, warned that the EU was "at 'war' with a Japan bent on world economic domination."[12]

With its increased economic presence on the European continent, and in keeping with its desire to assume a greater international role, Japan attended the NATO talks and the Conference on Security and Cooperation in Europe (CSCE). It also sought, and received, observer status at the latter conference in early 1992. Needless to say, some European nations were not welcoming of their new security "partner" from halfway around the globe. During his visit to Japan in 1990, French Defense Minister Jean-Pierre Chevenement reportedly told his hosts that "with regard to both NATO and the CSCE, the component nations and areas of scope are definitely limited; therefore, there is no room for Japan to be involved deeply."[13] Germany, on the other hand, suggested to Japan that they should have observer status at the CSCE.[14] And although along with the British they have promoted a more liberal policy toward Japanese foreign investment than have other EU nations, the Germans, particularly those in the automobile industry, are concerned about the short-term effects of lost competitiveness relative to their Japanese counterparts. One article in a German newspaper noted, "In view of the catastrophic position of the U.S. producers, many European manufacturers are lamenting the construction of [manufacturing] plants in previously well-insulated Europe."[15] Not only will Japan's transplant of operations throughout EC nations increase competition between Japanese and EU industries, but also between individual nations. In short, the writer concludes, "The competition in Europe will certainly be murderous."[16] As the above description makes clear, EU nations are hardly in agreement on a response to the challenge of Japan, a challenge that has seen the EU trade deficit with Japan widen. In the future we are likely to see both increased Japanese-EU economic friction, as EU nations demand more access to what they perceive to be a "closed" Japanese market for their exports, and increased friction among the individual nations of the EU, which have heretofore adopted their own polices— both economic and political—toward Japan.

What can Japan learn from the realities of Western Europe? There are indeed similarities between the regional roles and expectations assumed of both Germany and Japan. Both are expected to be the central force in regional economic development, whether economic relations are to be integrated by formal agreement, as is the case with the EU, or integrated through activity, as is the case with Asia. Although the problems facing the EU in its move toward integration are by no means insignificant, there is a high degree of similarity among the nations of Western Europe in terms of social structure, culture, and income levels. Europe has been divided for centuries, and perhaps integration is the only way to prevent a return to divisiveness.

In both the EU and Asia, one of the common security interests is reflective of history more than reality. As a German newspaper commented, "Internationally, both countries are struggling with the same problem: their neighboring states do not quite trust them."[17] The concern from within the EU is the economic "power" of Germany, and the potential for this economic power to be translated into military capability. The level of Germany's military makes this likelihood remote, unless quantitative and qualitative improvements were to go unchecked by the other EU member nations. This seems highly unlikely. For many Asian nations, as we noted in Chapter 3, Japan represents a potential military threat, and few would wholeheartedly wish to formally enter into an economic or military regional agreement in which Japan is the leading player, and more substantially, the leading decision-maker. It is unclear at this juncture whether the EU will, as a group, be more forthcoming than some Asian nations in its official dealings with Japan. Nevertheless, even though the major obstacle to "normalized" relations between Japan and its neighbors—history—will not be a divisive force in Japan–EU relations, it appears that many Europeans believe that history begins with today.

EASTERN EUROPE: MEASURED RESPONSE

Of all of Japan's regional roles analyzed in this study, that with Eastern Europe is at present clearly the least developed. The potential for regional economic integration and an increased role in maintaining regional security, two factors that weigh into Japan's Asia relationship, are nonfactors in its dealings with Eastern Europe. Nor is there a strong degree of interdependence in the relationship, a sense of a "shared fate," and thus the exigency of strengthening existent ties and developing new ones, as is the case with Japan's relations with the United States (which will be discussed in Chapter 6), and to a lesser extent Japan's relations with the nations of the EU. Even calls from abroad that Japan assume a major role in providing the financing to prop up an infant democracy, as is the case with Japan-Russia relations, are hardly heard regarding Eastern Europe.[18] In short, since the imperatives or pressures that often drive Japan's dealings with these other nations and regions are absent in its interest in Eastern Europe, one might wonder why Japan has shown any interest in the region in the first place. That is a question we will return to throughout this section.

Although Japan has shown limited though increasing interest in Eastern Europe to Eastern Europe Japan represents a potential savior if it plays the role that others have hoped for it as a financier of development. In the words of Czechoslovak Economics Minister Vladimir Dlouhy, "If we really want foreign investment, let's stop just pretending that maybe we want it.... Let us acknowledge openly we need to accumulate big capital which, within a short period of time, we cannot get from domestic resources."[19]

But while Japan has shown some interest in the region as a source of low-cost labor and destination for Japanese goods, the Japanese government and Japan's business leaders realize that both labor skills and markets are not developed overnight. In the short and medium term, the more established infrastructure of Western Europe (schools, roads, transportation), together with its more developed banking system, distribution networks, and relative political stability, make it a more attractive investment opportunity for Japanese capital than the nations of Eastern Europe. Save for occasional appropriations of humanitarian aid and high-risk venture capital (which is itself limited in supply), Japan will be cautious in increasing its presence in the region. It is not about to become the sole initiator in the effort of developing the region, and until there are indications that the economic and political instability of the region have abated, Japanese businesses will be averse to going it alone; nor will the government appropriate significant amounts of bilateral aid. On both fronts, whether through financial consortiums in the former case, or through multilateral agencies in the latter, shared risk and circumspection will be the norm. Once the initial uncertainties of a possible return to a command economy and widespread civil unrest have passed in the individual nations, together with their governments' and citizens' success at accepting the fundamentals of a market economy (stabilizing the value of the national currency, accepting letters of credit, and creating channels of distribution and exchange, to name a few), based on its track record in economically and politically "liberalized" nations, Japan will be a (if not the) leading foreign actor in the region.

Most readers would accept the proposition that in the long term Japan will play *a* leading role in the region; few, however, will be as willing to accept the notion that Japan will play *the* leading role. We believe that this is a likely scenario for three reasons. First, one could easily argue that the nations of Western Europe are in a more likely position than Japan to either pursue or assume the leading role in these nations because of their proximity to them, and because of their security concerns should these nations revert to authoritarian regimes. But with the exception of the integration of the formerly divided East and West German states, there has been limited initiative by the *individual* nations of Western Europe to promote the interests of their eastern neighbors or increase their presence in these new markets. For example, we have not seen the French invest in Hungary with abandon, nor have we seen a considerable increase of British interest in Romania. In large measure this is accountable to the preoccupation with plans for regional economic and political integration among the states of Western Europe itself. If Eastern Europe is eventually integrated into the EU, barring the end of the nation state system as we know it, the connection between the two regions will be multilateral on both sides. In other words, if Western European integration is successfully implemented (by whatever measure), the initiative to include in their grouping, or simply conduct relations with, Eastern Europe will be made by a body representing what are at present unitary states. For example, what would it mean to say that the "EU" represents the largest foreign economic interest in Eastern Europe? Would it not be more accurate to state the interests of the individual members of the EU? This raises the fundamental issue of how the EU will be referred to if Western Europe integration is successfully implemented (by whatever measure). If in the future we are to regard the states of the EU as a unitary actor and not as the autonomous states that they are now, Japanese interest in Eastern Europe will be secondary. If, however, we consider the individual actors as a consolidated whole (which is certainly not assured), then Japan's interest in the whole of Eastern Europe may be unmatched.

Secondly, although the Japanese are hardly awash in capital, they are in a much healthier financial state than are the nations of Western Europe. The traditional financial powerhouse of Europe—Germany—faces the expense of rebuilding an integrated nation, as its government leaders wrestle with ideas of how to create jobs for an expanded work force. The nations of Western Europe also face an array of domestic troubles, not the least of which is uninspired economic growth, and rehabilitation of their domestic economies will take precedence over constructing market economies where their adaptability is uncertain. On the security front, instability in Russia and the success of its democracy pose more of a challenge to the states of Western Europe than do the former communist satellite states of Bulgaria, Hungary, or Czechoslovakia. If money is allocated for the purpose of maintaining democracy and staving off a return to totalitarianism, the target will more than likely be Russia before it will be the smaller states of Eastern Europe. The reunification of previously partitioned East and West Germany was at the time considered a potential security threat by most Europeans who had experienced two world wars, or at least had an appreciation for the events of history. The other traditional threat to Western European security, Germany (during the Cold War, East Germany) is a major actor in plans for EU integration. Unless Germany determines that it is not in its best interest to continue plans for its participation in EU integration (which at this moment seems doubtful), and considering its limited military capability, Germany will not pose a security threat to its neighbors.

One additional factor leads us to believe that Japan may, in the future, play the leading role in Eastern Europe. Each of the nations of Western Europe are, by nature of geography and pending their votes of approval, included in the plans for economic integration. Corporate Japan's fears of the possibility of a restrictive, discriminatory trading group in Western Europe have been lessened by its positioning in the Eastern European market, a vantage point from which they hope to benefit from trade agreements favorable to products of Eastern European origin. The recent strengthening of the yen has also made location of production abroad more attractive, but again, each objective will be clearly articulated, all obstacles and opportunities carefully calculated, and each decision cautiously reached. Once the decision is made to allocate financial support for a particular government, or to locate business operations in any or all of these nations, we can expect the Japanese to be involved for the long haul.

Although the economic development of each nation in Eastern Europe similarly languished under the dictates of a command economy and a totalitarian leadership, we must avoid the potential pitfall of assuming that Japan's interest and experience in the region is uniform across nations, for this is clearly not the case. Indeed, there have been far-reaching initiatives of Japanese support for the reconstruction of Eastern Europe in the general sense, most notably Prime Minister Kaifu's repeated pledge during his trip to eight European nations that "Japan will aid Eastern Europe in its reforms," a pledge that led to a promise of $1.95 billion in aid. But just as Japan has shown a proclivity to prioritize its interest in certain nations of Western Europe, Asia, or North America over others, the same can be said of its dealings with Eastern Europe.

During his visit to Poland in October 1992, then Foreign Minister Watanabe Michio informed his hosts that Japanese businessmen would increase their interest in investing in their nation if the preferential treatment granted to Western European nations was also given to them.[20] A similar concession was requested of Hungary, which a Hungarian official viewed as Japan's attempt at making his nation "choose between [the] extremes" of Japan and Europe.[21] It is clear that neither the Japanese government nor Japanese firms are going to rush into Eastern European nations until they can prove their credit worthiness. Japan's manufacturers see the opportunity to supply Western Europe from Eastern Europe, especially if barriers are in place to restrict the level of imports of Japanese cars. Relatively low wages in Eastern Europe represent one way to offset barriers if they are to take the form of tariffs, but they are a non-issue if export quotas are applied. In this case, Japan hopes that local content laws will be favorable to products shipped from Eastern European nations, and it is this possibility that will in large part influence the extent of Japanese interest in the region.

NOTES

1. For the text of the Japan–EU joint declaration, see *FBIS*, WEU–91–141, July 23, 1991, p. 1.

2. The "third party" has rarely been the United States, however. Recent examples that were cause for Japanese concern were the Fall 1992 Uruguay Round discussions between the United States and the EU over agricultural subsidies and products (oil seeds among them); EU concern was evident with trade agreements reached between the United States and Japan in early 1992. For the latter, see "U.S.–Japan Trade Agreements Cited," *FBIS*, WEU–92–020, January 30, 1992, p. 8; "EU Expects Equal Trade Treatment From Japan," *FBIS*, WEU–92–006, January 9, 1992, p. 3; "EU to Seek Increased Access to Japanese Market," *FBIS*, WEU–92–100, May 22, 1992, p. 7; *London Times*, January 17, 1992, p. 19.

3. Huang Su'an, "United States and Japan Vie for Economic Supremacy," *CIIS Paper* (Beijing: China Institute of International Studies, 1990), p. 8.

4. Interview, Sugita Sadahiro, Deputy Director, Europe Division, International Trade Policy Bureau, Ministry of International Affairs and Industry, October 23, 1992.

5. *Mainichi Shinbun*, July 21, 1990, p. 9.

6. "Japan's Slow Approach to Europe Charted," *FBIS*, WEU–91–137, July 17, 1991, p. 27.

7. "Japanese Auto Makers' EU Strategy Analyzed," *FBIS*, WEU–91–120, June 21, 1991, p. 7.

8. Kuriyama Takakazu, "Taikenteki nihon gaikoron [Thoughts on Japanese Diplomacy, as Experienced]," *Chuo Koron*, November 1991, p. 116.

9. *London Times*, June 12, 1991, p. 23.

10. "Cresson Continues 'Attacks' on Japanese Policy," *FBIS*, WEU–91–106, June 3, 1991, p. 27.

11. "EU Fails to Agree on Relations with Japan," *FBIS*, WEU–91–073, April 16, 1991, p. 3.

12. "Delors: EU in 'Economic, Trade War' with Japan" *FBIS*, WEU–91–183, September 20, 1991, p. 3.

13. *Mainichi Shinbun*, April 23, 1990, p. 3.

14. "Foreign Minister Discusses Japan's Role in Europe," *FBIS*, WEU–92–032, February 18, 1992, p. 7.

15. "Japanese Auto Production in Europe Grows 'Rapidly,' " *FBIS*, WEU–92–224, November 19, 1992, p. 2.

16. Ibid.

17. "Press Assesses Helmut Kohl's Talks in Japan," *FBIS*, WEU–93–040, March 3, 1993, p. 7.

18. The only notable exception has been German Chancellor Kohl's request that Japan invest in the former East Germany, which can be viewed as more a solicitation by Germany for others to share in its burden of financing the development of its eastern region, rather than a suggestion that the fate of democracy throughout the world is contingent in part on Japanese economic support. See "Japan, Germany Split Over Aid to Soviets," *FBIS*, WEU–91–135, p. 7.

19. " 'Indifferent' Japanese Investment Attitude Viewed," *FBIS*, EEU–92–083, April 29, 1992, p. 15.

20. "Skubiszewski Criticizes Economic Ties With Japan," *FBIS*, EEU–92–193, October 5, 1992, p. 12.

21. "Official Explains Problems in Japan, EU Talks," *FBIS*, EEU–91–177, September 12, 1991, p. 19.

5

Russia and Japan

As to Russia, no one knows when and how that country will settle down. However, it is certain that the present state of anarchy cannot last forever, and someday Russia will settle down somehow. Countries other than Russia must first of all return to their normal condition before we can profitably think what to do with Russia. Anything we may do for Russia at the present moment would be merely a trial of doubtful nature recalling the spectacle of a near-sighted person searching for his lost eyeglasses. It may either accelerate or retard the settling of Russia in a manner which may be good or bad for the peace of the world. And yet we cannot help feeling instinctively that we must do something for Russia.[1]

The above passage was written in the early 1920s, a decade and a half after Japan's military victory over Russia in the Russo-Japanese War, and just a few years after the Tsarist regime's downfall that was in large part spurred on by Russia's military defeat to Japan. But it could just as easily have been uttered by a majority of Japanese seventy years later, in the post–Cold War period, which followed another Russian defeat (that of communism), a revolution that was just as monumental as Lenin's. Most Japanese, whether taxpayers or policymakers, see in Russia instability more than they do hope, and chaos more than they do cohesion. In the words of Gyoten Toyoo, "What Russia needs, first and foremost, is an economic road-map, because no one can start thinking about reconstruction until then."[2] Yet as members of a nation that has determined that it will pursue a greater role in the post–Cold War world, they believe that Japan should do something to address the problems of its neighbor that for most of their shared history has been Japan's antagonist more than it has been its ally. Exactly what Japan believes it should do, and the constraints that prevent it from doing so, will be the focus of this chapter.

If the economist's idea of comparative advantage has any merit, for Russia, a capital-scarce nation with significant natural resources, and Japan, a resource-scarce nation that uses capital as its major foreign policy tool, the opportunities for complementarity would seem unmatched. Economic laws, however, must always contend with political reality. For forty years, the Russians steamed over their loss to Japan in the Russo-Japanese War of 1904–1905, and for nearly fifty years following, Japanese emotions have simmered over the final days of World War II, when the Soviet Union abrogated the neutrality pact that it had signed with Japan in the early days of the war.

In analyzing Japan-Russian relations, no issue is perhaps as important between the two nations, yet as easily dismissed by foreign observers, as is their competing claims to four islands off the coast of Japan's northern island of Hokkaido. Arguments have been made by these "experts" that the existence of the issue has taken precedence over the value of the islands to either side, for they are insignificant "rocks" with little or no strategic, economic, or political value. Continuation of the dispute would therefore suggest that the two sides have agreed to disagree, for they must see some value in these islands that the rest of us do not. While we realize the islands may not have the strategic value they held during the Cold War, their political symbolism has nevertheless increased, and their potential economic value is hardly insignificant.

Politically, all Russian leaders (whether Boris Yeltsin or his successors, if the issue is not resolved during his term of leadership) will have to deal with the conservative element in Russia and their memories of the "great Soviet empire." The popular movements in the Baltic states, in the other non-Russian republics, and in Eastern Europe were a flood of independence euphoria that even the most concerted Russian military effort would have been powerless to dam, and with their independence went a significant chunk of the Soviet realm. In contrast, the Northern Territories issue (as it is referred to by the Japanese) lacks this independence component, and possession of the islands is in the firm control of Russia. Although the Japanese have awaited the return of the islands since shortly after the end of World War II, they have not made any military moves to retake what they claim is their inherent territory (à la Argentina and the Falkland Islands), nor does it appear that they will not wait another fifty years (or longer) until the issue is resolved, for they have few alternatives. On the one hand, Yeltsin's refusal to negotiate represents his attempt to quell his detractors and prolong his political life, while on the other hand he can hold out for a concession from the Japanese that would be more politically significant than the political consequences that would result from a return of the islands, in the end bolstering his political position.

Economically, under Russian administration, the islands have not been developed beyond the basic necessities of a small fishing community and a military garrison. If returned to Japan it is likely that their economic value would increase. The Ministry of Foreign Affairs is frank when it declares that the islands will become "the second Hokkaido" with hotels and apartment houses if returned to Japan,[3] and plans by Japanese developers to turn the area into anything from an "exotic" wilderness getaway for nature lovers to a tourist retreat have been proposed. Their value as an abundant fishing ground is well documented, and they are within easy reach of a fleet of Japanese commercial fishing vessels.

An alternative explanation for the impasse is that the two nations have not really liked each other in the past, and even if there was not a territorial dispute between them they still would not like each other. This explanation would suggest that the issue serves as an excuse by both sides to avoid having to normalize relations, or that the nations disagree for the sake of disagreement. This is also a possible explanation for the protracted nature of the dispute, but it loses a measure of validity when we consider what would happen if the stalemate was overcome and the islands were returned to Japan. Whether the Japanese would suddenly "like" the Russians if they returned what Japan considers to be its islands is an issue that can only be answered when an agreement is reached between the two sides. Yet it is clear that no action by either side could overcome the troubles in the bilateral relationship any more than this. Judging from the history between the two nations, the imperatives facing Russia, and the apparent unwillingness or inability of either side to offer a true compromise (i.e., one that cannot only be offered, but realized), we believe that this initiative will not happen any time soon.

Even if one accepts either or both of the explanations suggested for the longevity of the dispute, neither tells us how the issue evolved or why Japanese government officials and most of the Japanese public myopically view Russia through "territorial glasses." In short, to understand Japan's foreign policy towards Russia in the post–Cold War period, and its willingness or unwillingness to "do something" for Russia, requires an understanding of the Northern Territories dispute and the history that preceded it.

One could argue that a significant reason why Japan-Russia relations have rarely been amicable has been the primary role played by the United States in the foreign affairs of both nations. Since the end of World War II, American impressions of Russia and Japan have twice undergone a near about-face. During the Cold War, the perception of Russia had been transformed from wartime ally to ideological nemesis, and it was widely assumed that any international conflict that involved the United States would invariably draw the Russians (or the Soviets, as they were then referred) to the competing side. Although far from perfect, and not as positive to the extent that the image of Russia was negative, during the Cold War the American perception of Japan was no longer that of an insatiable imperialist nation, but instead Japan was given the moniker of "America's most loyal ally in the Pacific." In part because of these competing images, and the significant role played by the United States in the foreign affairs of both Russia and Japan, for more than forty years relations between Russia and Japan assumed a secondary status for both nations. And for most of these forty years, the perception that each had of the other was overwhelmingly negative because the relationship between the two during the two hundred years preceding the Cold War was at best neutral, but most often negative. The Cold War only served to solidify these negative sentiments.

With the end of the Cold War, Americans have felt "sympathy" for Russia and the plight of Russians, and have personalized the struggle for democracy—America's foreign policy yardstick—first in the person of Gorbachev and now in Yeltsin. It has been as if the collapse of the Berlin Wall and the slogans of *glasnost* and *perestroika* have erased our memories that less than ten years ago Russia was still termed the "evil empire," and that for more than forty years its foreign policy was based on the premise of a "final encounter" with the United States. It is only natural that the United States would expect Japan to share in its giddiness and enthusiasm with the slightest sign of "democratization" of its former enemy, for American foreign policy has often been tinged by short-sightedness and driven by idealism. Yet Americans should also expect that this enthusiasm, if not premature euphoria, may not be met by a similar response from Japan. It is somewhat ironic that just as easily as they have forgotten forty-five years of hatred of the former Soviet Union, Americans have been equally adept at selectively forgetting the strength of the U.S.-Japan relationship during this same forty-plus year period, but this is an issue that will have to wait for Chapter 6.

The threat posed by the Soviet military and their actions abroad throughout the Cold War were more credible than any other threat to Japan's security. But while the dislike of the other was (and for the most part remains) genuine among the citizenry of both nations, it is not a heated dislike similar to that which characterizes some potential and realized trouble spots in the world, for instance Israel's relations with some of its Arab neighbors (the 1993 Middle East declaration notwithstanding), or the near frequent boiling point between India and Pakistan. As with other relationships between nations that can be characterized by suspicion, aversion, and conflicting cultures, this one also has its historic element. And with no other issue between the two nations is history a more significant factor than that of their competing claims for islands off the northern coast of Hokkaido, hereafter referred to as the Northern Territories.

The Northern Territories (also referred to as the Southern Kuriles) comprise the islands ͵of Shikotan, Etorofu, Kunashiri, and the seven smaller islands of the Habomai group. Stretching in a northeasterly direction, the islands have a combined land area of 5,000 square kilometers, and the closest, Kaigara of the Habomai islands, is only 3.7 kilometers from Japan's northernmost island of Hokkaido. The waters around the islands benefit from a unique flow of warm and cold currents, and make up what is considered to be one of the three best fishing grounds in the world.[4] Though the Kuriles were regarded by some as islands that could serve as lands of fortune with their rich marine life, other minds were keenly preoccupied with their strategic location and their role as a potential buffer of Japanese and Russian interests. In 1746, Lieutenant Aleksei Chirikov proposed that a naval base be established in the Kuriles to preside over the eastern approaches to Siberia and the northern approaches to Japan.[5] Such foresight was particularly astute, recalling that at the time Japan was a non-warring nation that was by and large pursuing a policy of feudalism in an age of increasing innovation.

Diplomatic interactions between the two neighbors were non-existent, and neither nation was able to define its rights to the island chain or disclaim the presence of the other. It was this ambiguity regarding sovereignty over the islands which summoned Russian traders and statesmen closer to the coast of Japan, as their movements were left unchecked by the Bakufu (shogunal government) which was gradually losing its authority over areas under its rule. It must be remembered that during the Tokugawa period (1600–1868), the Japanese leaders proclaimed adherence to a policy of national isolation (even if it was not always followed, as noted in Chapter 1), and this seclusion policy was frequently challenged by Russian activity in the north.

EARLY TREATIES

When Commodore Perry arrived off the Japanese coast in July 1853, the "black ships" and superiority of Western innovation which they represented far outweighed any previous Russian provocation experienced by the Bakufu. Well aware of the continual Russian challenge to its northern border, the Japanese permitted American access to Hakodate, located in southern Hokkaido, hoping to play foreign interests off one another, if not to control Russian expansionism. Containment of the foreigners seemed to be the only solution available, and in this scheme the Americans were a more distant, and perceived to be a less hostile, menace. "United States envoy Townsend Harris lost no opportunity to suggest that ties with a distant United States would help protect Japan against pressure from her Russian neighbor . . . but probably no American of the time fully realized how long the Japanese had worried about the threat to their northern frontier."[6]

As Japan inked treaties of commerce and extraterritoriality with the United States and other nations, the government realized that postponement of defined territorial claims in the northern islands could not continue, for to do so would implicitly invite the Russians to all the territory they could occupy. The Treaty of Shimoda of 1855 declared Etorofu (Iturup to the Russians) and the islands south to be Japanese territory, while Uruppu (Urup) and those north would be under Russian sovereignty. This was the first formal territorial agreement between the two countries over the Kurile Islands, and the first legal recognition of the Southern Kuriles as Japanese territory. Any Japanese claim to the islands will cite this document to prove that from the time of mutual recognition, sovereignty over the Southern Kuriles rested with the Japanese. This position is strengthened by the two countries' signing of the Treaty of St. Petersburg twenty years later. Under this agreement, Japan received possession of all the Kuriles in exchange for cession of the southern half of Sakhalin Island (which previously had been divided north/south and governed by Russia and Japan, respectively) to Russia. It was not until the Russo-Japanese War of 1904–1905, brought on by their competing interests in Korea and Manchuria, that the two nations would clash.

One Japanese writer at the turn of the century captured the sentiments of his countrymen at the time when he reflected that:

The period from the close of the China-Japan War [1895] to the opening of the Russo-Japanese is to be looked upon as the days of "reclining on firewood and tasting liver," in the words of an old saying. Side by side with our just aspiration to redress the wrong done us by Russia, we had to think of the further encroachment of our northern neighbor across the

Sea of Japan. We had to prepare for the inevitable struggle from which there seemed to be no way of escape.[7]

The leaders of the Meiji governemnt, known as *genro*, were divided on the question of war with Russia. Some saw it as unavoidable if Japan were to receive recognition among the world's great powers and to them, Russian refusal to recognize Japanese priority in Korea, coupled with Russian advancements into Manchuria, justified the cries for war. To others, like *genro* Yamagata Aritomo and Ito Hirobumi, the war seemed unwinnable, and the result would be similar to the fate which befell China. In defeat, it was argued, unequal treaties with even harsher terms than those imposed on its neighbor would be forced upon Japan. Attempts at contacting the Russians to learn their intentions proved futile. "Despite Japan's many pleas for their views, it could only be assumed that they [the Russians], like the Japanese, were making last-minute preparations for war. By this time, the reluctant Ito had accepted that war was inevitable."[8]

THE SEEDS OF REVENGE

In a move that Josef Stalin would later refer to as a Russian version of "Pearl Harbor," Japanese forces made a surprise attack on Russian warships at Port Arthur, on China's Liaotung Peninsula, commencing the Russo-Japanese War. Beyond the military significance of this port to the Russians, it was somewhat fitting for the Japanese to attack this Russian holding. As noted in Chapter 1, Russia had joined France and Germany in "advising" Japan to return the peninsula to China following Japan's victory in the Sino-Japanese War of 1894–1905, and had subsequently occupied the territory three years later.

The war was an event of the first magnitude for the small island nation pitted against a naval colossus, seemingly nothing short of a life-and-death struggle. No one could have imagined that an Eastern country with a relatively young fleet would demolish an established naval power like that of Russia, but that is just what happened. Sixteen months after the start of the war, President Theodore Roosevelt would act as an intermediary and persuade both sides to the negotiation table in Portsmouth, New Hampshire. This diplomatic move earned Roosevelt the Nobel Peace Prize, and Japan the southern half of Sakhalin Island, Russian holdings in Manchuria, and a free hand in Korea.

The defeat came as a shock to Russians, and Japan's victory incited political discontent and was a significant catalyst in the downfall of the Tsarist regime. There were demonstrations, street riots, peasant insurrections, and defections in both the army and navy. In contrast, Japan's self-image was exalted as it basked in victory, for it too could now be considered a formidable military threat, never again having to passively accept Western imperialist ambitions. The victory over Russia altered the balance of power in Asia, and Japan's ability to defeat a great European power served to accelerate the development of nationalist movements in Asia. Perhaps a Japanese defeat would have nipped in the bud the aggressive, expansionist policies which Japan pursued until its defeat in World War II, or its participation in both world wars altogether. The point can be argued ad nauseam, but it is clear that the outcome of the Russo-Japanese War amplified Russian animosity toward Japan, as feelings of revenge and contempt would be carried with the Russian people until the end of World War II. Said Josef Stalin, "The defeat of Russian troops in 1904 in the period of the Russo-Japanese War left grave memories in the minds of our people. It was as a dark stain on our country. Our people trusted and awaited the day when Japan would be routed and the stain wiped out."[9]

THE UNITED STATES' UNWITTING ROLE IN THE DISPUTE

The United States, which had prioritized its World War II military efforts on the Pacific War, consistently defeated the Japanese in successive land and sea battles, most at sites which had recently been included in the Japanese empire. But instead of anticipating that the war was drawing to a close, many in Washington exaggerated the strength of the enemy, resulting in a blind pessimism of those in decision-making positions. Presidential adviser Charles E. Bohlen stated that "it would cost about 200,000 more in American casualties to assault the Japanese islands before rather than after Soviet entry into the Pacific War,"[10] while Secretary of State

Edward R. Stettinius, Jr. recalled that "the president [Roosevelt] was told that without Russia it might cost the United States a million casualties to conquer Japan."[11] It was this latter estimate which Roosevelt cited before a joint session of Congress on March 1, 1945. Stettinius did not state who supplied the president with this figure, nor the source for the informant's estimate. It is remarkable, however, that official estimates up to that time placed total American casualties since December 7, 1941 in the neighborhood of one million, and the same estimate was used in predicting future casualties without Russian participation. It was already March 1945. The war would end in five months.

Naturally, when the American public heard such alarming figures, Russia was perceived as the savior of the American soldier, and its participation the only way to ensure a speedy Allied victory. But as Rear Admiral Ellis M. Zacharias noted in his memoirs, "It was an altogether wrong estimate, its authors being deceived by a purely military and quantitative evaluation of the enemy, a treacherous trap into which the greatest military leaders are likely to fall occasionally."[12] According to Zacharias, the War Department had prepared two estimates regarding enemy strength rather than one, but "the more accurate and from our point of view optimistic evaluation of Japanese potentialities was pigeon-holed by a special intelligence outfit in the assistant secretary's office."[13]

At preliminary discussions convened at Yalta to win Soviet support for the Allied effort, Stalin requested initial supplies necessary for the Soviet army to effectively carry out the proposed intervention against Japan—"two months' supplies of food, fuel, transport equipment, and other needs for a force of 1,500,000 men, 3,000 tanks, 75,000 motor vehicles, and 5,000 aircraft."[14] The Americans delivered 80% of the Soviet demands, but this was only the beginning of the United States giving a rubber-stamp approval to Stalin's wishes. As Secretary of State James F. Byrnes wrote in his memoirs, *Speaking Frankly*, "Mr. Stalin [was] not bashful about making demands,"[15] and neither Byrnes nor his fellow diplomats was about to challenge forceful Stalinist ambitions. Writing in his memoirs, William D. Leahy, chief of staff to both Presidents Roosevelt and Truman, quoted Stalin in his "frank and appealing discussion" of Russia's part in the war against Japan.

"I want no reparations from Japan. Add to that Stalin's agreement to support the Chinese Government of Chiang Kai-shek and I do not see how anybody could object to the agreements made."[16] Leahy, too, was either ignorant of, or overlooked, in Stalin's words, the "special account" that Russia had "to settle with Japan"[17] as a direct result of the Russo-Japanese War of 1904–1905. This feeling of revenge that Stalin and Russians of his generation had carried with them would surface in the his later demands, yet they were not interpreted as signs of vengeance, and Stalin's "requests" were deemed reasonable. As Leahy later recalled,

Stalin repeated to the conference what he had told Roosevelt privately, namely, "I only want to have returned to Russia what the Japanese have *taken* from my country [emphasis added]." Roosevelt had said, "That seems like a very reasonable suggestion from our ally—they only want to get back that which was taken from them." It seemed very reasonable to me also, and no one was more surprised than I to see these conditions agreed to at labeled as some horrendous concessions made by President Roosevelt to an enemy.[18]

For fear of a Japanese first strike on Soviet cities, and as Japan and the Soviet Union were parties to a neutrality pact, no mention of the agreements reached at the conference could be made public. Stalin and Foreign Minister Mikhailovich Molotov said that if their conditions were met, it would be easier to explain to the Soviet public the reason for going to war against a country which did not attack them, unlike the case of Germany. The likelihood that a war declaration would be accepted by the Supreme Soviet would also be increased, Stalin noted, although everyone present knew that the "Supreme Soviet" was embodied in Stalin himself. But out of courtesy, no one dared challenge his claim. In the words of Charles Bohlen, "Even with all the advantages of hindsight, however, I do not believe that the Western Allies could have walked away from the attempt to reach an understanding with the Soviet Union. Nor do I believe that through harder bargaining we could have struck a better deal with Stalin."[19] In all honesty, however, most would agree that the Soviets were ridiculously overcompensated for their participation in the war effort against Japan. The U.S. position was epitomized in a note presidential aide Harry Hopkins passed to the president during the discussion of reparations: " 'The Russians have given in so much at this conference [Yalta] that I don't think we should let them down.' "[20]

The United States, it can be surmised, had its own intentions for the Kuriles. In a letter from President Truman to Stalin on August 17, 1945, a request was made for "air base rights for land and sea aircraft on some one of the Kurile Islands, preferably in the central group, for military purposes and for commercial use."[21] Stalin responded that "demands of such a nature are usually laid before. . . . a conquered state . . . or an allied state expresses readiness to grant its Ally an appropriate base [in return]."[22] When Stalin declared that the Soviets' desired base would be located on one of the Aleutian Islands, with the ultimate destination of Soviet planes to be Seattle,[23] the United States had no choice but to abandon its Kurile landing base scheme. "When you expect our support for your desire for permanent possession of *all* the Kurile Islands," wrote Truman to Stalin, "I cannot see why you consider it offensive if I ask for consideration of a request for landing rights on only one of those Islands [emphasis added]."[24] It was only at that time, when the U.S. government realized that its military plans for the islands would not materialize, that it questioned whether the Soviets had been "given" too much.

"During [a conversation between Molotov and Byrnes], Molotov kept returning continuously to his question as to what we proposed to do on U.S.–held islands in the Pacific, and each time Byrnes responded by asking what he proposed to do about the Kuriles and Sakhalin."[25] It is clear that this ambiguity and hedging on the part of the U.S. contingent revolved around its plans for Okinawa. Wrote James Byrnes: "The United States undoubtedly will stand by President Roosevelt's agreement on the Kuriles and Sakhalin. I see no objection to Japan's keeping the islands of the Ryukyu group north of Okinawa. From Okinawa south, it is my hope that the islands will be placed under a United Nations trusteeship. *For sentimental reasons*, the United States will want a trusteeship interest in Okinawa [emphasis added]."[26] The two countries had, in effect, agreed to honor their respective territorial interests; by accepting Soviet occupation of the Kuriles, American trusteeship of Okinawa would go unquestioned. Miraculously, the experience of a partitioned China fifty years earlier eluded a defeated Japan.

A day-long participation in World War II against the Japanese would give the Soviets their chance for revenge, but the most substantial gains would be garnered prior to their declaration of support for the Allied forces against Japan, and not on the battlefield. The American policymakers at the time were unaware of just how acute Soviet resentment toward Japan was, and in hindsight they were equally inept at clarifying their definition of the term "Kurile Islands," possession of which (among other spoils of war) would be granted to the Soviets for their superficial participation in the war effort against Japan. According to John Snell, the Americans arrived at Yalta with little or no appreciation for the issues of the day, or of the history which divided the Soviet Union and Japan. "It is by no means impossible," Snell writes, "that the Russians would have satisfied themselves with only the northern and central Kurile islands [for agreeing to enter the war against Japan]. But nobody ever raised the question."[27] It is interesting to note that Soviet occupation of the four southern islands lacked any historical basis. In fact, prior to the conclusion of the war, no attempts were made by the Soviets to assert their "rightful ownership" of the territories.

Following the atomic bombing of Nagasaki on August 9, 1945, the Soviet Union abrogated the neutrality pact that it had signed with Japan in 1941 and declared war on a nation which by most opinions had realized its defeat with the earlier bombing of Hiroshima. In the early morning hours of August 10, the United States received through the Swiss government a message from the Japanese that they were ready to accept the terms of the Potsdam agreement. While the devastation produced by the atomic bombs did not necessitate last-minute Russian "participation" in the war against Japan, it was evident to Stalin that the end of the war was imminent, and a sudden Japanese surrender to the Allied forces, which at the time did not include the Soviet Union, was possible. Failure to declare war against the Japanese could, therefore, "deprive" the Soviets of territorial gains which they had expected to receive. The former Soviet Union was never self-effacing when recounting its role in the war effort against Japan. An official Soviet version of the events stated that: "Even combined [aerial bombings and the U.S. blockade of Japan] they could not force a surrender out of Japan, which had powerful land forces. . . . Total victory over the Far Eastern aggressor . . . required powerful land troops with enormous combat experience. Such a force was the Soviet Army."[28]

THE DISPUTE TAKES SHAPE

One question most frequently asked by the Japanese . . . is how, under American democracy, the Yalta agreement was possible. One Japanese who lived for some time in the United States told this correspondent: "We are so used to important decisions being made without consulting the people, but we did not understand that this could be done under the United States system."[29]

Initially, the Americans could not be turned to for help, for jurisdiction over the Kuriles and the fate of their inhabitants rested with the Soviets. Virtually nothing was known of the destiny of the Japanese who, by virtue of a heretofore secret agreement, were now regarded as mere squatters on Soviet territory. When American interest in the matter was greater than characteristically scant appreciation, attempts at discovering Soviet plans for the residents proved futile, for six months after surrender, all communication with the islands ceased.[30] Almost immediately after the conclusion of the war, the Commission for Recovering Islands Attached to Hokkaido was formed, with the former mayor of a Hokkaido fishing village (who had been purged from his government post by the Allied Occupation forces for serving during Japan's militarist years) acting as its head. Three petitions asking for return of the islands to the Hokkaido fishermen were presented to General Douglas MacArthur, and whether the petitions received greater than superficial attention remains a matter in question. Nevertheless, the class action alerted the Americans that those Japanese with a vested interest in the issue believed the United States could effect a solution to a problem that many believed it had a hand in creating.

On December 22, 1949, the Japanese government presented its first policy statement on the Northern Territories before the Diet.

"The statement denied the Yalta decision and asserted Japan's claim to the Southern Kuriles. . . . Prime Minister Yoshida Shigeru reaffirmed this stand a month later, thereby becoming the first Japanese head of government to make an issue of northern irredentism."[31] The sincerity of the islanders' claim now carried with it governmental endorsement, and as American plenipotentiaries headed for San Francisco, there should have been no doubt in the minds of those in Washington regarding Japan's position, or the existence of the dispute. Above and beyond the ultimate ratification of a peace treaty, the San Francisco conference served as a forum for clarifying ambiguities relating to the Yalta meeting and for righting misunderstandings in interpretation. Through effective diplomacy, Japanese claims could have been realized, but save for a cursory display of opposition to the Soviet presence on the Kuriles and southern Sakhalin, maintaining a presence on several islands (including the Bonins, Ryukyus, and Okinawa) was the foremost American concern. This presence was maintained, despite heated opposition from the Soviets.

Forty-nine nations, including Japan, signed the treaty, while the Communist bloc, represented by the Soviet Union, Poland, and Czechoslovakia, refused (Japan and the Soviet Union subsequently signed a peace declaration, not a peace treaty, in 1956). The treaty went into effect on April 2, 1952, formally ending the Occupation of Japan. Japan admits that, according to the San Francisco treaty, it had relinquished its rights over the disputed territories, but argues that no provision had been made in the treaty indicating under which country's jurisdiction these areas would come. It seems an anomaly, note the Japanese, that the Soviets, who didn't even sign the agreement, should be in possession of the islands. The Japanese adamantly advance their position from both a legal and geographic perspective, noting the similar flora and fauna found on the islands and those of Hokkaido, together with pointing out that in all prior treaties between the two nations, the four southern islands had been neither mentioned nor occupied by the Soviets.

From the closing days of the war, however, the Soviet Union has kept a firm control over the islands which it claims had been "taken" by the Japanese, and subsequently "returned" to the Soviet Union as just compensation for its participation in the war

effort. Were the Americans at the San Francisco conference op-
erating under the dictum "possession is nine-tenths of the law,"
thereby regarding Soviet occupation of the islands as a foregone
conclusion? Their diplomatic actions, or lack of them, beg such
criticism,[32] and lend support to the argument that Soviet presence
on the Kuriles, including the Southern Kuriles, may have been
regarded as a quid pro quo if an American military presence on
the islands mentioned earlier was to be realized.

What Japan refers to as the "Northern Territories Dispute"—
pursued by Japan, but in the past often denied as existing by the
Soviet Union—has kept the two nations from signing a peace
treaty formally concluding the war. As Kimura Hiroshi, an expert
on the issue, stated in 1985, "Soviet diplomacy in the past has
been heavy-handed, clumsy, and inflexible, especially as regards
the so-called Northern Territories. Soviet attitudes must evidence
greater flexibility and a willingness to negotiate before the relationship can be significantly improved."[33] In 1985, one could have
justifiably argued that the existence of the Cold War was the primary obstacle to ending the dispute. Although the ending of the
Cold War may have softened Russia's inflexible attitude on the
issue it hardly guaranteed a resolution, while at the same time it
also created new difficulties.

To many Japanese, the islands represent a symbolic issue, but
to the Russians all symbolism ends with their strategic and political importance. Cold War or no, all nations have minimal, if not
essential, security concerns. Entrance to the open sea for Russian
vessels is restricted to the Korea Strait (located between South
Korea and Kyushu, and the site of American patrol ships), and
through the channels that run between the Kurile islands. Relin-
quishing the rights to any or all of these islands would invite the
American naval presence in the Sea of Okhotsk, which is a virtual
Russian lake contained within the natural boundary afforded by
the islands. Stalin was well aware of the islands' strategic significance when he exhorted, "From now on [the Kuriles] will not
serve as a means for isolating the Soviet Union from the ocean
and as a base for Japanese attacks on our Far East."[34] How militarily "significant" are these islands? Few may realize it today,
but on November 26, 1941, a sizable Japanese flotilla departed
from Hitokapppu port on Etorofu Island, one of the Southern

Kuriles. Few can forget, however, the destruction that this same fleet would bring to Pearl Harbor on the morning of December 7, 1941.

More recently, in the 1980s, a landing strip was constructed on the island of Etorofu (which is twice the area of Okinawa), which served as the base for twenty-five to thirty Soviet MiG 23s. Returning the islands to Japan outright would forfeit Russian use of the runway, and would result in the loss of a squadron within minutes from the main islands of Japan. Additionally, in 1980 the *London Times* reported accusations by Japan that the Soviets had moved nuclear weapons onto the islands,[35] a charge that was countered by Soviet allegations that Japan had allowed the United States to station nuclear arms on Okinawa.[36] It is impossible to determine that had it not been for the presence of U.S. forces in Japan, during the Cold War the Soviets would have turned their aversion of Japan into military action. Yet even though an unprovoked Russian strike against Hokkaido may now seem highly unlikely, the scenario is still on occasion raised in Japan and abroad.

The second factor which must weigh into Russian acceptance of Japanese claims involves the possibility that return of the islands might result in a further territorial domino effect against them. Even though the ending of the Cold War brought with it the liberation of those states that had been absorbed by the then Soviet Union after World War II, there are still competing claims over territorial boundaries between the Russian republic and its neighboring nations, particularly the People's Republic of China. The internal border disputes between the former Soviet republics have only heightened Russian sensitivity regarding the consequences of border modifications.

Third, many observers believe that Russia is using its possession of the islands as a "bargaining chip" in its relations with Tokyo, holding out until the price is right, which implies massive infusions of Japanese capital into antiquated Russian industries, or development of the Siberian wilderness. Japan, however, is in no rush to pursue such ventures. For nearly the past ten years, pundits had predicted that with an appreciated yen and protectionism from abroad, Japan would be eager to "develop" the Russian market. But even as the yen has appreciated still further, and protectionism has not diminished, Japan's interest in Russia has increased only marginally. The imperative for oil, and the attractiveness of Siberian resources, have become less pressing with the restructuring of Japan's productive capacities away from heavy industry and toward the tertiary level of service and technology, and Japan-Russian trade remains a very small percentage (approximately 2%) of Japan's total trade.

EFFORTS AT SETTLING THE DISPUTE

Considering the characteristic coolness of the Russians towards the Northern Territories issue, it seems an anomaly that Russian initiative brought the two sides together in 1956. As could be expected, both arrived at the negotiation table with competing proposals and contradictory historical recounts of sovereignty over the islands. The Japanese based their claim on historical sovereignty and the principles of "law and justice," while the Soviets referred to the recently inked San Francisco Peace Treaty (even if it lacked their signature), and possession of the islands, which was in their favor.

Believing that the process of compromise would whittle down their claim to something less than the Southern Kuriles, the Japanese delegates opened the talks with their nation's claim to the entire Kurile chain and the southern half of Sakhalin island, territories that were included in its wartime empire. Initially, the Soviets maintained an unyielding stance on their own claim to all of the islands, but their position softened as they offered to relinquish their rights to the two territories closest to Japan, the island of Shikotan and the smaller Habomai islands. Japanese representatives were divided on whether they should assume an "all or nothing" stance, but the leaders of the then recently merged LDP, as well as public opinion, were nearly unanimous in the view that Japanese interests could not be compromised. Negotiations stalled, but in October of the same year the two nations still signed a joint declaration providing for diplomatic relations, and "in the absence of a peace treaty, it is still the sole basis for diplomatic relations" between the two countries.[37]

To the Japanese, the 1956 Russian proposal, which was repeated in 1966, is an indication that if hard-pressed, the Russians might return all four islands if Japan practices "patient diplomacy" (which is equivalent to waiting). With the larger and adjacent islands of Kunashiri and Etorofu in Soviet possession, these lesser islands have relatively little military importance, which is why the Russians have at times hinted to their return under certain conditions. However, under threatening "advice" provided by the United States in 1956, which declared that "if Japan abandoned her claims to Kunashiri and Etorofu in favor of the Soviet Union, the United States would ask Japan to confirm Okinawa as American territory,"[38] the Japanese refused the Soviet proposal. The Soviets attached a corollary to their pledge of four years earlier to return the Habomai islands and Shikotan: If Japan signed the Security Treaty with the United States, the proposal would be withdrawn. Almost simultaneously, Foreign Minister Andrei Gromyko proposed his own scheme, one which linked the return of the islands to the removal of all American bases in Japan.[39]

Until recently, the Japanese had firmly maintained their "no compromise" position, and the Russians declined to again present their 1956 proposal. The latter's position was adamantly summarized in 1978 in the words of then Soviet Ambassador to Japan Dmitrii Polyansky, who proclaimed that "the Soviet Union has no intention of transferring to Japan a single piece of stone, let alone an island."[40]

It is not as if the Japanese allowed such comments to deter their efforts. In 1973, attempting to bolster his international image while his domestic rating was already high, Prime Minister Tanaka visited Moscow and repeatedly brought to the surface his real reason for making the trip—to solve the territorial dispute. His Soviet counterpart, Leonid Brezhnev, was reportedly so angered by Tanaka's incessant one-sided debate over the issue that he exploded in a fit of rage. Again, until recently, in the twenty years since the encounter between Tanaka and Brezhnev, the Russian side has maintained its characteristically hard-line attitude, while Japan has refused to let an opportunity slip by to raise the issue in their meetings with the Russians.

THE "INTERNATIONALIZATION" OF A BILATERAL ISSUE

As should be apparent from the earlier sections of this chapter, the United States played an unwitting role at best, and the primary role at worst, in the creation of the Northern Territories dispute. Yet throughout the Cold War, the United States maintained that the dispute was a "bilateral problem" in which it had "no direct involvement."[41] This position is somewhat curious, for had the issue been "resolved" (i.e., if a resolution was adopted which explicitly terminated any Japanese claims to the islands or resulted in Soviet acceptance of the Japanese claim), the United States, as well as other interested onlookers (notably those regions which would be "liberated" from the Soviet empire in the late 1980s and early 1990s, not to mention the PRC) would have been directly affected. But this does not mean that Japan did not have its supporters.

China expressed unqualified support for the Soviet claim until 1964, when Mao Tse-tung was reported to have said that "Communist China, in principle, is in favor of Japan's demand to the Soviet Union for return of the Northern Islands."[42] Following the Sino-Soviet clashes across the Ussuri River in 1969, China became a vocal supporter of Japan's territorial claim. Chinese Premier Chou En-lai gratuitously offered to "send troops" to the Northern Territories to help defend Japan's claim, and in his annual speech to the Congress of the Chinese Communist Party exhorted: " 'If you [the Soviet Union] are so anxious to relax world tension, why don't you show your good faith by doing a thing or two—for instance, withdraw your armed forces from Czechoslovakia or the People's Republic of Mongolia and return the four northern islands to Japan—China has not occupied any foreign countries' territory.' "[43]

Sase Masamori commented on this surge of official Chinese support:

On the following day all the leading Japanese newspapers triumphantly played up Chou's reference to the northern territories. None of them even hinted that the rhetorical reference in a world forum by a third nation to a bilateral problem between Japan and the Soviet Union was misplaced and embarrassing to Japan. Nor did they evidence the awareness that the remarks might make the return of the islands more difficult than before. On the contrary, they appeared to welcome the emergence of what might be described as a powerful "cheering section" supporting Japan.[44]

China's unsolicited endorsement of Japan's position, which was both a reflection of its ideological rift with the Soviet Union and support for its own territorial claims, served to polarize even further Japan's relations with the Soviet Union. A supposedly "bilateral" dispute between the Soviet Union and Japan acquired new meaning in Beijing's relations with Moscow, and indirectly aligned China, Japan, and the United States. As the *Washington Post* noted in 1980, "The Soviets fear that the combination of Chinese manpower, American technology and Japanese industry may prove virtually unbeatable in any confrontation."[45] Soviet concern was evident in 1978 "when the Soviet Union unilaterally published a draft treaty of friendship with Japan (which the Japanese summarily rejected) and the Chinese and Japanese signed a peace treaty (which took on added significance the following year when China refused to renew its treaty of friendship with the USSR)."[46]

For the duration of the Cold War, then, the issue was primarily defined in bilateral terms as Japan's "problem" with the Soviet Union, as interference from other nations did nothing to "internationalize" the issue but in the end only created a greater hindrance for resolution. Japan has always believed that the more support it can mount on its side the better will be the chances that the Russians will act on the issue. And in the post–Cold War world, largely because of Japan's efforts, the issue has in fact become internationalized. It is not as clear, however, whether turning the dispute into a global problem will produce the desired result for Japan any sooner (or any more certainly) than if it had remained a purely "bilateral" issue. By most accounts, the Japanese government is appreciative that the rest of the "advanced world" has finally taken up its cause, but even if it had wanted the issue to remain a bilateral one, it is doubtful that Japan would have had much choice.

The Japanese government pledged that it would continue its policy of "the inseparability of economics from politics" (i.e., no bilateral economic aid to the former Soviet Union until the dispute was resolved),[47] but following President Bush's avowed support for Russian reform at the U.S.–USSR Summit talks (the "Malta talks") in December 1989, many in Japan believed that it would not be long before the United States would rethink its support of Japan's position, or Japan would become isolated among the "Western side."[48] In effect, the independent stance of Japan's foreign policy towards Russia was being questioned by both Japan and its allies, and Japan would feel compelled to reformulate a decades old policy that was both a part of the Cold War and at the same time independent of it. In exchange, Japan believed, the issue would become an international one, with the world's major industrialized nations declaring their support for Japan's position. The Japanese government was elated when the participants at both the Houston Summit of 1990 and the London Summit (Advanced Nations Summit conferences) agreed to mention the issue and their support of Japan's position in a few lines of the conferences' declarations. Kaifu and the Ministry of Foreign Affairs must have thought it was somewhat of a coup to have their position on the issue included in these declarations, and the forums in which to tell the leaders of the world's leading industrialized nations that the territorial issue was the "biggest reason for Japan's not falling in step with the other nations of the world regarding financial assistance to the USSR."[49] Then again, Bush referred to the issue in his opening address at the Kremlin during his Soviet trip in July 1991, linking it with the stability of the Asia-Pacific. But there was a clear reason for this support.

During the London Summit of 1991, German Prime Minister Helmut Kohl reportedly told then Japanese Prime Minister Kaifu that discussions between G-7 nations and then Soviet leader Gorbachev "must not end in 'any form of failure' to prevent Gorbachev's restructuring efforts from collapsing."[50] Kaifu responded that Japan would not be forthcoming with financial assistance until there was "concrete evidence" of market reforms in the Soviet Union, which exemplified both a realistic and circumspect appraisal of the conditions then facing the Soviet Union. The Japanese position was also in keeping with the government's policy of the "inseparability of politics and economics" in its relations with Russia, which was clearly a policy limited to, and created in response to, the Northern Territories dispute, for it was a policy often sidestepped when the "politics" of another nation would seem to conflict with Japan's own (i.e., China, Cuba, North Korea). But beyond these two explanations for Japan's limited interest in supplying capital to Russia, Japan has not been as receptive as have the nations of Western Europe, or the United States, to link the success of democracy with the decrease of security threats. There are three possible explanations to account for Japan's unwillingness to do this.

The first is that Japan has yet to notice (or believe) there has been a perceptible change in the security threat posed by the Russian republic, regardless of its pledge of democracy. For Japan to support a nation that it still perceives as a security threat would be counter to its own interests. As Keidanren (Federation of Economic Organizations) Chairman Nukazawa Kazuo commented, at present Russia is asking for something similar to a "Marshall Plan." When Japan was the beneficiary of foreign aid after World War II, he noted, it handed over its weapons to Occupation forces; contrastingly, Russia had taken no initiative in this direction.[51]

The second explanation is that every nation has different security concerns, and it should be expected that those for Japan are different than those for the nations of Western Europe and the United States. This was clearly reiterated in 1991 when then Japanese Foreign Minister Nakayama Taro reminded his German counterpart, Hans-Dietrich Genscher, that "as an Asian country neighboring China and various developing nations, [Japan] has to take a different approach to the security issue from that of Germany in Europe."[52]

The third explanation for Japan's reluctance to commit a substantial amount of funds to Russia in the name of "democracy for security" is a combination of the previous two. While Russia (or more accurately, the Soviet Union) represented the greatest threat to Japan's security during the Cold War, the perceived threat still may not have been as great as that perceived by the United States and Western Europe, which were the assumed primary targets of Soviet nuclear warheads. One could hypothesize that when it is perceived that a threat to a nation's security has abated, support of the source for that threat reduction will be encouraged, especially if the source appears to be something familiar to the threatened nation. In this case, the source has been identified as "democracy," whatever its form and however ill-defined, and leaders in both Western Europe and the United States have framed the support of Russian democracy as not only a national security objective, but a world security objective. Perhaps not only

do Japan's leaders believe there has not been a significant reduction of the Russian threat, but they may also believe that Russia
is "experimenting" with something less than, or different than,
democracy. This perception factor seems as significant as the existence of the Northern Territories dispute and the circumspection
of plunging into an undeveloped market economy, for explaining
Japan's reluctance to substantially increase its financial support of
the Russian republic. A variant of the previous explanation is offered by Keidanren Chairman Nukazawa: "Europeans believe it
is strange that Japan is engrossed in a boundary dispute when
their next-door neighbor is on fire. [Yet] it seems that Russia's
efforts at self-help have been minimal."[53]

It is clear that the leaders of the other G-7 nations believe that
Japan's economic support of the Russian experiment in democracy is essential if Yeltsin's efforts are to succeed, and to them for
Japan to allow a territorial issue to get in the way of something
of such "monumental" significance seems somewhat selfish on Japan's part. Undoubtedly, Japan had no choice other than to
change its position. As part of Japan's "flexible response" on the
issue, Foreign Minister Watanabe Michio proposed the "two stage
reversion formula" in April 1992, whereby the smaller islands
(and those lying closest to Japan) of Shikotan and the Habomai
group would be returned to Japan upon conclusion of a peace
treaty, while Russian administrative rights over the other two islands would be recognized by Japan until their formal reversion.
Watanabe's "new" proposal had earlier been included in the
Japan-Soviet Joint Declaration of 1956, and at the time it appeared to be a likely step towards resolution. However, with the
intensity of the Cold War came a change of strategy by Japan,
and until the Watanabe statement the official position of the Japanese government was to accept nothing short of the simultaneous
reversion of all four islands. To support the viability of his proposal, Watanabe cited the case of U.S. administrative control over
Okinawa until its reversion to Japan in 1973. Yet no mention was
made of the continued U.S. military presence on the island, and
whether this arrangement would extend to Russia when and if the
islands are reverted to Japan.[54] The reason for Japan's change in
policy seems clear. As a commentary in the *Nihon Keizai Shinbun*
suggested, if Japan was to maintain its hard-line stance over the

territorial problem, it risked "isolation among the advanced nations,"[55] all of which in principle supported Russia's political and economic reform measures, and none of which had a territorial claim against Russia. Compared to the preceding decades of stalemate, the change in the Japanese position was remarkable, as was the position of Yeltsin when he visited Japan in October 1993.

A "NEW LOOK" RUSSIAN POLICY?

Initially, Mikhail Gorbachev did little to change the perception of the "hard-line Soviets" when he announced to a Japanese visitor to Moscow in 1985 that "there is no [territorial] issue [between Japan and the then USSR]."[56] (Perhaps as evidence of the policy of "openness" which he espoused, Gorbachev would later acknowledge the existence of the dispute, and in 1988 a Soviet representative to the World International Economic Conference held in Tokyo suggested that the islands of Etorofu and Kunashiri could be shared if Japan signed a formal peace treaty.[57] The proposal was unacceptable to Japan, which maintained its "no compromise" policy for the simultaneous return of all of the islands).

In his meeting with Foreign Minister Aleksandr Bessmertnykh, which was to pave the way for the first trip to Japan by a Russian or Soviet leader (Gorbachev), former Prime Minister Kaifu Toshiki raised the territorial issue, and noted the "historic significance" of Gorbachev's pending trip. Kaifu even told his guest that he and all of Japan were "expecting" Gorbachev to "make a political decision" on the territorial issue during his visit.[58] For his part, not only did Bessmertnykh acknowledge the existence of the territorial issue, but he even referred to another issue of contention between the two nations, that of Japanese prisoners of war who, it is charged, were not repatriated following World War II.[59] With the apparent headway made by the Bessmertnykh visit, the Japanese press and prominent government leaders alike played up the "significance" of Gorbachev's visit, and anticipated (if not hinted) that the Soviet leader would come armed with a settlement plan.[60] Few seemed to remember that less than one year earlier, Gorbachev reiterated his position that a territorial dispute did not exist between the two nations, and anticipating that Japan might press him on the issue, told the Speaker of Japan's Lower House that "if Japan–USSR relations are to worsen with my trip to Japan, perhaps it would be better if I did not make the visit."[61]

On the eve of Gorbachev's trip, a *Tokyo Shinbun* poll found that more than 70% of respondents in Japan expected that his "historic" visit would lead to some kind of settlement of the territorial issue.[62] Considering Kaifu's hope for a breakthrough on the issue during Gorbachev's visit in April 1991, "based on the strong desire of the Japanese people who want to drastically settle Japan–USSR relations through settlement of the territory problem,"[63] it is only understandable why there was a letdown when progress on the issue was relatively minimal. True, during a speech before the Japanese Diet, Gorbachev inserted words not in the draft copy to the effect that the Soviet Union was trying to "fully coordinate" various problems that it faced, including the "demarcation of territory."[64] Yet there was an unrealistic appraisal on Japan's part of the opportunities for resolution, which in Japan's case (and which Kaifu reaffirmed) was the return of all four islands. From Gorbachev's perspective, there was little room (if any) allowed for compromise by the Japanese side. Since Gorbachev's visit, Japan has changed (or felt compelled to change) its position, yet for Gorbachev's successor, Boris Yeltsin, the inability to compromise on this (and other issues) may no longer be Japan's, but his. As a Ministry of Foreign Affairs official involved in the dispute noted,

During the Gorbachev visit, the Japanese press and media became hysterical with anticipation of an announcement by Mr. Gorbachev that the Soviet position had changed. But we learned from that experience. On the other hand, in Russia people went crazy over Mr. Yeltsin's planned trip to Japan, fearing that it would serve as the moment for a significant announcement on the issue. In fact, when Mr. Yeltsin announced his proposed trip, the "Northern Territories Dispute" was on the front page of Russian newspapers, while announcement of the establishment of the Commonwealth of Independent States, which would seem to have been a more significant story, was on page two.[65]

When Yeltsin abruptly canceled his September 1992 trip to Japan, it was as much a shock as the disappointing result of Gorbachev's earlier trip. But during his October 1993 visit to Tokyo, Yeltsin announced that his government would honor agreements and treaties concluded by the former Soviet regime, which would include the 1956 Joint Declaration (although he did not specifically mention the document by name), and honor the principles of "law and justice." To the Japanese, this was a step in the right direction for normalized relations with Russia, as was their guest's unexpected reference to the Soviet Union's "inhuman" treatment of Japanese prisoners following the conclusion of World War II. It appeared that Japan's initiatives, including its flexibility on the "inseparability" policy, and its spearheading a $48 billion aid package to Russia during the April 1993 Tokyo Summit, were paying off. Certainly, Yeltsin's visit to Japan went a long way in promoting good will between two nations that needed nothing as much as that, yet on the territorial issue the accomplishments were minimal. Even the most optimistic analyst must surely realize that Yeltsin's domestic position is so tenuous that he could not even mention the 1956 declaration by name, and even the most optimistic must realize again that presently Yeltsin is in no position to see his "offer" to the Japanese appease his domestic opposition.

What can we predict for the future course of Japanese-Russian relations? On the territorial issue, which we believe, unfortunately, is the major issue that links the two nations, the internationalization of the issue has seen Japan lose a substantial degree of leverage. Although Japan has maintained that it will limit its bilateral aid to Russia until the dispute is settled, pressure from the other G-7 nations has compelled Japan to contribute to Russia's experiment with democracy through international organizations. Interviewed for an article that appeared in *Chuo Koron*, Vice Minister for Foreign Affairs Owada Hisashi stated,

Obviously, we [Japan] cannot agree that because the G-7's support for Russia is of emergency importance, bilateral problems can be temporarily shelved, and the Japanese government has taken such an attitude. On the other hand, it is not proper to say that because the territorial issue is not settled Japan will not extend cooperation at all for Russia's reform efforts. It is necessary to forcefully promote both, simultaneously. This is the government's view.[66]

Without Japan's economic contributions, the plans of the world's "leading nations" for Russia could not materialize, yet the same Japanese bilateral aid (if not the combined economic resources of all the G-7 nations) is insufficient to meet the massive capital demands for a *construction* of the Russian economy (*reconstruction* implies that it was constructed in the first place, which is arguable). Japanese bilateral aid has therefore become a nonissue, while the internationalization of Japan's territorial dispute assures that Japan will contribute to an effort that is, by Japan's estimates (if not the estimates of others), questionable at best. It is only fitting that the comments of Deputy Foreign Minister Matsuura Koichiro made in 1993 resemble those cited at the beginning of this chapter: "The Russian problem is important, but since the fall of last year Japan has taken the initiative in proposing to the other G-7 nations that the problem of the developing nations ought to be discussed comprehensively."[67]

NOTES

1. Fujisawa Rikitaro, "The Monroe Doctrine and the League of Nations," in K.K. Kawakami, ed., *What Japan Thinks* (New York: Mac-Millan, 1921), pp. 40–41.

2. Interview, Gyoten Toyoo, November 20, 1992.

3. Interview, Kanehara Nobukatsu, October 14, 1992.

4. *Japan's Northern Territories* (Tokyo: Ministry of Foreign Affairs, 1982), p. 5.

5. John J. Stephan, *The Kuril Islands* (Oxford: Clarendon Press, 1974), p. 102.

6. Douglas H. Mendel, *The Japanese People and Foreign Policy* (Berkeley: University of California Press, 1961), p. 195.

7. Fujisawa Rikitaro, *The Recent Aims and Political Development of Japan* (New Haven, CT: Yale University Press, 1923), p. 174.

8. Ian Nish, *Japanese Foreign Policy, 1869–1942* (London: Routledge and Kegan Paul, 1977), p. 71.

9. Josef Stalin, "Victory Address: We Have Waited Forty Years," September 15, 1945, *Vital Speeches of the Day*, vol. 11, no. 23, p. 711.

10. Charles E. Bohlen, *The Transformation of American Foreign Policy* (New York: W.W. Norton, 1969), p. 35.

11. Edward R. Stettinius, Jr., *Roosevelt and the Russians: The Yalta Conference* (Garden City, NY: Doubleday, 1949), p. 304.

12. Ellis M. Zacharias, *Behind Closed Doors: The Secret History of the Cold War* (New York: Putnam, 1950), p. 56.

13. Ibid.

14. F.C. Jones, Hugh Borton, and B.R. Pearn, *Survey of International Affairs, 1939–46*, vol. VII (London: Oxford University Press, 1955), p. 127.

15. James F. Byrnes, *Speaking Frankly* (New York: Harper & Brothers, 1947), p. 43.

16. William D. Leahy, *I Was There* (New York: McGraw-Hill, 1950), p. 318.

17. Josef Stalin, "Victory Address," p. 711.

18. Ibid.

19. Charles E. Bohlen, *Witness to History, 1929–1969* (New York: W.W. Norton, 1973), p. 200.

20. Robert E. Sherwood, *Roosevelt and Hopkins, an Intimate History* (New York: Harper, 1948), p. 860.

21. U.S. Department of State, *Foreign Relations of the United States, 1945*, vol. VI, p. 670.

22. Ibid., p. 687.

23. Ibid., p. 699.

24. Ibid., p. 692.

25. Walter Mills, ed., *The Forrestal Diaries* (New York: Viking Press, 1951), p. 233.

26. Byrnes, *Speaking Frankly*, pp. 224–225.

27. John J. Snell et al., *The Meaning of Yalta* (Baton Rouge: University of Louisiana Press, 1956), p. 162.

28. Summary of official history in *Izvestia*, July 8, 1980, from *World Press Review*, September 1980.

29. *New York Times*, February 2, 1946, p. 5.

30. Ibid.

31. Rajendra Kumar Jain, *The USSR and Japan 1945–1980* (Atlantic Highlands, NJ: Humanities Press, 1981), p. 55.

32. The strong protest made by the government of India was one among several. *See Department of State Bulletin*, September 3, 1951, pp. 386–388.

33. Kimura Hiroshi, "Moscow and Tokyo: An Uneasy Peace," *Annals of the American Academy of Political and Social Science*, vol. 481 (September 1985), p. 61.

34. Josef Stalin, "Victory Address."

35. *London Times*, February 23, 1980, p. 4.

36. *Japan Times Weekly*, International Edition, April 23, 1983, p. 12. Andrei Gromyko produced shock waves and raised suspicion in Japan in

1983, when he stated that " 'there are huge nuclear weapons facilities in Okinawa.' " *London Times*, April 6, 1983, p. 5.

37. Kamiya Fuji, "The Northern Territories," in Donald S. Zagoria, ed., *Soviet Policy in East Asia* (New Haven, CT: Yale University Press, 1982), p. 132.

38. John J. Stephan, "Japan and the Soviet Union: The Distant Neighbours," *Asian Affairs*, October 1977, p. 283.

39. Recorded in *Pravda*, January 29, 1960; translated in *Current Digest of Soviet Press*, February 24, 1960, pp. 19–20.

40. *Mainichi Daily News*, November 25, 1978, p. 1.

41. Personal Correspondence, John K. Ward, Political Officer, U.S. Embassy, Tokyo, October 22, 1984.

42. *New York Times*, July 13, 1964, p. 2.

43. *New York Times*, September 1, 1973, p. 6.

44. Masamori Sase, "The Northern Territories in International Politics," *Japan Echo*, no. 2, 1976, p. 55.

45. *Washington Post*, August 10, 1980, p. 9 (*Parade* magazine).

46. Kataoka Tetsuya, "Japan's Northern Threat," *Problems of Communism*, March/April 1984, p. 14.

47. *Nihon Keizai Shinbun*, December 4, 1989, p. 2.

48. *Nihon Keizai Shinbun*, December 5, 1989, p. 2.

49. *Asahi Shinbun*, July 10, 1990, p. 2.

50. "Japan, Germany Split Over Aid to Soviets," *FBIS*, WEU–91–135, July 15, 1991, p. 6.

51. "Nihon wa Ajia, Taiheiyo no daihyoo toshite no koodoo o [Japan as a Representative of the Asia–Pacific]," *Gaiko Forum*, May 1993, p. 37.

52. "Differences Remain Unsettled," *FBIS*, WEU–91–135, July 15, 1991, p. 7.

53. "Nihon wa Ajia," p. 31.

54. *Asahi Shinbun*, March 24, 1992, p. 2.

55. *Nihon Keizai Shinbun*, April 19, 1992, p. 2.

56. Yoshinari Daishi, "Hoppo Ryodo, Sato Eisaku no Ofureko Danwa [The Northern Islands—Sato Eisaku's Off the Record Conversation]," *Bungei Shunju*, December 1985, p. 129.

57. Wada Haruki, "Niso 'dakkyo' de hoppo ryodo mondai wa kechaku suru [Japan–Soviet Union Compromises for Settlement of the Northern Terrories Problem]," *Ekonomisuto*, November 15, 1988, p. 61.

58. *Asahi Shinbun*, March 31, 1991, p. 4.

59. Bessmertnykh stated that there were "some Japanese" who were "unable to return home" following the war, and pledged that his government would investigate the possible locations of remains, names of detainees, etc. *Nihon Keizai Shinbun*, March 31, 1991, p. 2.

60. *Tokyo Shinbun*, March 31, 1991, p. 2.

61. *Nihon Keizai Shinbun*, July 26, 1990, p. 1.

62. *Tokyo Shinbun*, April 5, 1991, p. 2.

63. *Sankei Shinbun*, April 19, 1991, p. 7.

64. *Nihon Keizai Shinbun*, April 18, 1991, p. 2.

65. Interview, Kanehara Nobukatsu, October 14, 1992.

66. Owada Hisashi, "Korega Roshia shien ronrida [This Is the Logic of Support for Russia]," *Chuo Koron*, July 1993, p. 34.

67. *Gaiko Forum*, May 1993, p. 31.

III

RELATIONS WITH THE UNITED STATES

6

Japan and the United States: Bilateral and Global Dimensions

IN SICKNESS AND IN HEALTH

Thus far, we have examined Japan's inclusion as a member of the international community as defined by the West following centuries of its intentional nonparticipation in that system, and the resultant challenges faced by Japan, the successes it achieved, and the failures it experienced. We have also related what a group of Japan's leaders believe will constitute, in broad terms, the post–Cold War world and Japan's role in it, as well as analyzed Japan's changing relations with Asia, its developing relations with the nations of Eastern and Western Europe, and its tenuous relations with Russia. Throughout this study, while having focused on the contemporary, we hope that we have also imparted to the reader a necessary appreciation of the past, for we believe that in the study of international affairs, terms that signify a supposed revolution in the way that nations relate to one another, be it "Cold War" or "post–Cold War," may inaccurately express a detached break from the past. Rarely does the dawning of a new era present a clean slate on which to diagram foreign policy, and it almost goes without saying that in U.S.–Japan relations this continuity also applies.

It is undeniable that the U.S.–Japan relationship is unmatched by any other for Japan, and that most people in Japan admit that their nation will suffer enormous hardship if relations with the United States should turn increasingly acrimonious and, ultimately, unmanageable. To avert this worst-case scenario, officially Japan has maintained its policy of near-assumed accommodation with the United States in terms of the bilateral relationship itself, while it also has gone beyond this exclusive relationship with the United States in accepting a more inclusive definition (whether their own or that of others) of what constitutes international responsibility. Even though the United States remains the "linchpin" for Japanese foreign, economic, and political relations, in the post–Cold War world Japan has not pursued better relations with the United States at the expense of developing its international role, nor has this increased international role necessarily been pursued in the framework of U.S.–Japan relations, although these two components of Japan's foreign policy clearly overlap. It used to be said that when the United States sneezes Japan catches a cold, not only emphasizing the dependence of Japan on the well-being of the United States, but suggesting that ultimately Japan is the recipient of the worst of any situation facing the United States. In a world characterized by a high level of economic interdependence between two nations (exceeded only by the U.S.–Canada tie as a percentage of world trade, and representing more than half of the world's GNP), one could say that a sickness for both would create an epidemic in the world trading system as we know it. The emphasis of whose actions affects whom more still lies with the United States. Most recently, President Clinton's statement during his April 1993 meeting with Prime Minister Miyazawa that he would "tolerate" a higher yen, in the belief that appreciation of the yen would alleviate the U.S. trade deficit with Japan, promptly sent the value of the yen upward and created havoc for Japan's financial institutions and exporting firms.[1]

On the other hand, whether or not Americans like to admit it, for the United States the repercussions of an estrangement with Japan would far outweigh those of a similar scenario with Canada, its largest trading partner. Yet while Japan is with concern facing the challenge of deteriorating bilateral relations head-on, the United States has done its part to add fuel to a smoldering fire. The end of the Cold War changed the thinking of many Ameri-

Figure 6.1
***Asahi Shinbun* Opinion Poll (conducted in November 1991 and December 1992)**

	Japan		I	United States		
	Nov.	Dec.	I	Nov.	Dec.	
	1991	1992	I	1991	1992	
Going Well	39	30	I	5	3	GoingWell
Don't Think So	37	47	I	33	48	Not Very Well
Can't Say Which	18	16	I	56	35	So-So
N.A./Others	6	7	I	1	3	N.A./Others

cans in the sense that, at least until the next "revolution," economics will be prioritized over military strategies, but with this change in perspectives has come the rise of what many view as a new enemy. For example, an ABC/Washington Post poll conducted in February 1989 indicated that 50% of respondents considered the military threat of the Soviet Union to be a bigger threat to the national security of the United States than was the economic power of Japan (44%), though one year later the same organizations conducted a poll that showed that only 28% of respondents believed the Soviet military was the greater threat, while 66% felt more threatened by Japan's economic power.[2] While we acknowledge that public opinion data are not beyond skepticism, we also believe they cannot—nor should they—be rejected as a useless barometer to gauge the degree to which perceptions that Americans and Japanese have of each other and of each nation change over time, as well as highlight possible problems in the relationship. Public opinion polls conducted in November 1991 and December 1992 by the *Asahi Shinbun* (see Figure 6.1) are reflective of this change.[3]

Of course, polls administered at different times and under different circumstances could have expressed results that do not coincide with those above. But we believe that despite momentary blips and apparent changes either negative or positive, the underlying sentiment between the United States and Japan during the post–Cold War period has not been one that suggests partnership.

Our interest in this chapter is not to present an all-encompassing analysis of the myriad components of the U.S.–Japan relationship, for this would be an exercise beyond the limits of this study and one doomed to superficiality. Rather, we have chosen to focus on what we believe are those key issues that are not only significant for both sides of the U.S.–Japan relationship, and for the rest of the world, but that also present differences in cultural norms, expectations, political and social exigencies, and a memory of history that at times has been selectively employed by each side. An analysis of these issues—Japan's rice market, the U.S.–Japan security arrangement, and the broader issue of trade—will highlight the challenges in the U.S.–Japan relationship, and illustrate that it is nearly impossible to any longer consider U.S.–Japan relations in purely bilateral terms.

RICE: A STICKY, INFLATED ISSUE IN U.S.–JAPAN RELATIONS

Most industrialized nations with vestiges of an earlier, agrarian-dominated economy usually adopt agricultural subsidy programs for reasons of "food security" or because of political partisanship toward a still powerful voting bloc. The retaliatory aspect of subsidization, in which a government supports its farmers in response to like programs of other governments, has also been employed. "Sympathy" for the rural population, which is often a nostalgic longing for days gone by, or an attempt to narrow the differential between rural and urban incomes, is a further reason. Even in the United States, which prides itself as the eminent "free trade" nation, the practice of granting agricultural subsidies is so widespread that many policymakers are more concerned with the emphasis and degree of subsidy programs, rather than arguing about the merits and rationality of such programs.

Curiously (though perhaps naturally), American farmers, who are themselves beneficiaries of government-allocated, taxpayer-financed supports, are quick to point the finger at similar practices by foreign governments. Foreign agricultural programs are labeled "unfair" if they restrict American access to, or prevent equal opportunity in, foreign markets. In recent years, perhaps no country has been a greater target of American farmers' accusations of agricultural "improprieties" than has Japan.[4] For most of the 1980s, beef and citrus made nearly as many trade dispute headlines as did semiconductors; yet even for these agricultural products the Japanese market was not impenetrable, and at least for beef, the Japanese government gave preferential status to the American product relative to other import competitors.[5]

In the United States, if only for their numbers, cattle and citrus farmers are influential groups within an interest group, and their eventual penetration of the Japanese market was hailed as the opening of the spigot for alleged competitive, and higher quality, American agricultural goods. What most people failed to realize, however, was that Japan was already the largest single market for American agricultural produce, purchasing more throughout the 1980s than Mexico and the nations of Latin America combined.[6] Given the lofty expectations, for all but a select few farmers whose products had previously been restricted in the Japanese market, it is a boom that has yet to materialize. In the postscript to the beef and citrus controversy, it is now access to Japan's closed rice market, and American criticism of Japan's government-supported rice program, which have taken on a symbolism that previous disputes lacked. In the United States, the rice issue has gone beyond the sole interest of the U.S. Rice Millers Association, which represents U.S. rice growers, and has been inflated to include the images of closed Japanese markets in general and Japanese special-interest politics. Rice is often disussed in the same breath with disputes over supercomputers, satellites, and intellectual property rights, and in an environment of growing bilateral trade friction, rice has become the most visible symbol for both sides.

For American producers, no matter which goods they are peddling, the Japanese government's inflexible attitude on the rice issue is thrust before the United States public to demonstrate an inherent "unfair playing field" in Japan which discriminates against foreign competition. The American media has followed suit, and it is not unusual for Americans, even those who live in states that are major suppliers of other agricultural goods to the Japanese market, to believe that Japan's market is closed to farm products.[7] For the Japanese, it is *gaiatsu* (literally "pressure from the outside") at its worst. Editorials in Japan have frequently compared the image of persistent Americans hawking the rice issue in Tokyo with that of Commodore Perry's "opening" of Japan more than one hundred years earlier, an opening that Japan was powerless to prevent. Many Japanese note that rice and rice products hold a sacred place in many life-affirming rituals of the Shinto faith, including births, marriages, and even the dedication of new businesses. Among the many arguments advanced by the Japanese is one which states that the American demands fail to adequately consider the cultural dimension of Japan's position. In a resolution passed in September 1988, the Japanese Diet declared that rice is "closely related to the Japanese culture" and "helps to maintain and develop the wholesomeness of Japanese society."[8]

American rice farmers contend that the Japanese market is effectively closed to imports, and in their efforts to penetrate the market they have based their case on what they view to be economic rationality and political morality. On economic grounds, the United States side claims that the system of rice subsidies, price supports, and market closure (1) results in economic inefficiency through prices five to ten times higher than the world price, a discrepancy which must be borne by the Japanese taxpayer and rice consumer, ultimately decreasing the welfare of both Japanese citizens and American rice farmers; (2) exacerbates the inflated price of land in Japan, particularly in urban areas where the conversion of unproductive plots (often located on the edges of highways and between buildings) to other uses would improve transportation and lead to the expansion of productive facilities;[9] and (3) leads to surplus stocks of rice accumulated by the Japanese government as a result of rice subsidy programs, excesses which are then dumped on the world market at prices below the world price. From a political standpoint, foreign critics of Japan's rice program assume that the LDP has been reluctant to challenge the present arrangement for fear of alienating a significant bloc of their electoral support—the rural sector.[10] The rice support program was instituted in the tumultuous postwar years, in an effort to encourage rice production and alleviate hunger. It was during these years that the LDP and its predecessors emerged as the ruling party of Japan, earned its reputation as a rural-based party, and benefited from the absence of realistic redistricting that would have been more reflective of rural to urban population shifts. If the U.S. perception were true that the Japan's position on the rice issue has been maintained for political reasons, most notably to appease the supporters of the LDP, then there would be an apparent shift in Japan's position since the LDP lost its majority in the July 1993 election. A policy shift has indeed occurred, namely Japan's announcement in November 1993 that it would allow limited liberalization of its rice market at levels that exceeded the expectations of the United States. But it is not certain that this change in policy can be attributed solely to a change in political leadership at the national level, although this no doubt was a considerable influence. Rather, we believe that Japan's decision to open the rice market, however slight at first this may be, is an indication that Japan's leadership is serious about their nation's responsibility as a member of the international community, while realizing that perhaps their nation has more to lose than either the United States or the members of the EU if impasses similar to that of the protracted Uruguay Round of GATT talks are to continue. Japan's concession on ending its virtual ban on the importation of rice was the most significant initiative in reviving the stalled international trade talks, which reached a near deadlock over the issue of agricultural subsidies, especially those granted by EU member nations.

COSTS, CONSEQUENCES, AND CONSIDERATIONS OF AGRICULTURAL SUBSIDIZATION

The American rice farmer perceives the Japanese market to be one of the most lucrative in the world, if not the savior to reverse a trend of steadily decreasing profits and lost market share to foreign competitors.[11] However, it is a market that has been virtually closed to foreign competition. In 1985, the amount of rice allowed into Japan by the Japan Food Agency represented less than 0.2% of the total Japanese consumption.[12] Specifically, in the talk of trade negotiation, which in this instance is clear enough for a layman, the U.S. side charges that Japan's virtual ban on rice imports "unfairly and unreasonably" restricts U.S. commerce. Market penetration is the principal American objective, and charges of Japanese dumping of surplus rice on the world market have normally been tolerated so as not to risk potential access to the Japanese consumer. This approach characterized the position of the U.S. Rice Millers Association (hereafter referred to as RMA) in the latter two of three petitions filed with the Office of the U.S. Trade Representative (USTR) alleging Japanese violation of the spirit and intent of Section 301 of the United States Trade Act of 1974. The first 301 petition filed by the RMA attacked the dumping allegation head-on, and was in direct response to a clearly defined sequence of events that began in 1979.[13]

In April 1979, the Japanese government began to dispose of 6.5 million tons of surplus short grain rice stocks accumulated from years of its domestic price support program.[14] Disposal was to be in the form of animal feed and increased sales to industries which use rice as an input (beer, baby food, soups, cereals, etc.), with Japan promising the United States that only 200,000 tons would be earmarked for export. Coincidentally, also in April 1979, South Korea announced that its domestic rice production would fall shy of expectations, and the Korean government expressed its intention to purchase 500,000 tons of rice from the United States. The first installment of this total was to be delivered in a shipment of 90,000 tons, but South Korea suddenly canceled 55,000 tons of this amount for no apparent reason. It was later learned that the recipient turned to Japan for 200,000 tons of rice at a seemingly cut-rate price.

Later in the year, shipments of lower-priced Japanese rice totaling 350,000 tons found their way to Indonesian markets (traditionally an American customer), and for that year Japanese export totals exceeded the predicted total by 640,000 tons. In April 1980, the RMA filed a 301 complaint charging Japan with violation of GATT, which specifically prohibits subsidies of the kind promoted by the Japanese government. The principle advanced by the RMA was that subsidies for agricultural exports which displace U.S. commercial sales are illegal. Just one week after the petition was filed with the Office of the U.S. Trade Representative, an agreement was reached between the two governments limiting Japanese rice exports to 1.6 million tons over a four-year period.

Japan had heretofore been an insignificant presence in the world rice market, while the United States produced all but a fraction of its short grain rice (preferred in most Asian nations over the long grain variety common in the West) for export abroad. In the view of the RMA, the agreement legitimized Japan's unfair trading practices while it increased Japan's market share at the expense of American producers. The U.S. government, on the other hand, believed the agreement was intended to make Japan a residual supplier of rice in the world market, and if nothing else would serve to control any Japanese plans of becoming a world rice supplier. The U.S. government persuaded the RMA to withdraw its 301 petition, citing a Japanese pledge to consider the possibility of allowing rice imports, and a promise to restrict export activity to the agreed levels. The RMA somewhat reluctantly complied with Washington's request, but believed the agreement to be too vague and too lucrative for a market newcomer.

From the start, the agreement was the subject of controversy, most of which centered around a provision granting emergency exceptions to Japan's level of exports, contingent upon American approval. The RMA saw this exception clause as a source of future squabbles and possible discrepancy in the determination of what would constitute an emergency situation, and which bureaucratic department in Washington would decide when such a situation did in fact exist. Almost as soon as the agreement was inked, Korea approached the United States and requested that Japan be allowed to sell them 88,000 tons of rice, since Korea's harvest had fallen short of expectations and Japan's quota had already been met. Since Korea is the number one purchaser of American rice, as well as its political ally, the exception was granted. Actually, approval of the Korean request did not divert business from the United States because its stockpiles of short grain rice had already been depleted.

In the summer of 1980, Korea contracted to buy 600,000 tons of U.S. rice, with the price to be negotiated. Shortly thereafter, and with the price on the American contract still not finalized, Korea announced that it was facing a massive food shortage and would need more rice than the United States could supply. Their request to the United States for an emergency exception was summarily granted, but this time the amount was staggering: one million tons of rice, representing 8% of the annual world traded total, seemed too large a request to be above the suspicion of the RMA. Although the United States did not want to be accused of prohibiting grain inflows to a hungry nation, especially an ally, many U.S. agriculturalists believed that Japan would be unloading part of their rice reserves below the world market price to a more than willing customer, which also happened to be the primary export market for the United States.

With exceptions to the agreement routinely granted, the RMA believed the United States response served only to approve of Japanese actions, and failed to challenge a feared penetration into the world market, an American domain. According to Congressman Vic Fazio of California, U.S. producers could have met the Korean demand, yet neither their association nor members of Congressional or Senate subcommittees were approached for their input.[15] The decision to grant exceptions floundered between the Department of Agriculture, which claimed to represent the interests of producers, and the State Department, which considered such matters to be more of diplomacy and national interest. In fact, the State Department did not fully investigate the emergency situation claimed by Korea, nor the United States and Japanese abilities to meet the request, and was apparently unaware that a contract between the United States and Korea had yet to be finalized.[16] The State Department decision to allow Japan to sell rice at a lower price clearly could have jeopardized the U.S. bargaining position during price negotiations with Korea.

In a front page *New York Times* article in March 1989, Robert Pear wrote that after dozens of interviews with experts on Japan, he concluded that "the United States is unable to pursue a coherent policy toward Tokyo because of a series of 'turf wars' among Federal agencies. On key issues, the agencies do not communicate, much less coordinate."[17] Ronald Morse, an expert on Japan at the Library of Congress and a frequent contributor to scholarly journals, wrote that "the degree of ignorance about Japan in the U.S. Government is shocking. Each agency negotiates with the Japanese in isolation and tries to cut a deal on its own issues."[18] This lack of coordination and the excessive expectations of the United States in its dealings with Japan are two related issues that Japan must address in its future relations with the United States, and they will be discussed further in the chapter.

How was Japan, a nation virtually closed to rice imports, and in which the price of rice is approximately five to seven times the world price, able to sell at such a low price abroad? The answer, argues the U.S. government (particularly the USTR, the Department of Agriculture, and the Department of Commerce), is through a system of subsidies and government purchasing programs that serve to benefit the Japanese farmer at the expense of the Japanese consumer. Originally, price supports were intended to narrow the widening income gap between farmer and city worker, the income of the latter having appreciated 30% relative to that of his rural counterpart from 1952–1960. The conclusion reached by many in the United States is that Japan's virtual one-party dominance had been dependent on the support of the Japanese farmer, whose vote in the rural district had been given "electoral clout" without a proper reapportionment of districts following the exodus of workers from the countryside to the cities since the war. As noted in the latter part of Chapter 2, this argument is not entirely accurate.

American farmers find something grossly "unfair" about the idea of Japan's rice market being closed to foreign competition, and the Japanese government subsidizing its farmers; yet as a United States Department of Agriculture bulletin noted in 1984:

[in the United States] the ratio of Government expenditures to the farm value of rice has increased significantly. . . . In 1980, this ratio was 6 percent: Government expenditures totaled $118 million, but the farm value of rice production was a record $1.87 billion. By 1983, however, the ratio rose to 92 percent: total Government expenditures were estimated at $794 million, but the farm value of rice production dropped to $862 million.[19]

Agricultural subsidies are by no means cheap, and awarding them results in an inefficient use of resources, stockpiles of food products that are scarce in less developed nations, and depressed prices for exports. The cumulative monetary cost to the industrialized nations adopting such programs was estimated in 1987 at $140 billion annually.[20] Clearly, as is apparent from the protracted Uruguay Round of the GATT talks, the issue of agricultural subsidies has become an international political quagmire, while national involvement in agricultural decisions has been pursued for increasingly non-economic ends. Following his January 1992 diplomatic-turned-trade mission to Japan, President Bush "defended U.S. agricultural programs as necessary until other nations stop subsidizing their farm products" before the American Farm Bureau convention in Kansas City. "I will not put our farmers at an unfair disadvantage" he exhorted before the nation's largest organization of farmers.[21]

Most of the recipients of U.S. agricultural subsidy programs, rice farmers included, sell their produce on the world market. Japan's rice subsidy program, on the other hand, is a political perquisite enjoyed by a mostly part-time agrarian sector. Its objective is not to pervade the world market, although with steadily decreasing levels of domestic consumption[22] and no change in production, government purchase programs would inevitably require a foreign market with unmet demand. This is exactly what precipitated Japan's seeking an outside market (Korea) in 1980. Since that time, however, programs rewarding acreage idling have resulted in a noticeable downtrend of production, and Japan's infrequent participation in the world market has most often been brought about by Korean requests following floods and typhoons. If there is a violator of subsidizing agricultural exports to the world market in an attempt to capture market share from a nonsubsidized competitor, it has not been Japan but the United States. Sixty-five to seventy percent of world short grain rice exports are supplied by just five nations: the United States, Thailand, Burma, Pakistan, and China. The United States and Thailand normally account for half of the rice exported to the world, but in 1993 Thailand displaced the United States as the leading export nation, mainly because of noncompetitive U.S. rice prices.

In 1986, the U.S. government initiated a policy aimed at recapturing the lost market share. In essence, it encouraged American farmers to sell rice to export markets at the then current price of $4 per 100 pounds, with the U.S. government providing the difference between what the farmers would have received if the government had purchased the rice, at that time $8 per 100 pounds. Although they were not underselling the market, the U.S. farmers' participation in the world market was subsidized by the government. Naturally, Thai farmers, who do not receive any subsidies from their government, were not pleased.[23]

Frequently justifying that their subsidy benefits are necessary to make their product competitive in the world market and to combat the government subsidies earned by foreign competitors, American rice farmers also point to the cost of their capital intensive operation, making it the highest of any crop in the United States. In contrast, Japan's rice market is highly labor intensive, with about two-thirds of farming households being part-time farmers who derive more than half their income from other sources. "This category of part-time households cultivates about 40% of all agricultural land. In 1975, more than 70% of those engaged in farming were either men over 60 [years of age] or women,"[24] figures that have since remained steady, if not having slightly increased. Because of the high percentage of part-time older farmers and the realities of Japan's topography, the methods of rice cultivation are not nearly as advanced as those in the United States, as noted by a *Washington Post* reporter traveling in Japan. "On the steep slopes above the narrow roads [in Kumamoto prefecture] we saw farmers in big straw hats stooping to their work in terraced rice paddies—exactly like the old photos in the fourth grade geography book."[25]

Given these statistics and images, American rice farmers view their Japanese counterparts as either not as devoted, not as efficient, or not as professional. California rice growers are more than four times as productive as the Japanese, and based solely on the economics of comparative advantage and specialization, the U.S. farmer should be represented in the Japanese market, if not dominate it. But that is just what the Japanese government fears.

Japan's self-sufficiency in grain has consistently fallen during the past two decades, and is the lowest of any advanced nation. To a U.S. industry "literally on [its] knees," according to one of its representatives, the Japanese market represents the elixir for the malady plagued U.S. rice farmer, and access to it would relieve some of the pressure on the U.S. government (and financing taxpayer) to provide costly subsidy programs. Even with the image of the poor American farmer fighting for his self-proclaimed survival against a tide of Japanese protectionism, it does not mean that the U.S. rice farmer has endeared himself to the American public. In drought-stricken California, the state's rice farmers, who use more water than all the households in Los Angeles and San Francisco combined, refused to sell their water to an emergency

water bank that would redistribute the scarce commodity to the
worst affected regions. As the *New York Times* reported in 1991,

under decades-old agreements, the farmers pay the government as little
as $7 for the water they consume on each acre of land. [In 1991] the state
offered about $450 for that amount of water. But accepting the offer
would force farmers to idle land, thus losing income from rice. Some
farmers would also lose a $260 Federal subsidy for each idled acre.....
The Federal program allows thefarmers to idle half their land and still
get 92 percent of their total subsidy payments.[26]

Since both the Japanese and American rice farmer are recipients of government subsidy programs, the issue is actually not one
of "free trade" but "fair trade." In an attempt to penetrate the
Japanese market, the RMA filed two 301 petitions with the Office
of the USTR in 1986 and 1988. Press accounts said the millers
later offered what they considered a compromise: withdrawal of
the first petition in return for a commitment by Japan to buy a
set amount of rice for aid to third countries and for use in proc-
essed form in Japan. The RMA would not have to wait for a
response from the Japanese, for USTR Clayton Yeutter dismissed
their petition after pledging he would "urge Japan to roll back its
rice import restrictions in line with the broad commitment of the
General Agreement on Tariffs and Trade to reduce trade barriers."[27]

Yeutter had not discussed the RMA petition with the White
House which, as head of a supposedly autonomous office, he was
not required, or expected, to do. He insisted, "I did not decide
this case on political grounds. I did it on the basis of what is in
the best interest of both countries, and more important, what is
in the best interest of the rice growers."[28] After waiting two years
for some indication that the Japanese government would remedy
the situation, the RMA refiled their petition in the fall of 1988,
alleging barriers to United States commerce. The complaint was
the first to be filed under the "Super 301" provision of the Omnibus Trade Act of 1988 which, in the words of the *Wall Street
Journal*, "strengthened the role of the trade representative as the
nation's chief spokesperson on trade."[29] When the Senate Finance
Committee's trade subcommittee was drafting the Super 301 pro-

vision, certainly, stated subcommittee chairman Max Baucus of Montana, "Japan was on the minds of us all."[30] The provision mandates a formal investigation and up to eighteen months of negotiation with a nation cited as an "unfair trader." The violating country must then remove its trade barriers within three years, or face American retaliation in the form of tariffs up to 100% on selected imports from the cited nation.

The timing of this second petition was meant to coincide with the presidential election campaign of front-runner George Bush, and force the Republican hand to prove its tough-talking free trade policy platform. Although Bush publicly called for Yeutter to follow through on the petition, it was once again rejected. In Yeutter's view, pursuing a politically entrenched issue such as access to the Japanese market might result in a tide of anti-American sentiment, and he was "convinced that the best way to open Japan's rice market was through current multilateral trade talks [Uruguay Round]."[31] Yeutter notified the RMA that he had won assurances from Japan that the issue would be on the table at the talks, but they were not satisfied. Yet among the American farming sector, there was dissension over the RMA's insistence on pushing the issue of market liberalization. As a *New York Times* editorial stated, "wheat farmers and major farm organizations opposed their rice-growing brethren, fearing that a crackdown on Japan would result in still stiffer Japanese curbs on other U.S. products."[32]

The Japanese also did their own lobbying on this side of the Pacific. Zenchu, one of Japan's politically powerful agricultural cooperatives, announced that it "would send representatives to the United States to seek support from American farmers."[33] Prime Minister Takeshita "personally appealed to President Reagan in a letter, addressed 'Dear Ron,' urging rejection of the petition,"[34] and promising to put rice quotas on the table during the Uruguay Round of GATT talks. This seemed to Yeutter to be a step in the right direction. The RMA and Democratic presidential nominee Michael Dukakis were not as easily appeased, however. Yeutter's decision was criticized by both Dukakis and the president of the RMA, who suggested that his delegation rethink their support for the Republican Party in the upcoming election.[35]

In any event, the issue of agricultural protectionism has become

a central point of deliberation during the Uruguay Round, and
Yeutter was replaced as USTR by Carla Hills. When Hills came
before the Senate Finance Committee for her confirmation hearing in early 1989, she said her strategy as USTR would be to open
foreign markets "with a crowbar or a handshake."[36] Appropriately, when he swore in his new appointee, President Bush presented her with a crowbar. The symbolism of that event should
have been apparent, for what can be termed the "crowbar approach"—one that seeks and may achieve immediate results, but
one that leaves noticeable destruction in its less-than-refined
methods—has been the defining characteristic of U.S. efforts in
penetrating the Japanese market since the end of the Cold War.
For her part, Hills was judged tough but fair, and this image of
prudence carried through in the spring of 1990, when she rejected
protectionist sentiment in the United States and refrained from
listing Japan's closed rice market in violation of the Super 301
provision, even though the Japanese anticipated the worse of two
outcomes.[37] "I think Japan has moved further this year than any
other country,"[38] she responded to lawmakers in justifying her
decision. As we will see further along, however, although rice was
spared mention from Super 301, Japan as a nation was not.

The Uruguay Round has presented a conundrum for trade ne-
gotiators, even though Hills declared in 1989 that its conclusion
by December 1990 was "the highest priority."[39] Although envisioned as a forum for delegates of the world's industrialized
nations to conduct trade negotiations on high-tech matters on the
eve of the next millennium, the talks have been mired over issues
more representative of the early 1900s. Foremost among these has
been the insistence of the EU to continue its system of agricultural
price supports, and, until recently, Japan's refusal to abolish its
rice barrier. As has been noted, although it criticizes the practice
of farm subsidies, the United States is also a practitioner of them.
In a U.S. Department of Agriculture publication that understandably presents the U.S. position at the Uruguay Round in the most
favorable light, the choices were made clear to the rest of the
world: continuation of agricultural protectionism, or the risk of a
"trade war and its likely effects on the world economy."[40] According to the Department, "The U.S. proposal to tie trade negotiations to reform of domestic agricultural policies was a historic

step beyond the traditional agenda for trade talks . . . the United States placed all of its policies on the table."[41]

One could argue that the U.S. initiative has actually hindered progress on issues more significant than agricultural policies, although the response of other nations (as well as the response of many farmers in the United States) indicates that this is also an important issue. As has been discussed, rhetoric and reality are often two different commodities, especially when the former is uttered by a politician. Partisanship and the reality of facing the electorate are as politically imperative in Japan as they are in the United States, and many in both nations predicted that foreign pressure would eventually erode the barriers to Japan's protected rice market. Such a move, it was suggested, might be in the context of the United States approaching Japan to make concessions on the rice issue as a member of what Japan likes to call "the global partnership," a term that the United States once also used, though its use has been limited in favor of the term "the new world order." Even then, the United States use of the phrase "global partnership" usually has only been applied in discussions with Japan, making one wonder how seriously the United States has taken either the terms "partnership" or "global" in its recent relations with Japan.

U.S. Ambassador Michael Armacost used both the "global partnership" and bilateral approaches when he reportedly stated that "if Japan [made] a new proposal on something such as the rice issue that would get member nations back to the negotiating table, it would make a contribution to the promotion of Japan–U.S. relations as well as [revive] the stalled [Uruguay Round] talks,"[42] a conclusion that had already been reached by Prime Minister Miyazawa Kiichi.[43] One editorial linked Japan's concession on the rice issue to the intent of the Tokyo Declaration of 1992, which stated that "both nations will increase their cooperation in the undertaking of helping build a fair, peaceful, and prosperous world as it moves toward the 21st century."[44] The *Yomiuri Shinbun* echoed this sentiment, stating that it would be "unavoidable for Japan to make some concession or other in order to have the [GATT] negotiations succeed."[45] It appears that Japan's decision to partially liberalize its rice market may have been motivated by the combined effects of U.S. pressure, the defeat of the

LDP, and certainly natural occurrences such as typhoons, torrential amounts of rainfall, and a rice plant blight that produced the worst rice harvest in Japan since the end of World War II, leaving an unmet demand of 2 million tons.[46] Nevertheless, each of these factors that threatened the maintenance of Japan's rice policy has been faced before.

U.S. pressure for Japan to allow an open market for imported rice has ebbed and flowed in the past, and at times the challenge to Japan's policy has been blatant. Fully aware that violators of the foreign rice prohibition could face up to two years in prison and a fine of ¥3 million, U.S. trade officials displayed samples of American grown rice at a food trade show in Chiba, east of Tokyo. "Agriculture Ministry officials sent to the show angrily told American officials that the samples had to be removed,"[47] a response that drew criticism from both U.S. Commerce Secretary Robert Mosbacher ("an unfortunate incident")[48] and Agriculture Secretary Edward Madigan ("a serious affront").[49] Although the LDP has been the primary beneficiary of infrequent redistricting, the members of the Diet are a diverse group of politicians representing a diverse group of interests, not all of which are agricultural. And ultimately, Japan's agricultural support policies have to be explained to the electorate, the real financier of these programs. Even within the bureaucracy, both sides of any policy issue are advanced through ministerial battles that are waged with as much zeal and conviction as they are in the United States, and on the rice issue it is no different. Japan's bureaucrats may epitomize the notion of public servants, if only for their generally elite educational background and devotion to government service, but unanimity of opinions, especially between ministries, is hardly the norm.

The point to be made here is that there has always been considerable pressure, both internal and external, for Japan to liberalize its rice market. Rice liberalization for Japan is not only an issue of economics, it is one of potential sacrifice that few can now foresee, but none can disregard. As stated, we believe that the decision for liberalization was not a reactive response to U.S. pressure, but an expression to the rest of the world that Japan is prepared to make the ultimate sacrifice, if necessary, to assume a share of world leadership. At the same time, if Japan's narrow self-interest was the priority, it could have continued its closed rice market policy.

The world rice market is notoriously volatile, but it is doubtful that the long-term thinking Japanese will be assuaged by temporary lower prices if future supply can not be guaranteed. Some Japanese agricultural analysts believe that the demand for rice will increase with the lower price brought about by market liberalization, and few doubt that Japanese consumers would rather pay a lower price for rice which "half the participants in a widely publicized taste test by a Japanese television station could not differentiate between Japanese and [American] rice."[50] But while they are knowingly paying a relatively exorbitant price for what many regard as a dietary staple, a high percentage of Japanese express nationalist sentiment when it comes to the rice issue. In a 1991 poll conducted by the *Yomiuri Shinbun*, when asked to list "good points" of liberalization, 46.3% of respondents said "inexpensive rice will come in," but when asked to list "bad points," 67.6% said "rice-planting farmers will suffer a serious blow." Perhaps more interestingly, when asked if (1) Japan's position in international society should be given priority over protection of Japan's domestic agriculture, or (2) Japan's protection of domestic agriculture should be given priority over its position in international society, 27.3% answered the former, and 56.7% the latter. Similarly, the Japan Housewives' Association, which was instrumental in organizing females to vote against LDP candidates in the July 1989 Upper House election in protest of the sex scandalous former Prime Minister Uno Sosuke and the enactment of a 3% consumption tax in 1988, was a vocal opponent of market liberalization. "About 47.5% said they were against liberalization,"[51] continuing a trend which began in 1987, and they cite safety reasons (less stringent pesticide restrictions abroad) and a decrease in Japan's food self-sufficiency rate among their concerns. The primary concern facing the government is the extent to which market liberalization will see agricultural land, not just land for rice cultivation, converted into nonagricultural uses, thus increasing Japan's dependence on foreign suppliers for its agricultural products.

In the 1300s, the Ashikaga military leaders (the only semblance of government in Japan during four hundred years of internal

warfare) urged the peasantry to adopt new crop enhancing tech-
niques to alleviate shortages and increase crop-based tax revenue.
Since that time, rice producers and the government have provided
a steady supply of rice for the population, and on most occasions
when the government claimed that it could not meet demand, rice
riots would be waged, followed by the "miraculous" appearance
of rice. These attempts at price manipulation were rarely successful, and if the government was truly intent on raising revenue,
rather than restricting supply to increase price they simply raised
the proportion of crops to be paid in taxes. More protests would
ensue, but for different reasons. As long as the peasant was not
pushed below the subsistence level, increased tax rates were in-
tolerable and despised, but accepted as inevitable; starvation,
however, was not.

There have been times, however, when the government was
simply unable to ensure that demand would be met. Memories of
hunger and starvation in the closing days and aftermath of World
War II are still vivid among the late-middle and older generations
in Japan, who remember that Occupation rations of rice, while
well intentioned, could nevertheless not be guaranteed. The
United States is a nation of boundless fields of plenty, feeding its
own citizens and a large proportion of the world. Arguments
against full market liberalization are not solely for reasons of self-
sufficiency and food security, however.

In 1991, the then ruling LDP formulated a three-point policy
which it presented to the United States, as conditions for a limited
opening of the rice market. Two of these were economic "exchanges." The United States would agree to decrease its own
number of items covered by the GATT waiver clause (objects
exempt from liberalization), as well as repeal the U.S. Meat Import Act, which limits the importation of beef. The second measure was a bit of an irony, considering that, along with oranges,
beef exports to Japan were headline grabbers in the United States
in the early and mid-1980s. But it was also an attempt to challenge
the United States to open up what Japan considered to be a "sacred" market for the United States, one free from foreign competition, which was parallel to the demand that Japan faced. The
most significant request submitted to the United States in ex-

change for limited liberalization of the rice market, however, was the third—that the United States would "positively promise not to ban food exports"—a reflection of the food security concern.[52] Of course, many Japanese have memories of the war, but many more have memories of President Nixon's decision to place an embargo on the export of soybeans to Japan (and the rest of the world) in the summer of 1973. Nixon's justification was that the United States was faced with a lower than normal soybean reserve, and there was concern that there would be a shortage of feed for cattle, hogs, and poultry in the United States. But domestic difficulties faced by its major supplier is not the only possible impediment to guaranteed shipments. Withholding American agricultural plenty is a weapon of international relations that knows no party lines and does not discriminate between ally and enemy recipient. In response to the Soviet invasion of Afghanistan in 1980, President Carter's decision to withhold 17 million metric tons of grain (out of a planned shipment of 25 million metric tons) was an initiative followed by some U.S. allies, and rejected by others.[53] In the end, it did not appear that this policy produced the response Carter had hoped for, namely the withdrawal of its troops from Afghanistan. But Carter's decision to suspend grain exports to the Soviet Union, itself a major producer of agricultural products, must have evoked among the Japanese memories of seven years earlier, and reinforced their vulnerability.

It may be very tempting for Americans to dismiss the food security concern that was one reason for Japan's continued ban on foreign rice. It is true that compared to their American counterparts many Japanese rice farmers are relatively inefficient, that Japan already relies on other nations for a high percentage of its agricultural products, and that the consumption of rice has been slowly decreasing as the Japanese have changed both their diet and demand for easily prepared, ready-when-wanted food. When the Allied Occupation forces arrived in Japan in the aftermath of World War II, the biggest hurdle they faced was not anti-American or anti-peace sentiment, it was starvation. Rice rationing, and the effort to provide each family with a minimum amount of rice, was not a program undertaken by the victorious to solely satisfy the dietary preferences of the defeated. It was in keeping with the widely-held belief that under the most severe circumstances, a person's life, although it would become malnourished, could be maintained with nothing but rice.

We can speculate about the future, but we can hardly predict it. Long after the authors of this study and most of its readers have left this world, is there not the possibility that Japan could be involved in another international conflict, perhaps involving the United States? We say this because at the time few anticipated there would be a sequel to World War I, which was named only when the world had witnessed World War II. Was this really the "war to end all wars"? In this light, Japan's decision to begin liberalization of its rice market may prove to be the greatest commitment of all to seeing the continued stability of the international system, or it may prove to be a sacrifice far greater than any of us at present can envision.

Japan's decision to liberalize its rice market is an initiative of both bilateral and international significance, for the rice issue, as we have noted, is one of the most visible barriers to trade, if not one of the most overemphasized by the United States. From an international perspective, Japan's decision will put pressure on the EU at the Uruguay Round to address its agricultural subsidy programs. What therefore may have been viewed as a bilateral issue by many Americans will in fact have far greater international implications. A year before agreement was reached to allow for limited liberalization of the Japanese rice market, Sato Hideo believed that, "It is not enough for Japan to wait for the United States and Europe to settle a bilateral issue [which at that time was oil seeds]. Japan always waits and sits. . . . If you are a Prime Minister willing to risk your political life, you can do it. If you want to effect change in the short and medium run, political leaders can do it. If not, Japan will be on the defensive at all times."[54]

There are other issues in the U.S.–Japan relationship that have overwhelmingly been viewed in bilateral terms, but these too will assume a larger international dimension in the post–Cold War world. Two of the most important are (1) Japan's defense and its role in international security, and (2) trade.

ON MATTERS OF DEFENSE AND
INTERNATIONAL SECURITY

One way to avoid a repeat of the past is for the United States to show its commitment to the stability of the international system by working with Japan on matters of defense within the framework of the U.S.–Japan Security Treaty, and by involving Japan in closer consultation over military matters determined to be of international import. It may be difficult to achieve either of these objectives, however, because of the inconsistency and unrealistic expectations on the part of United States. For instance, in 1989 both the U.S. House of Representatives and the U.S. Senate passed bills seeking Japan's shouldering of the total "direct expenses" of U.S. forces stationed in Japan. Although the Senate declared that salaries of U.S. military personnel would be excluded, it did not present a list of specifics as to what would be covered, or what Japan would be expected to pay.[55] The bill was in direct contradiction to the U.S.–Japan Status of Forces Agreement (which is renewed every few years as a stipulation of the U.S.–Japan Security Treaty), which states that maintenance expenses are to be paid by the United States, while Japan will provide the facilities and areas of operation. This 1989 request would be followed by another in 1990, by which the United States sought Japan to bear the total amount of yen-based expenses for U.S. Forces in Japan. As the *Nihon Keizai Shinbun* perceived the situation, the U.S. initiative for these bills was trade friction between the two nations.[56] But the issue has gone far deeper than trade friction. It is a realization that relative to those that face Japan, the structural problems that confront the United States, particularly its massive federal budget deficit, have necessitated cost-saving measures. Testifying before the U.S. House of Representatives Defense Burden sharing Panel in 1988, Rear Admiral Gene R. LaRocque, Director, Center for Defense Information, stated:

Our allies are rich. They are powerful, and they are not threatened by anybody. It is a big burden for the United States and a big burden that we ought to look at carefully today, because our Treasury is broke, flat broke. There is not a penny in the United States Treasury. The country is rich, but the Treasury is broke, and we borrow $3 billion every week just to pay our Government bills and to keep those forces in foreign countries.[57]

The burden sharing issue has eclipsed matters of defense, as it has raised comparisons between social conditions facing each nation, and questioned the priorities of each nation's government. To continue with the views of LaRocque:

[R]ecently we have decided that if we can persuade our young people to serve four years in the military . . . we promise them a college education or at least a lot of help toward a college education. So we get a kid in the military, man or woman, and we send them to Japan to defend the Japanese. When they get to Japan, what do they find? They find the Japanese children, young people, are in college while our kids are being promised to go to college if they serve for 4 years to defend the Japanese. That is true in Europe and in the other countries as well. In fact, the Japanese can afford to send their kids to college because they lend us the money to pay for our deficit. They buy our bonds and we pay them interest, which they can then pay to have their children go to college. Japan has become a powerful nation in the area with self-defense forces and there is a lot to learn from that example. . . . When we went into Japan, I don't think anyone ever thought that we intended to stay there in perpetuity. I think everyone agrees that some day we are going to take our armed forces out of Japan. So it is just a question of when.[58]

But it is precisely because of the existence of the security alliance between the United States and Japan that Japan can assume a wider responsibility in the world. In the words of an official in the Japanese government, "It gives us the credibility that as long as U.S. forces are stationed in Japan, we won't act independently. I think we see the same argument regarding Germany—that it should remain in the NATO alliance for the same reason."[59] Despite assurances from the highest ranking Japanese officials that their nation will never again pursue a policy of militarism and aggression, some Asian nations believe that the end of the Cold War is all the more reason for continuation of the U.S.–Japan Security Treaty. During the Cold War, the emphasis was on protecting Japan from the threat of the Soviet Union, but now a justification that was of secondary importance during the Cold War—that the agreement protects Japan from its neighbors—has come to the fore. On the other side of the equation, even if the United States believes that "Japanese host nation support for U.S. service personnel is overstated,"[60] it is undeniable that as long as the United States maintains its economic presence in the region, which considering President Clinton's remarks during the APEC meetings held in Seattle in November 1993 it intends to do, there is no more efficient means for the United States to meet its security interests than through its military presence in Japan. Host nation support provided by Japan is still the largest of any American ally, and the U.S. General Accounting Office notes that Japan has been more responsive to U.S. burden sharing initiatives than the European allies.[61]

Clearly, on the issue of defense burden sharing the level of Japan's host nation support is approaching that of total support, and it should be considered whether the United States desires a situation in which support resembles that given to a mercenary army. But on other issues of security, the United States has been less than receptive in including Japan in the decision-making process. Commenting on the Kuwaiti reflagging operation, undertaken during the bombing of neutral ships sailing through the Persian Gulf during the Iran–Iraq war, the Burden Sharing Panel somewhat presciently noted that:

The United States went in with a large military force without first reaching agreement with the allies on whether they would participate and in what way. According to some observers—including former Ambassador Jeane Kirkpatrick—the result of this "high profile" has been somewhat counterproductive. *The United States might have gotten more equitable burden sharing from the allies had we consulted them before announcing our own commitment. The Panel believes that a lower U.S. profile might be preferable in future Gulf operations* [emphasis added].[62]

In the words of the committee, the operation was "a case in point on how not to get equitable burden sharing [from U.S. allies]," but for the most part their recommendations were unheeded two years later by Bush's decision to near unilaterally "draw a line in the sand" against Iraq on behalf of "peace-loving peoples" throughout the world. Ironically, just weeks before Iraq's invasion of Kuwait in August 1990, the U.S.–Japan Security Consultative Committee (SCC) was upgraded to a Security Ministerial Conference (composed of the foreign minister and the Japan Defense Agency director general from the Japanese side, and the secretary of state and secretary of defense from the U.S. side) for "consultations on the fluid Asian security situation after the Cold War."[63] But that cooperation was not extended to include joint consultation on military matters involving other regions of the world. The Japanese government confirmed that there was indeed prior notification from the United States to Japan regarding dispatch of troops to Saudi Arabia,[64] but the United States hardly maintained a lower profile in this "Gulf operation," nor did it discuss or suggest at the outset what would be the contribution expected of Japan. In retrospect it was this very point that for the world would reinforce an image of Japan as indifferent to its international responsibility. Without a clear articulation by the United States of how much Japan was expected to contribute, among non-Arab nation contributors, its financial support was exceeded only by that of the United States. Speaking of Japan's role in the Allied coalition, President Bush would later remark, "Japan stepped up and did what Japan was asked to do,"[65] although what was perceived as its delayed response would serve to popularize the dislike of Japan in the United States, a dislike which for the most part had previously been limited to those knowledgeable about issues of trade and industry.

Perhaps the biggest problem facing Japan in its defense relations with the United States is the competing images of Japan's defense capability and the contributions expected of it. On the one hand, as stated by Senator John McCain of Arizona, Japan's revival of militarism is not a factor, but rather "Japan's negative pacifism is a problem."[66] The other image is of a Japan that harbors aspirations of remilitarization. In a public opinion poll conducted on the fiftieth anniversary of Japan's attack on Pearl Harbor, when asked if Japan is an ally that can be trusted militarily, 40.1% of Americans responded that they did "not think so at all."[67]

There have been positive steps taken by the United States to involve Japan in issues of international security, and we believe that sincere consultation with Japan is one way in which the United States can alleviate this negative image of Japan's military capability, or inability. Sincere consultation does not mean unilateral decision-making and subsequent bill collecting. For example, one would not likely have seen a high-ranking representative of the Japanese government invited to a White House ceremony on matters that do not appear to be within Japan's direct sphere of influence. But in September 1993, Foreign Minister Hata Tsutomu was conspicuously present in the front row of dignitaries at the signing of the Mideast Declaration between Israel and the PLO. Of course, a large proportion of Japan's contribution for international security operations will be financial, but that should not imply that Japan should have no input in the policymaking process. Similarly, it appears that the United States and Japan have put the animosity of the FSX tactical fighter plane issue behind them, as the U.S. Department of Defense and the Japan Defense Agency have agreed to jointly develop military technology, most recently and notably regarding a new type of missile, as well as a duct rocket engine. Defense experts suggest that more cooperative defense-related projects are in the planning stages, and with positive results and subsequent publicity of these efforts, we believe that the spirit of the U.S.–Japan Security Treaty will only be strengthened.

THE POLITICS OF TRADE

For more than twenty years, trade conflicts have been an ever-present component of the U.S.–Japan relationship. Considering the ad hoc, often contradictory nature of U.S. trade policy towards Japan, especially that since the late 1980s, there is no reason to believe that this conflict will abate. As noted in Chapters 3 and 4, Japan has developed its trading relationships with both Asia and Europe not only because of increased economic opportunity in these regions, but also because of trade friction with, and increasing demands raised by, its leading trading partner. Our interest here is the trade credo that the United States has applied in its post–Cold War relations with Japan, and how the inability of Japan to meet these changing, often unrealistic and presumptuous expectations has resulted in unwarranted criticism of Japan, and has thus weakened the U.S.–Japan relationship on both sides of the Pacific.

The Omnibus Trade and Competitiveness Act of 1988, which addressed questions of trade more than it did U.S. competitiveness, was the last major piece of trade legislation enacted by the United States during the Cold War. In part, the Congressional committee charged with studying the issue declared that "our [U.S.] trade and economic relations with Japan are complex and cannot be effectively resolved through narrow sector-by-sector negotiations."[68] Strangely enough, this has been the emphasis of the U.S. trade position in dealing with Japan ever since, as has been the notion that Japan is the cause of lost American jobs and world market share for a variety of products. Speaking before the U.S. House of Representatives Subcommittee on Trade in 1989, convened to consider which nations would be cited for application of the "Super 301" provisions of the 1988 Trade Act, Howard Lewis of the National Association of Manufacturers stated that "more than any other country, Japan has become a symbol of our frustration over the erosion of U.S. international competitiveness."[69] Similarly, while President Bush was following through on his illconceived and ill-fated trip to Japan, U.S. Representative John Dingell asserted that Japan "had brought the U.S. recession."[70] These views are in stark contrast to those of the American emissary Townsend Harris more than one hundred years earlier, who remarked "In all my travels, I have never seen a people so wellfed, clad and lodged and so little overworked as the Japanese."[71] The "problem" for many Americans is that the Japanese work too much, they save too much, and they spend too little, and U.S. officials have usually felt no compunction in prescribing policies for Japan, including an increase in the spending habits of Japanese consumers and a decrease in their savings rate to narrow the trade deficit between the two nations.[72]

Based on testimony presented at the 1989 hearing, Japan was cited as one of three unfair trading partners that would face trade sanctions if stated issues were not addressed. The fact that the other two nations cited were Brazil and India, neither a significant trading partner of the United States, suggests that they were included to deflect possible criticism that the intent of the Super 301 provision was to target Japan, an intent which we believe is clear from the testimony before the committee and the anti-Japanese sentiment that was widespread on Capitol Hill. Brazil was cited for restrictive licensing of both agricultural and manufactured products, India for barriers to investment and for its prohibition on the sale of insurance, and Japan for exclusionary government procurement of satellites and supercomputers, and standards and technical barriers for forest products. Agreement with Japan was reached on all three products, as was the goal of 20% market share for foreign manufactured semiconductors in the Japanese market, as stipulated under the U.S.–Japan Semiconductor Agreement. With these sectorial successes, the United States has intensified its efforts at "breaking down" barriers to trade in other sectors. At the same time, it has sought Japan's continuation of its VER (voluntary export restraint) for automobiles, and has pressured Japan to pursue a program of VIE (voluntary import expansion). This is the latest in a long line of American trade strategies in dealing with the problem of Japan's "competitiveness."

Initially, the United States requested that Japan lower its tariff barriers, and it complied to the extent that its rates were the lowest among developed nations. Then the U.S. strategy of the day suddenly turned to currency manipulation. The Plaza Accords of 1985 were designed to bring about realignment of the Japanese yen and German mark in relation to the dollar, and thus eliminate the U.S. trade surplus with these two nations. Half of the desired result was ultimately achieved, though indirectly. Germany's surplus has been eliminated, mostly because of the cost of its national reunification. But even though the value of the yen relative to the dollar increased dramatically overnight, which would have made Japanese products more expensive in the United States and U.S. products cheaper in Japan than before the currency change, the U.S. trade deficit with Japan ballooned. Simultaneous with the experiment in currency engineering, and subsequent to it, import restrictions imposed by the Reagan administration exceeded those of the previous six administrations combined, and by 1990 more than two-thirds of Japan's exports to the United States were included in some type of quota, special tariff, "voluntary trade restraint" or other barrier. These efforts may have mitigated the trade deficit with Japan, but it was hardly eliminated. Searching for a third explanation, soon to become a prioritization, "structural impediments" became the new buzzword. Could an explanation for the U.S. trade deficit with Japan be found in Japan's distribution system, in its dual economy of large scale, multinational business on the one hand and small subcontractors with less than one hundred employees on the other, or in the infamous but much misunderstood *keiretsu*? Japan entertained the fair trade curiosity of the United States, as Prime Minister Kaifu was a prime motivator behind the Structural Impediments Initiative talks that would raise attention to the suspected culprits for the economic woes of the United States.

With the postponement from November 1991 to the following January of his trip to Japan, the objective of which was to solidify a "U.S.–Japan Compact for Global Partnership," Bush redefined his objectives and suddenly became "more of a trade minister than the leader of the world's sole superpower."[73] Declaring that the objective of his trip could be summarized in three words, "jobs, jobs, and jobs," Bush's 1992 diplomatic journey-turned-trade mission to Japan was more memorable for the verbal outbursts by his corporate traveling companions (Lee Iacocca among them), and his visceral outburst on the lap of Prime Minister Miyazawa, than for what it accomplished. With the enthusiasm of a political candidate on a stump, which in fact he was at the time, Bush proclaimed that the opening of a Toys-R-Us store in Japan was "the first time that a large U.S. discount store has opened here, and it's blazed a trail. And now all kinds of companies can come on in, from toy stores to high-tech outlets."[74] The fact that the "Big Three" leaders of the U.S. auto industry were included in Bush's entourage was not a coincidence, as automobiles and auto parts account for two-thirds of the U.S. trade imbalance with Japan. But by unveiling his "Action Plan," which called for voluntary import proposals worth billions of dollars and increased U.S. content for Japanese cars made in the United States,[75] Bush failed to realize that Miyazawa, even more so than previous prime ministers because of his low approval rating, was in no position to deliver. Nor is it likely that Bush's plan would have amounted to billions of dollars, as he claimed. As the *Tokyo Shinbun* reminded its readers more than a year after Bush's trip, and after more sectorially targeted demands had been made to Japan, what Bush and his advisors should have understood is that "Japan is not a socialist nor planned economy nation, and so the government cannot decide on import quantities of certain commodities."[76] The U.S. "request" that Japan raise its purchase of U.S.–manufactured auto parts from the 1990 figure of $9 billion to $19 billion by 1994 was agreed to by Japan as a target figure, not a pledge, as USTR Mickey Kantor would discover in the Japanese reply to his charges that the Japanese were not fulfilling the terms of the agreement. (Considering the U.S. attitude that Japan must be "confronted" over trade issues, it was only fitting that when deciding who to appoint to his cabinet, then President-elect Clinton considered the advice of those Kantor dealt with during the campaign that he would to be too contentious for the chief of staff post, so he was tapped as the USTR, the chief negotiator on U.S.–Japan related trade issues).

Rather than there being a change in trade policy toward Japan with a change in presidential administration, Clinton has continued where Bush left off, and has intensified his efforts. Many in Japan view Clinton's trade agenda toward Japan as an extension of the Reagan and Bush administrations, which flew the banner of free trade but operated behind a veil of managed trade. Clinton is just much more forward and open about what his plans are. In the words of Okamoto Yukio, former official at the Ministry of Foreign Affairs and now a consultant to business clients in the United States and Japan:

This may be a bad example, but the Republican administration said to Japan, "Make donations on your own initiative," and pinched money from Japan in a rather forcible way. The Democratic Party, on the other hand, will put a hand in the other person's pocket and take his wallet. [Laughs] It is only a matter of style. The amount of money taken will be the same in either case."[77]

The biggest concern for Japan is that the new U.S. administration is aiming at managed trade in order to produce quick results,[78] as the notion of sectorial access has become the rallying cry of trade hawks and "fair traders" in the United States. Representative of this "emphasis on the sectorial" is Laura D'Andrea Tyson, head of the President's Council of Economic Advisers, who has written of the "utility" of numerical targets.[79] For those sectors that are not easily quantified as to units or monetary amount of U.S. share, a "trend indicator" was suggested.[80]

In April 1993, the travel obligations were reversed and Miyazawa journeyed to the United States. Before departure he viewed his upcoming visit to Washington for the U.S.–Japan Summit Talks as an opportunity to shape post–Cold War history with the United States, and understandably hoped that economic issues would not dominate the agenda. But faced with the reality of a trade deficit with his nation's second largest trading partner, Clinton viewed the summit as an opportunity to discuss economic problems between the two nations. This is not to imply that Japan would rather not discuss economic issues or address the concerns of the United States. Japan realizes perhaps more than any other nation that one of the tasks that the two nations will have to tackle cooperatively is the rehabilitation of the U.S. economy, for its strength or weakness affects the prosperity of the world. There are some Japanese, however, like Professor Muroyama Yoshimasa, who argue that Japan's economic support of the United States "means the preservation of the imbalance of the U.S. economy, the weakening of incentives for self-help, and a delay in efforts at rehabilitation."[81] And certainly, resolution of bilateral trade issues is one part of the rehabilitation process. But Japan must be growing weary of the "changing agenda diplomacy" of the United States, in which issues of international concern have been routinely mentioned only after trade issues have been addressed and prioritized in discussions with Japan. In his request of the prime minister that the Japanese government continue its measures for the expansion of the domestic market, Clinton did not seem to consider the domestic economic stimulus package— the largest in Japan's history—that had earlier been approved by the Diet. To Japan, the U.S. requests must question whether its real commitment is to national interests or to world leadership.

Clinton has differed from his immediate presidential predecessors in that together with his administration's efforts at expanding U.S. commerce by identifying barriers to trade present in the Japanese marketplace, he has more seriously addressed what the Japanese have been saying all along—that most of the structural impediments to U.S. trade and a lack of competitiveness can be found within the borders of the United States. In a December

1991 interview with *Mainichi Shinbun* editor Sato Rikuo, then Governor and yet undeclared Presidential candidate Bill Clinton stated that,

over the long run, the incomes of [Americans and Japanese] will grow only insofar as we can expand the size of the global economy. But it is difficult for us to do that unless we believe that we are being treated fairly. That is we know that we have in America, for example, two problems that you don't have in Japan: a much more diverse population and it is more difficult to train all of them up to international standards. We know that. We also know that through most of our history we have not been a trading nation. That is, we have sold a lot of things but mostly when we did not have much competition.[82]

One way that the United States has attempted to face foreign competition, particularly that posed by Japan and the EU, is through conclusion of NAFTA. As mentioned in various contexts throughout this study, it is not certain to anyone—especially the Japanese—how this new trading regime will affect Japanese exports, although Japan clearly faces the prospect of NAFTA with "less than whole-hearted enthusiasm."[83] Publicly, both Japanese business and government leaders echoed the official rhetoric advanced by Clinton during the 1993 APEC meetings that the agreement will create a freer international trading system. Privately, however, many of these same leaders admit that a true "free trade" arrangement would not require such a voluminous document, and note that Clinton has implied that NAFTA may be used to increase the bargaining position of the United States in trade discussions with the EU, and especially with Japan. But that line of reasoning is nothing new. During his January 1992 trip to Japan, Bush declared, "This trip is not simply about jobs and business. This is a terribly important part of it. . . . But now we've got to follow through. We've got to be specific. We've got to get to as much as we can, set tables, limits, let's do it by then. And I think we can do it. . . . we've got to iron out these differences between us so that we can go forward without tensions mounting and dividing up the world into trading blocs.[84]

Considering the U.S. promotion of NAFTA, which is exclusionary in its membership if not intent, U.S. criticism of an Asian trade agreement that is still at the speculation stage is hypocritical at best. In the words of Omori Takashi, an official at the Economic Planning Agency,

Why is the United States opposed to the proposal for the EAEC [East Asian Economic Caucus], put forward by Dr. Mahathir Mohamed of Malaysia? Why does it feel such antipathy towards his plan, especially since it has itself entered into a free trade agreement, that at least on paper appears to be more restrictive than that put forward by the Malaysian Prime Minister?[85]

The United States is clearly concerned should an Asian trade grouping be formed without its sharing the benefits, and to some extent it has created NAFTA to threaten discrimination of Asian—particularly Japanese—products if it is shut out of the region. But NAFTA, unlike proposed Asian trade agreements, is well beyond the rhetorical stage, and the Japanese government considers its enactment a foregone conclusion. On the other hand, the big issue of concern for Japan as it watches, step by step, the possible erection of a "fortress America," is local content, for which there are two components. The first is the rule of origin as it applies to the automobile sector. The requirements of the value content ratio for cars sold in Canada will be changed from 50% to 62.5% after five years. To Japan, according to trade official Tanabe Yasuo, this is an indication of a worsening investment climate in Canada.[86] The second issue involves *maquiladoras*. Japanese companies in *maquiladoras* can now enjoy duty-free access of parts and components from Japan to Mexico to be exported to the United States, but this benefit will be lost under NAFTA. With NAFTA, will companies that have been importing labor-intensive goods from Southeast Asia because of the low wage levels shift resources to Mexico, where wages are comparable? It remains to be seen whether Japanese companies will relocate from Mexico, and if decreased opportunities for trade will force Japan to consider participation in its own trade grouping (perhaps involving Southeast Asian nations). In the words of then Arkansas Governor (and not yet presidential candidate) Clinton, "if you do nothing, you're still affected by the global economy. It's just that you always lose."[87]

A GLOBAL PARTNERSHIP

In this chapter we have discussed specific issues that appear to be bilateral in nature, but have shown how each holds a larger implication for the world community. It should have come as no surprise that one week to the day after Japan decided to "commit the unthinkable"—liberalization of its rice market—South Korea, itself a nation that had barred rice imports, followed suit. Almost simultaneously with the Korean initiative, the EU and the United States announced that "significant progress" had been made on the agricultural impasse at the Uruguay Round. In retrospect, it is unlikely that either of these decisions would have been reached had Japan maintained its stand. On matters of defense and international security as well, we have repeated throughout that any change in the defense arrangement between Japan and the United States will have an immediate, and almost certainly disastrous, effect on the stability of Asia. Likewise, on the broad issue of trade between the two nations, it can no longer be said that the prosperity of one is the engine that drives the economic growth of the world. Only with time can we evaluate with certainty whether NAFTA will lead to discrimination against the products of outside nations, which we believe it will. How readily will both nations pursue a "global partnership" if this is the case?

Yet the problems that confront the world are now in many ways more serious than those of the Cold War. Nuclear proliferation through a fire sale of the Soviet arsenal never happened to the extent predicted, yet the number of nations on the edge of acquiring the technology, and the materials needed to realize it, increase each year. Newly democratizing states plan a course for economic development that resembles that of the already industrialized West, yet it is uncertain that the earth's resources are able to sustain the ambitions of all. Ethnic and religious tensions reach the level of mass slaughter, yet as outsiders we feel powerless to act. Kitaoka Shin'ichi commented that,

People say that the end of the Cold War was a victory for the market mechanism—that the strong wins and the weak loses—that it was a victory for liberal democracy. But every government can become selfish and inward looking. . . . The next problem will not be interference by the developed world in the developing world, but too little interaction, or indifference."[88]

In early 1993, Sato Yukio, director general of the Ministry of Foreign Affairs, North American Affairs Bureau, contributed an article to *Gaiko Forum* in which he proposed areas of international policy that could lead to greater cooperation between Japan and the United States. In part, he wrote that

Japan and the United States ought to cooperate with each other on issues related to the peace and prosperity of the post–Cold War world, such as the poverty problem in developing nations, settlement of regional disputes, the proliferation of weapons of mass destruction, and the strengthening of UN abilities to deal with problems that transcend national borders, such as the environment, refugees, population growth, narcotics, and AIDS. It is also the task for Japan, in this new Japan–U.S. age, to be the first to take concrete measures in these fields. This will lead to expanding the scope of Japan–U.S. cooperation.[89]

Sato's proposal for U.S.–Japan cooperation is similar to that of Japan's international role advanced by his predecessor, Kuriyama Takakuzu, which was published in the same journal almost three years earlier (and discussed in Chapter 2 of this study). The crucial difference, however, is that instead of presenting to the world "Japan's" new foreign policy as one of three members of a leadership trilateral with the EU and the United States, a relationship in which it admittedly and willingly assumes the least significant role, the emphasis in this proposal is clearly on enhanced cooperation with the United States as a partner in solving international problems.

The first step for U.S.–Japan cooperation on all of these issues is, of course, dialogue and consultation, and one means by which to address these issues is through the appropriation of foreign aid. Is an "aid partnership" possible, in which there is consensus on objectives and methods between the United States and Japan? As previously noted, the United States has never been reluctant to "suggest" possible aid policies to Japan.[90] And at times, it has been direct in its requests. As reported by the Japanese press, following the announcement by Kaifu, President Bush sent an

"unprecedented letter requesting [Japanese] cooperation" on aid
to Nicaragua, to which the Japanese government gave its assent.[91]
Japan has also recently increased its level of "non-developmental"
aid to Russia in the name of fulfilling its international responsibility, even though Japan has historically vowed to restrict or at
best limit aid to Russia until the territorial dispute between the
two nations is resolved. For Japan, therefore, the purpose of foreign aid is multidimensional. It allows Japan to meet its security
objectives, to actively contribute to the international system in a
non-military manner, and also presents the possibility of closer
collaboration with the United States on international issues. The
concept of joint collaboration on aid as it relates to security was
first proposed at the 18th Japan–U.S. Administrative Level Security Consultations, but Japan and the United States are also
applying aid appropriations to the solution of global problems. In
April 1989, the Japanese government announced that it would
unveil a ¥100 billion "Green Fund" that would for the most part
be targeted for the development of technology to eliminate chlo-
rofluorocarbons, and a swap of the debt of rain forest nations for
local currency, which is then applied to environmental protection
projects in these nations. In a 1992 *Tokyo Shinbun* editorial that
preceded the Rio Summit, and President Bush's ill-fated trip to
Japan, United Nations statistics were cited to show that the
United States is the nation with the highest total emissions and
the highest emissions per capita, but it "has not yet officially formulated a target for the reduction" of these wastes.[92] Anticipating
that Bush would request Japan's financial support of the Super-
conducting Super Collider project (and certainly not predicting
the diplomatic-turned-trade mission that Bush was to take with
U.S. automobile executives later that month), the editors wrote,
"On the issue of cooperation, it should be evident which is more
urgent: the construction of the SSC, or the protection of the environment of the earth." Judging from the consultations of the
Rio Summit, however, industrialized nations are hardly in agreement on what the problems of the world are, and how to solve
them. As is clear from the different perspectives on aid to China
and on environmental issues, there is no guarantee that Japan's
vision will be shared by the rest of the world, especially the
world's lone superpower. Nevertheless, there is an increased like-

lihood that Japan and the United States can cooperate on environmental issues to a greater extent than previously, because the Clinton administration (especially Vice President Gore, who is respected by the Japanese) has shown more interest on these issues than have Bush and Reagan. The United States is also reconsidering its China policy, and has softened its hard-line stance toward Vietnam. On all three issues, Japan is the one that has taken the lead.

Although the two nations have approached agreement on these issues, problems of perception between them are still evident and will hinder any intentional move beyond a strictly bilateral relationship (we hesitate to use the term "global partnership"). And while in the future both nations may proclaim their "global partnership," the term implies more of a new *relationship* between them, rather than a *partnership*, per se. The level of agreement on a breadth of issues may indeed be high but, lest we forget, Japan and the United States are two autonomous nations that, perhaps more than any other nations, must struggle with the demands of the national and the international. Conflicts between them are undesirable but inevitable, and images, whether of oneself or of others, are not changed as easily as the drafting of proclamations. For the near term, because of these images, perceptions and conflicts, we can expect the United States and Japan to continue exhibiting behavior more reminiscent of their positions during the Cold War. But as time guides our move from the subjective to the objective, so too will the reality of this new relationship come to light.

When asked what he thought of the proposals put forward by Kuriyama, Shiina Motoo replied,

Those are all good, but who can disagree with them? Foreign direct assistance and all of that is good—but it is like saying we have to believe in God [cynical laugh]. Before you discuss the specifics, the most important international public good will be to jointly set the agenda. What I call it is "perception sharing"—some say burden sharing or responsibility sharing—but if we do not share the perception, we Japanese cannot feel responsible. For Japan, closer cooperation in setting the agenda is the most important task. . . . The United States is very unique in its ability of agenda setting, but you know, sometimes you ignore people. For instance,

Japan can give very useful pieces of advice. . . . The cooperation of the two countries is vital—it can't just be an extension of the past forty-seven years.[93]

NOTES

1. *Nihon Keizai Shinbun*, April 20, 1993, p. 1. As Francis McCall Rosenbluth argues, the Ministry of Finance has as much control over the decisions made by Japanese investment firms, banks, and insurance companies that the Securities and Exchange Commission, the Interstate Commerce Commission, and the Department of the Treasury have over counterpart institutions in the United States. Japanese brokerage houses purchase U.S. government securities just as readily as American firms purchase the obligations of foreign governments on behalf of their customer, the U.S. government. But while for analytical simplicity it may be tempting to assert a "Japan, Inc." model of orders given by the central government, and orders obeyed by its financial agents, this is a view that is largely inaccurate. Francis McCall Rosenbluth, *Financial Politics in Contemporary Japan* (Ithaca, NY: Cornell University Press, 1989).

2. Appreciation to John Benson, the Roper Center for Public Opinion Research at the University of Connecticut, for supplying these figures.

3. *Asahi Shinbun*, December 28, 1992, p. 2.

4. With the possible exception of the EU, taken as a whole, which is not a single nation.

5. The Japanese restrictions on imported beef allowed for a higher percentage of corn, hay, and roughage-fed cattle, which is considered higher quality, and is the U.S. practice. This is in contrast to the beef of Australia and New Zealand, which is usually grazed and therefore of lower quality. The agreement reached between Japan and foreign producers eliminated this distinction, and has since led to an increase in the Australian/New Zealand market share. Discussion with Dr. Larry Berger, Department of Animal Sciences, University of Illinois, February 17, 1992.

6. *Statistical Abstract of the United States, 1991*, "Agricultural Exports," p. 663. As Kashiyama Yukio, a staff writer for the *Sankei Shinbun*, and at the time a visiting fellow at Columbia University, noted, "The United States condemns Japan because its agricultural market is closed. But as a matter of fact, Japan is America's best customer for agricultural products. Japan buys $8.1 billion of American produce every year, amounting to 20.2% of U.S. annual agricultural exports. Do Americans who criticize Japan for its closed agricultural market know this? Kashiyama Yukio, *To Avoid the Coming War: A First Hand Observation of US–Japan Relations* (New York: East Asia Institute, Columbia Univer-

sity, 1991), p. 12. In 1990, Japan was the destination for 20.5% of the value of U.S. agricultural exports. *Statistical Abstract of the United States,* 1992, p. 659.

7. Martin E. Weinstein, "Japan and Fair Trade," Focus 580 (Radio Broadcast), WILL-AM, Champaign, IL, January 24, 1992. Even in the heart of America's soybean belt, for which Illinois is the source for a majority of Japan's supply of soybeans, a phone–in caller stated, "My understanding is that Japan is a fairly closed market to virtually all U.S. agricultural products," whereby Weinstein replied, "Japan imports more agricultural products from the United States than any other country in the world. Japan is America's biggest agricultural product, bar none."

8. *New York Times*, October 26, 1988.

9. Robert E. Weigand, "No Open Door for Foreign Rice in Japan," *Food Policy*, August 1988, p. 232.

10. David Rapp, *How the US Got into Agriculture, and Why It Can't Get Out* (Washington, DC: Congressional Quarterly, 1988), p. 163.

11. In 1983, Thailand replaced the United States as the world's leading exporter of rice, a position it has since maintained.

12. *Review of Japan's Policy Concerning the Importation of Rice, Including a Petition Filed by the United States Rice Millers Association.* Hearing Before the Subcommittee on Cotton, Rice and Sugar of the Committee on Agriculture, House of Representatives. October 1, 1986, p. 45.

13. *Review of United States–Japan Rice Agreement.* Hearing Before the Subcommittee on Cotton, Rice, and Sugar of the Committee on Agriculture, House of Representatives. February 26, 1981. Specifics of the 301 petition can be found in this document, which has been summarized in the text.

14. Otsuka Keijiro and Hayami Yujiro, "Goals and Consequences of Rice Policy in Japan, 1965–80," *American Journal of Agricultural Economics*, August 1985, p. 529.

15. *Review of the United States–Japan Rice Agreement*, p. 23.

16. Ibid.

17. *New York Times*, March 20, 1989, p. 1.

18. Ibid.

19. U.S. Department of Agriculture, Economic Research Service, *Rice: Background for 1985 Farm Legislation*, Information Bulletin 470, September 1984, p. 28.

20. Allen Wallis, *US Agriculture and the Global Context: A Time for Action*, U.S. Department of State, Current Policy Paper 950, May 1987, p. 2.

21. *Washington Post*, January 14, 1992, p. A6.

22. *Rice: Background for 1985 Farm Legislation*, p. 15.

23. Please refer to the following *Wall Street Journal* articles for further reading on this issue: February 10, 1986, p. 30; April 28, 1986, p. 24; September 11, 1986, p. 46.

24. Michael W. Donnelly, "Conflict Over Government Authority and Markets: Japan's Rice Economy," in Thomas P. Rohlen, et al., eds., *Conflict in Japan* (Honolulu: University of Hawaii Press, 1984), p. 340.

25. *Washington Post*, December 14, 1986, p. H 5.

26. *New York Times*, April 7, 1991, p. 20.

27. *Wall Street Journal*, October 23, 1986, p. 50.

28. *Washington Post*, October 24, 1986, p. F 2.

29. *Wall Street Journal*, February 23, 1990, p. 1.

30. *New York Times*, April 24, 1989, p. D 4.

31. *Wall Street Journal*, October 31, 1988, p. A 15.

32. *New York Times*, November 2, 1988, p. A 26.

33. *New York Times*, September 20, 1988, p. D 6.

34. *New York Times*, October 29, 1988, p. 37.

35. Ibid. In the words of RMA president J. Stephen Gabbert, "We are shocked, disappointed, and dismayed." Rice farmers will have to think about what party protects their interests."

36. *New York Times*, January 28, 1989, section III, p. 4.

37. Hills did in fact tell Japanese reporters that Japan would be among a list of thirty-four nations so identified, but she reversed her decision. "Nation Labelled 'Unfair' US Trade Partner," *FBIS*, EAS–90–059, March 27, 1990, p. 2.

38. *Wall Street Journal*, April 26, 1990, p. A 16.

39. *USTR Identification of Priority Practices and Countries Under Super 301 and Special 301 Provisions of the Omnibus Trade and Competitiveness Act of 1988*, Hearing Before the Subcommittee on Trade of the Committee on Ways and Means, House of Representatives, June 8, 1989, p. 7.

40. Jane M. Porter and Douglas E. Bowers, *A Short History of US Agricultural Trade Negotiations*, U.S. Department of Agriculture, Economic and Research Service, Agriculture and Rural Economy Division, 1989, p. 20.

41. Ibid.

42. "Nakayama, Armacost Discuss USSR, Gulf, GATT," *FBIS*, EAS–90–249, December 27, 1990, p. 2.

43. *Japan Times Weekly International Edition*, February 3–9, 1992.

44. *Japan Times Weekly International Edition*, January 20–26, 1992.

45. *Yomiuri Shinbun*, December 7, 1991.

46. The rice crop index for the 1993 harvest season was 80 (100 is

normal), necessitating the first large scale import of rice since 1984, when 150,000 tons were imported from South Korea. *Nihon Keizai Shinbun*, September 30, 1993, p. 2.

47. *New York Times*, March 13, 1991, p. D 6.

48. "Meets LDP Leaders, Others," *FBIS*, EAS–91–064, April 3, 1991, p. 11.

49. *Washington Post*, March 27, 1991, p. A 18.

50. *New York Times*, July 24, 1988, III, p. 8.

51. "Poll on Rice Liberalization Issue Reported," *FBIS*, EAS–91–102, May 28, 1991, p. 14. In a poll conducted by the JHA, out of 1000 contacted (with a 90% response rate), 38.1% were in favor of liberalization.

52. *Nihon Keizai Shinbun*, April 15, 1991, p. 1.

53. Australia followed the U.S. lead, while Argentina's decision to supply the Soviets was criticized in Washington.

54. Interview, Sato Hideo.

55. *Asahi Shinbun*, November 1, 1989, p. 2; also August 4, 1989, p. 2.

56. *Nihon Keizai Shinbun*, June 7, 1990, p. 2.

57. *Common Security Interests in the Pacific and How the Costs and Benefits of Those Interests Are Shared by the US and its Allies*, Hearing Before the Defense Burdensharing Panel of the Committee on Armed Services, House of Representatives, One Hundredth Congress, Second Session. Hearing held April 19, 1988 (Washington, DC: U.S. Government Printing Office, 1989), p. 3.

58. Ibid., p. 4.

59. Interview, Japanese government official, October 14, 1992.

60. *Report of the Defense Burdensharing Panel*, August 1988, p. 8. The committee cited the widely quoted figure of $45,000 per U.S. soldier, which it noted includes " 'non-outlays' like estimates of the value of land provided without charge to U.S. forces, and foregone revenues as a result of waiving taxes, landing and port fees, customs duties and so forth."

61. Ibid., p. 9.

62. Ibid.

63. *Asahi Shinbun*, June 25, 1990, p. 2.

64. *Nihon Keizai Shinbun*, August 9, 1990, p. 2.

65. "Remarks with Prime Minister Miyazawa of Japan to the Presidential Business Delegation in Tokyo," *Weekly Compilation of Presidential Documents*, vol. 28, no. 1, January 6, 1992, p. 52.

66. *Sankei Shinbun*, June 9, 1990, p. 5.

67. *Nihon Keizai Shinbun*, December 7, 1991, p. 9.

68. *Omnibus Trade and Competitiveness Act of 1988*, specifically Section 1306, "Trade and Economic Relations with Japan," U.S. House of

Representatives, Conference Report to Accompany H.R.3, April 1988, p. 81.

69. *USTR Identification of Priority Practices*, p. 43.

70. *Nihon Keizai Shinbun*, January 6, 1992 (evening edition), p. 5.

71. Sakanishi Shio, ed., *Some Unpublished Letters of Townsend Harris* (New York: Japan Reference Library, 1941), letter 2, p. 4.

72. The remarks of Clinton Yeutter, at that time U.S. trade representative, are typical of this "suggestion" diplomacy. See "Kono mamadewa hogoshugi hooanga seiritsu suru [Under These Circumstances, Protectionist Bills Will Be Enacted]," *Ekonomisuto*, September 10, 1985, esp. pp. 50–51. In response to whether he had any "requests" to make of Japan, Yeutter admitted to his Japanese interviewer that he was an "outsider" and his suggestions might therefore be considered impudent. Succeeding U.S. officials have not been as self-effacing as Yeutter in their "requests."

73. *Nihon Keizai Shinbun*, December 18, 1991, p. 2.

74. "Remarks at the Opening of Toys-R-Us in Kashihara, Japan," January 7, 1992, *Weekly Compilation of Presidential Documents*, vol. 28, no. 2, January 13, 1992, p. 50.

75. "The President's News Conference with Prime Minister Miyazawa of Japan in Tokyo," January 9, 1992, *Weekly Compilation of Presidential Documents*, vol. 28, no. 2, January 13, 1992, p. 60.

76. *Tokyo Shinbun*, April 18, 1993, p. 6.

77. *Gaiko Forum*, "Nichibeikankeiwa retorikku kara aideia e [Moving the US–Japan Relationship from Rhetoric to Ideas]," January 1993, p. 11.

78. *Nihon Keizai Shinbun*, March 31, 1993, p. 2.

79. Laura D'Andrea Tyson, *Who's Bashing Whom?* (Washington, DC: Institute for International Economics, 1992).

80. *Nihon Keizai Shinbun*, April 18, 1993, p. 1.

81. Muroyama Yoshimasa, "Posuto nichibeianpo no senryaku koosoo [Post US–Japan Security Treaty Strategic Concept]," *Sekai*, February 1993, p. 236.

82. Sato Rikuo, editor of *Mainichi Shinbun*, unpublished interview with Governor Clinton, Little Rock, Arkansas, December 1991.

83. Haraguchi Koichi, consul general of Japan at Los Angeles, "Remarks on NAFTA," Panel Discussion, Los Angeles World Trade Center Association, October 22, 1992.

84. "Remarks with Prime Minister Miyazawa of Japan to the Presidential Business Delegation in Tokyo," *Weekly Compilation of Presidential Documents*, vol. 28, no. 2, January 13, 1992, pp. 51–52.

85. Interview, Omori Takashi, October 19, 1992.

86. Interview, Tanabe Yasuo, October 23, 1992.

87. Sato Rikuo, interview with Governor Clinton.

88. Interview, Kitaoka Shin'ichi, November 11, 1992.

89. Sato Yukio, "Motomerareru nihonno hasso tenkan [Change in Japan's Way of Thinking Required]," *Gaiko Forum*, January 1993, p. 34.

90. For example, see *Report of the Burdensharing Panel*, in which it was suggested that "Japan should increase its development assistance budget substantially and should target more untied aid to countries with both economic need and strategic importance to Japan and the United States (e.g., Turkey and the Philippines)," p. 9.

91. *Yomiuri Shinbun*, May 20, 1991, p. 2. In part, the report stated that "[Japan] has taken action for full scale aid, believing that positive cooperation will be necessary from the viewpoint of the Japan–U.S. global partnership."

92. *Tokyo Shinbun*, January 7, 1992, p. 5.

93. Interview, Shiina Motoo, November 19, 1992.

Conclusion

To say that the course of world events during the past five years has been monumental in significance might be a cliche, but it is a point well worth contemplating. Few analysts would have predicted that the Berlin Wall would collapse, and that the event would be met by the encouragement of the Soviet Union, or that the Soviet Union itself would implode. Even fewer analysts would have concluded that peace between Israel and its neighbors, tenuous though that peace may be, would transpire before the end of the century, if at all. Yet even if some of these same analysts believe that peace may be "breaking out all over" in some parts of the world, armed conflict is hardly absent in other parts of the world, and the dichotomy between the world's haves and have-nots in terms of wealth creation and population growth are joined by the global issues of environmental degradation and the continued strain on limited resources.

Similarly, just as unlikely (and just as unforeseen) as the collapse of the international system's biploar structure, five years ago virtually no one would have anticipated the end of Japan's two party structure, or the reality that the the LDP and its chief opposition—the SDPJ—would join forces to create a coalition government or, even more unlikely, that a Socialist would be chosen to lead that strangest-of-bedfellows coalition. As is clear from the fall from grace of Prime Minister Hosokawa, himself an avowed "reformer" who was propelled to the position on an anticorruption agenda but who was eventually implicated in political scandal after less than a year in office, it would be a mistake to assume that with the fall of the LDP, political corruption will ever be a nonissue in Japan, or that because Japan's voters voted out the LDP in 1993 they are any less conservative than they have always been. An analysis of pre- and post-election support for conservative parties belies such a hasty conclusion, for voter support of conservative parties, made up of the LDP and former party members who broke ranks to form their own political parties, was greater after the election than it was before. Rather than falsely expressing a nonexistent revolutionary fervor among Japanese, the polls showed that many Japanese voters merely wanted a non-LDP conservative alternative, and the newly created splinter parties filled that need. Election results showed the biggest victim of the "sea change" in Japanese poltics was not the conservative-thinking prties, but the "progressive" minded SDPJ. Ironically, following the 1993 election, parliamentary maneuvering and a coalition government made up of non–LDP party members assured the SDPJ that as the party with the greatest number of seats among coalition members, even if it had lost a significant number, its power to influence the policymaking process would be greater than at any time in the past three decades. That coalition government has since been replaced by the LDP–SDPJ arrangement, which has caused an ideological quandary among many SDPJ members and calls for party dissolution into two distinct camps. Clearly, just as one cannot assume that with the end of the bipolar international structure peace will be inevitable, one also cannot assume that Japan's political "revolution" will bring domestic political stability. Nor should one expect a significant change in Japanese foreign policy until the domestic political situation is less fluid, if at all.

However, we do believe that in the post–Cold War world Japan's foreign policy will continue to be characterized by the elements of identity, adaptability, and resolve, and that Japan will not try to construct the rules and determine the expectations made on other members of the international society of states, but will contribute to the maintenance of these rules and will continue as a pivotal member of that society. Corporate Japan will augment its already visible economic presence throughout Asia and, as expressed by the Japanese government's announcement of a $1 billion program for historical studies and educational and scholarly exchanges with Asian nations to "atone" for Japan's wartime aggression, the Japanese government is attempting to deflect criticism from the rest of Asia that Japan has tried to "selectively forget" its militarist past. As evident by dispatches of Self Defense Forces personnel to participate in peacekeeping activities in Mozambique and humanitarian relief efforts in Zaire, an event that was once considered taboo—sending SDF forces overseas—is no longer an issue, but has become accepted both at home and abroad as a tool of Japanese foreign policy. The next issue, of course, and one that Japanese officials have been discounting, is whether the noncombat role of the SDF will be breached and they will no longer solely play a peacekeeping-humanitarian role, but will instead be forced to participate in peace making.

There are three distinct strengths which Japan believes it can offer as a member of the international society, two of which it openly acknowledges and one of which most Japanese—whether or not members of the government—subscribe to, but with exception and obvious reason, few will publicly advance. First, both Japanese elites and masses realize that Japan's economic resources, both in the form of export of capital (primarily through loans, ODA, foreign direct investment, and financial support of international organizations) and access to Japan's markets, will continue to be its most visible and (most easily called upon) strength. Of course, for the past five years this economic capability has lost some of its vitality with Japan's protracted recession, yet Japan still remains the world's second largest economy and it still possesses the human capital that made economic development possible. But instead of assuming what has in the past appeared by many to be a disinterested attitude that has relied on economic contributions, Japan is resolved that it should, and will, play a greater role in policy formulation on international issues. Japan's pursuit of a permanent seat on the UN Security Council is one example of this resolve, a position that has been strengthened by its ability to send SDF forces overseas, and by the work of two Japanese in influential UN positions (UN High Commissioner on Refugees Ogata Sadako and UNTAC head Akashi Yasushi). Whether that resolve will be met with the approval of other nations is, for reasons previously discussed, problematic.

The second distinct strength that the Japanese believe they can offer to the world is embodied in the ideals of their "peace constitution," which, it has been advanced by the government, allows Japan to take an objective view of conflict between other nations. Nevertheless, because Japan lacks the means of the United States to influence other nations, its opinions will not always be considered, nor will its economic prowess allow Japan to be seen as an "objective" outsider on most issues. It is therefore understandable why Norweigian Foreign Minister Johan Jorgen Holst oversaw the secret talks that led to the agreement between the PLO and Israel, recognizing Israel's right to exist and renouncing the PLO's renunciation of terrorism. Japan, the EU, the Scandanavian nations, and the United States pledged economic aid to further the peace process, but it was apparent that in bringing the two sides together any Norweigian claim to objectivity on the issue would have been stronger than any made by Japan. Paradoxically, the source of Japan's foreign policy strength is also the source of its greatest weakness. Until the rest of the world is convinced, if it ever can be, that Japan's motives in assuming a greater world role are not necessarily economic driven, what the preamble of the Japanese Constitution states is Japan's "desire to occupy an honored place in an international society striving for the preservation of peace" will be consistently overlooked.

Third, most foreigners are unaware that the Japanese population is not as homogeneous as many Japanese themselves believe. A select few of these foreigners have even adopted a "holier than thou" attitude in their disdain for the Japanese government and Japanese society in general for their lack of consideration of the claims of minority groups in Japan, as if their own nations are a testament to the tolerance of others and examples of perfect social equality. Perhaps Japanese social norms and expectations of conformity may inhibit these groups from making more vocal and more visible demands on the government and on the rest of society, reinforcing this sense of Japanese homogeneity, but most Japanese consider their shared cultural and ethnic identity to be an asset both domestically and abroad. Ongoing armed conflict in

Eastern Europe and the riots in Los Angeles (following the Rodney King trial) in the United States are just two examples of racial and ethnic strife in both developing and developed nations that were watched by the Japanese public, and some Japanese have concluded that the increase in crime in their formerly safe, virtually crime-free neighborhoods is in large measure attributable to the wave of foreigners in their nation. A nation that was once offered to the world as a model of social harmony has for the past ten years been faced with demands from abroad that it "internationalize," yet is has been difficult for some Japanese to see the benefits of such a policy.

Until the world can clearly identify what constitutes the "new world order," Japan will cope with both domestic and international instability, and its foreign policy may at times reflect the uncertainty and fluidity of these distinct, yet overlapping, realms.

References

INTERVIEWS

Gyoten Toyoo, Chairman, Bank of Tokyo
Kanehara Nobukatsu, Director of the Northern Territories Problem Section, Russian Division, Ministry of Foreign Affairs
Kitaoka Shin'ichi, Professor of Law, Rikkyo University
Kuroda Makoto, Managing Director, Mitsubishi Corporation
Nishizaki Fumiko, Associate Professor of History, Faculty of Law, Seikei University
Okamoto Yukio, President, Okamoto Associates
Omori Takashi, Director, Second International Affairs Division, Economic Planning Agency
Sato Hideo, Professor of Political Science, Tsukuba University
Sato Seizaburo, International Institute for Global Peace
Shiina Motoo, Member, House of Councilors
Sugita Sadahiro, Deputy Director, Europe Division, International Trade Policy Bureau, Ministry of International Trade and Industry
Tanabe Yasuo, Director, North America Policy Planning, Ministry of International Trade and Industry
Tanaka Akihiko, Associate Professor, School of Oriental Cultures, University of Tokyo
Yoshino Bunroku, Chairman, Institute for International Economic Studies

PERSONAL CORRESPONDENCE

John Benson, The Roper Center for Public Opinion Research, University of Connecticut, October 15, 1991.

John K. Ward, Political Officer, U.S. Embassy, Tokyo, October 22, 1984.

RADIO BROADCAST

Martin E. Weinstein, "Japan and Fair Trade," Focus 580, WILL-AM, Champaign, IL, January 24, 1992.

NEWSPAPERS

Asahi Shinbun
Department of State Bulletin
Foreign Broadcast Information Service (FBIS)
Japan Times
Japan Times Weekly International Edition
London Times
Mainichi Daily News
Mainichi Shinbun
New York Times
Nihon Keizai Shinbun
Sankei Shinbun
Tokyo Shinbun
Wall Street Journal
Washington Post
Yomiuri Shinbun

BOOKS AND PERIODICALS

Anonymous. "The 'White' Problem in Asia," in K.K. Kawakami, ed., *What Japan Thinks*. New York: MacMillan, 1921.

Beasley, W.G. *Select Documents on Japanese Foreign Policy, 1853-1868*. London: Oxford University Press, 1955.

———. *The Meiji Restoration*. Stanford, CA: Stanford University Press, 1972.

Bohlen, Charles E. *Witness to History, 1929-1969*. New York: W.W. Norton, 1973.

———. *The Transformation of American Foreign Policy*. New York: W.W. Norton, 1969.

Brown, Harrison. *The Challenge of Man's Future: An Inquiry Concerning the Condition of Man During the Years that Lie Ahead.* Boulder, CO: Westview Press, 1954.

"Bush kusen no amerika daitoryosen. Matamata chutoga kinakusakunatte kita! [Bush's Hard Fight in the American Presidential Election. Once Again, Something Smells in the Middle East!]." *More,* December 1992.

Byrnes, James F. *Speaking Frankly.* New York: Harper & Brothers, 1947.

"China Aid to Be Resumed." *Japan Economic Survey,* vol. 14, no. 8, August 1990.

Chung, Henry. *The Oriental Policy of the United States.* New York: Fleming H. Revell Co., 1919.

Current Digest of Soviet Press, February 24, 1960.

Daishi Yoshinari. "Hoppo Ryodo, Sato Eisaku no Ofureko Danwa [The Northern Islands, Sato Eisaku's Off the Record Conversation]." *Bungei Shunju,* December 1985.

Donnelly, Michael W. "Conflict Over Government Authority and Markets: Japan's Rice Economy," in Thomas P. Rohlen et al., eds., *Conflict in Japan.* Honolulu: University of Hawaii Press, 1984.

Economic Eye: A Quarterly Digest of Views from Japan, Vol. 10, No. 1, Spring 1989. Tokyo: Keizai Koho Center.

Endo Shusaku. *Silence.* New York: Taplinger Publishing Co., 1969.

Fujisawa Rikitaro. *The Recent Aims and Political Development of Japan.* New Haven, CT: Yale University Press, 1923.

——. "The Monroe Doctrine and the League of Nations," in K.K. Kawakami, ed., *What Japan Thinks.* New York: MacMillan, 1921.

Fukuzawa Yukichi. *The Autobiography of Fukuzawa Yukichi,* trans. Kiyooka Eiichi. Tokyo: Hokuseido, 1934.

Garten, Jeffrey E. *A Cold Peace.* New York: Times Books, 1993.

Generalissimo Chiang Assails Konoye's Statement. Chungking, China: China Information Committee, 1939.

Gifford, Prosser, and William Roger Louis, eds. *France and Britain in Africa: Imperial Rivalry and Colonial Rule.* New Haven, CT: Yale University Press, 1971.

Goto Shimpei. "The Anti-Japanese Question in California." *Annals of the American Academy of Political and Social Science,* January 1921.

Griffis, William Elliot. *Matthew Calbraith Perry, a Typical American Naval Officer.* Boston: Houghton Mifflin, 1890.

Hamada Takujiro. "Opinion: Japan's International Role." *Japan Economic Survey,* vol. 13, no. 6, June 1989.

Hanubasa Masamichi. "Fueling Success: Japan's Economic Aid Programs in Asia." Speech delivered at Princeton University, September 29, 1989, as reported in *Speaking of Japan*, vol. 10, no. 109, January 1990. Tokyo: Keizai Koho Center.

Haraguchi Koichi, Consul General of Japan at Los Angeles. "Remarks on NAFTA." Panel Discussion, Los Angeles World Trade Center Association, October 22, 1992.

Harris, Townsend. *The Complete Journal of Townsend Harris*. New York: Charles E. Tuttle, 1930.

Hawks, Francis L. *Narrative of the Expedition of an American Squadron to the China Seas and Japan*, vols. I and II. Washington, DC: U.S. Senate Printing Office, 1856.

Hishida, Seiji G. *The International Position of Japan as a Great Power*. Ph.D. thesis, Columbia University, 1905.

Huang Su'an. "United States and Japan Vie for Economic Supremacy." *CIIS Paper*. Beijing: China Institute of International Studies, 1990.

International Monetary Fund. *Summary Proceedings of the Forty-Seventh Annual Meeting of the Board of Governors*. Washington, DC, 1992.

Jain, Rajendra Kumar. *The USSR and Japan 1945–1980*. Atlantic Highlands, NJ: Humanities Press, 1981.

Jansen, Marius B. *China in the Tokugawa World*. Cambridge, MA: Harvard University Press, 1992.

————. *Sakamoto Ryoma and the Meiji Restoration*. Princeton, NJ: Princeton University Press, 1961.

Japan International Training Cooperation Organization. *An Overview of the JITCO: Providing Information to Support and Promote Training Programmes in Japan*, 1992.

Japan Statistical Yearbook. Tokyo: Statistics Bureau, Management and Coordination Agency, 1992.

Japan's Northern Territories. Tokyo: Ministry of Foreign Affairs, 1982.

Jones, F.C., Hugh Borton, and B.R. Pearn. *Survey of International Affairs, 1939–46*, vol. VII. London: Oxford University Press, 1955.

Kamiya Fuji. "The Northern Territories," in Donald S. Zagoria, ed., *Soviet Policy in East Asia*. New Haven, CT: Yale University Press, 1982.

Kashiyama Yukio. *To Avoid the Coming War: A First Hand Observation of US–Japan Relations*. New York: East Asia Institute, Columbia University, 1991.

Kataoka Tetsuya. "Japan's Northern Threat." *Problems of Communism*, March/April 1984.

Kimura Hiroshi. "Moscow and Tokyo: An Uneasy Peace." *Annals of the American Academy of Political and Social Science*, vol. 481, September 1985.

Kissinger, Henry. "Kissinger-Nakasone Forum." Tokyo, October 22, 1992.

Komiya Ryutaro. " 'Nihon kyoiron' no meimo [The Fallacy of the 'Japan Is a Threat' Argument]." *Chuo Koron*, January 1991.

Kuriyama Takakazu. "Gekido 90 nendai to nihon gaiko no shintenkai [The Great Upheaval of the Nineties and Japan's New Diplomacy]." *Gaiko Forum*, May 1990.

————. "Taikenteki nihon gaikoron [Thoughts on Japanese Diplomacy, as Experienced]." *Chuo Koron*, November 1991.

————. *New Directions for Japanese Foreign Policy in the Changing World of the 1990s.* Tokyo: Ministry of Foreign Affairs, 1990.

Leahy, William D. *I Was There.* New York: McGraw-Hill, 1950.

Management and Coordination Agency, Japan. *Japan Statistical Yearbook*, Tokyo, 1992.

Mendel, Douglas H. *The Japanese People and Foreign Policy.* Berkeley: University of California Press, 1961.

Mills, Walter, ed. *The Forrestal Diaries.* New York: Viking Press, 1951.

Ministry of Foreign Affairs, Japan. *Diplomatic Bluebook 1991.* Tokyo, 1991.

Ministry of Justice, Japan. *Summary of Statistics Related to Immigration Control*, as cited in Japan External Trade Organization (JETRO), *Japan Economic Databook*, Tokyo, 1991.

Moss, Joanna, and John Ravenhill. *Emerging Japanese Economic Influence in Africa: Implications for the United States.* Institute of International Studies, Policy Papers in International Affairs, Number 21. Berkeley: University of California Press, 1985.

Muroyama Yoshimasa. "Posuto nichibeianpo no senryaku koosoo [Post U.S.–Japan Security Treaty Strategic Concept]." *Sekai*, February 1993.

"Nichibeikankeiwa retorikku kara aideia e [Moving the US–Japan Relationship from Rhetoric to Ideas]." *Gaiko Forum*, January 1993.

"Nihon wa Ajia, Taiheiyo no daihyoo toshite no koodoo o [Japan as a Representative of the Asia-Pacific]." *Gaiko Forum*, May 1993.

Nish, Ian. *Japanese Foreign Policy, 1869–1942.* London: Routledge and Kegan Paul, 1977.

Oba Osamu. *Edo jidai ni okeru Chugoku bunka juyo no kenkyu* [The Demand for Chinese Culture in Tokugawa Japan]. Tokyo: Shohan, 1984.

Otsuka Keijiro and Hayami Yujiro. "Goals and Consequences of Rice Policy in Japan, 1965–80." *American Journal of Agricultural Economics*, August 1985.

Owada Hisashi. "Korega Roshia shien ronrida [This Is the Logic of Support for Russia]." *Chuo Koron*, July 1993.

Porter, Jane M., and Douglas E. Bowers. *A Short History of US Agricultural Trade and Negotiations.* U.S. Department of Agriculture, Economic and Research Service, Agriculture and Rural Economy Division, 1989.

Rapp, David. *How the US Got into Agriculture, and Why It Can't Get Out.* Washington, DC: Congressional Quarterly, 1988.

"Remarks with Prime Minister Miyazawa of Japan to the Presidential Business Delegation in Tokyo." *Weekly* Compilation of Presidential Documents, vol. 28, no. 1, January 6, 1992.

Rix, Alan. "Japan's Foreign Aid Policy: A Capacity for Leadership?" *Pacific Affairs,* vol. 62, no. 4, Winter 1989–1990.

Roosevelt, Theodore. *Theodore Roosevelt, an Autobiography.* New York: MacMillan, 1914.

Rosenbluth, Francis McCall. *Financial Politics in Contemporary Japan.* Ithaca, NY: Cornell University Press, 1989.

Royama Masamichi. *Foreign Policy of Japan, 1914–1939.* Tokyo: Japanese Council, Institute of Pacific Relations, 1941.

Sakanishi Shio, ed. *Some Unpublished Letters of Townsend Harris.* New York: Japan Reference Library, 1941.

Sase Masamori. "The Northern Territories in International Politics." *Japan Echo,* No. 2, 1976.

Sato Rikuo. Unpublished interview with Governor William Clinton, Little Rock, Arkansas, December 1991.

Sato Seizaburo. "Jidaino henka ga yori kyokona domei o motomeru [Changes in the Times Call for Still Stronger Alliance]." *Chuo Koron,* March 1990.

———. "Imakoso nichibei domei no kyoka o [Now is the Time to Strengthen the U.S.–Japan Alliance]." *Chuo Koron,* June 1988.

Sato Yukio. "Motomerareru nihonno hasso tenkan [Change in Japan's Way of Thinking Required]." *Gaiko Forum,* January 1993.

Sherwood, Robert E. *Roosevelt and Hopkins, an Intimate History.* New York: Harper, 1948.

Shidehido Toshio. *The Economic Development of Japan,* as cited in Zhang Peiji, "China's Strategy and Policy on Utilizing Foreign Capital," in Richard D. Robinson, ed., *Foreign Capital and Technology in China.* New York; Praeger, 1987.

Snell, John J. et al. *The Meaning of Yalta.* Baton Rouge: University of Louisiana Press, 1956.

Solomon, Robert. *The International Monetary System, 1945–1981.* New York: Harper and Row, 1982.

Stalin, Josef. "Victory Address: We Have Waited Forty Years." *Vital Speeches of the Day,* vol. 11, no. 23, September 15, 1945.

Stephan, John J. "Japan and the Soviet Union: The Distant Neighbours." *Asian Affairs*, October 1977.

———. *The Kuril Islands*. Oxford: Clarendon Press, 1974.

Stettinius, Edward R., Jr. *Roosevelt and the Russians: The Yalta Conference*. Garden City, NY: Doubleday, 1949.

Tahara Soichiro. "Nichibei anpojoyaku wa ippotekini haki sareru [The U.S.–Japan Security Treaty Will Be Abrogated Unilaterally]." *Ushio*, January 1990.

Takeda Isami. "A New Dialogue for Japan, ASEAN and Oceania." *Japan Echo*, vol. XX, special issue, 1993.

Takeuchi Tatsuji. *War and Diplomacy in the Japanese Empire*. Garden City, NY: Doubleday, 1935.

Toby, Ronald P. *State and Diplomacy in Early Modern Japan*. Princeton, NJ: Princeton University Press, 1984.

Tsunoda Ryusaku et al. *Sources of the Japanese Tradition*. New York: Columbia University Press, 1958.

Tyler, Sydney. *The Japan-Russia War: The Greatest Conflict of Modern Times*. Philadelphia: P.W. Ziegler, 1905.

Tyson, Laura D'Andrea. *Who's Bashing Whom?* Washington, DC: Institute for International Economics, 1992.

United Nations Handbook, 1994. Wellington, New Zealand: Ministry of Foreign Affairs and Trade, 1994.

Urata, S. "The Rapid Globalization of Japanese Firms in the 1980s: An Analysis of the Activities of Japanese Firms in Asia," as cited in Fukasaku Kiichiro, *Economic Regionalization and Intra-Industry Trade: Pacific-Asian Perspectives*. Research Program on Globalization and Regionalization, OECD Technical Papers, no. 53, February 1992.

U.S. Department of Agriculture, Economic Research Service. *Rice: Background for 1985 Farm Legislation*. Information Bulletin 470, September 1984.

U.S. Department of Commerce. *Statistical Abstract of the United States* (years as cited).

U.S. Department of Defense. *A Strategic Framework for the Asian Pacific Rim: Looking Toward the 21st Century*. 1990.

U.S. Department of State. *Foreign Relations of the United States, 1945*, vols. V & VI. 1955.

U.S. House of Representatives. *Common Security Interests in the Pacific and How the Costs and Benefits of Those Interests Are Shared by the US and its Allies*. April 19, 1988.

———. *Report of the Defense Burdensharing Panel of the Committee on Armed Services*. August 1988.

————. *Review of Japan's Policy Concerning the Importation of Rice, Including a Petition Filed by the Rice Millers Association.* October 1, 1986.

————. *Review of United States–Japan Rice Agreement.* February 26, 1981.

————. *USTR Identification of Priority Practices and Countries Under Super 301 and Special 301 Provisions of the Omnibus Trade and Competitiveness Act of 1988.* June 8, 1989.

Wada Haruki. "Niso dakkyo de hoppo ryodo mondai wa ketchaku suru [Japan–Soviet Union Compromises for Settlement of the Northern Territories Problem]." *Ekonomisuto*, November 15, 1988.

Wallis, Allen. *US Agriculture and the Global Context: A Time for Action.* U.S. Department of State, Current Policy Paper 950, May 1987.

Wang, Ching-chun. "Theodore Roosevelt and the Monroe Doctrine." *Pacific Affairs*, vol. 9, no. 1, 1936.

Weekly Compilation of Presidential Documents, vol. 28, no. 2, January 13, 1992.

Weigand, Robert E. "No Open Door for Foreign Rice in Japan." *Food Policy*, August 1988.

White, John. *Japanese Aid.* London: Overseas Development Institute, 1964.

Whiting, Allan. *China Eyes Japan.* Berkeley: University of California Press, 1989.

Woodruff, William. *The Struggle for World Power, 1500–1980.* New York: St. Martin's Press, 1981.

World Press Review. Summary of Official History in *Izvestia*, September 1980.

Yeutter, Clinton. "Kono mamadewa hogoshugi hooanga seiritsu suru [Under These Circumstances, Protectionist Bills Will Be Enacted]." *Ekonomisuto*, September 10, 1985.

Zacharias, Ellis M. *Behind Closed Doors: The Secret History of the Cold War.* New York: Putnam, 1950.

Index

About the Authors

RICHARD D. LEITCH, JR. is a Visiting Assistant Professor in the Department of Political Science and East Asian Languages and Cultures at the University of Illinois at Urbana-Champaign. He has recently completed a research project for the Japan Foundation Center for Global Partnership in Tokyo.

AKIRA KATO is a Professor at the National Institute for Defense Studies in Tokyo. He is also the author of *Gendai Sensoron*.

MARTIN E. WEINSTEIN, Professor of Political Science, University of Montana, is well known for his numerous studies of Japanese politics, including *The Human Face of Japan's Leadership* (Greenwood, 1990).

ISBN 0-313-29731-2

HARDCOVER BAR CODE